Taming the Unpredictable

Real World Adaptive Case Management:
Case Studies and Practical Guidance

Excellence in Practice Series

Taming the
Unpredictable

Real World Adaptive Case Management:
Case Studies and Practical Guidance

Foreword by
Tom Koulopoulos

Excellence in Practice Series 2011

Published in association with the
Workflow Management Coalition

Workflow Management Coalition

18 Years of Thought-Process Leadership

Edited by
Layna Fischer

Future Strategies Inc.
Lighthouse Point, Florida

Taming the Unpredictable
Real World Adaptive Case Management: Case Studies and Practical Guidance

Published by Future Strategies Inc., Book Division

3640-B3 North Federal Highway #421, Lighthouse Point FL 33064 USA
+1 954.782.3376 Fax +1 954.719.3746
www.FutStrat.com; books@FutStrat.com

All book titles are available at quantity discounts for corporate and academic education and training use in both Print and Digital Formats.

Publisher's Cataloging-in-Publication Data

Library of Congress Catalog Card LCCN No. 2011937017
SAN: 299-9374

Taming the Unpredictable
Real World Adaptive Case Management: Case Studies and Practical Guidance

/Emily V Burns, Dave Duggal, Frank Michael Kraft, John T Matthias, Dermot McCauley, Nathaniel Palmer, Max J Pucher, Bruce Silver, Keith D Swenson (authors)

/Layna Fischer (editor)

p. cm.

Includes bibliographical references, appendices and index.

ISBN-13: 978-0-9819870-8-8

1. Management Science. 2. Technological Innovation. 3. Case Management. 4. Organizational Effectiveness. 5. Business Process Technology. 6. Knowledge Management.7. Adaptive Computing Systems. 8. Strategic Planning 9. Business Process Technology. 10. Workflow Management Coalition

Table of Contents

Award-Winning ACM Case Studies

Appendix

Foreword

Beyond the Breaking Point

In the early 1930s military pilots were starting to experience a strange and often fatal phenomenon—black-out. As the aircraft of the time became faster and more maneuverable the G-forces they exerted would exceed the ability of the pilot to maintain consciousness as blood drained from the brain. Yet it was not until after World War II that the first generally available G-suits were used, enabling pilots to fly at up to nine times the force of gravity.

Throughout most of WWII pilots simply had to deal with the extreme G-forces using maneuvers that would contort and squeeze their torso to push blood back into the brain. Not all had the physiology to do so—let's just say that being a pilot was a bit of a self-selective process. But even those who could withstand extreme G-forces were barely able to focus on anything other than maintaining consciousness. Their mission objective and piloting skills were somewhat secondary at these critical times when their machines exceeded their capability. To be short, speed was their nemesis. It distracted them from what they were best at, flying. Ironically, speed was also their goal.

Yet, we've all been to that precipice of panic where the amount to do far exceeds the time to do it, or the resources needed. In those moments, hours or days time seems to accelerate, we feel far less than adequate and collaboration reaches a frenetic pace where a team's ability to communicate and execute needs to be nearly flawless, despite the intensity of the situation.

There is nothing new about that. Every enterprise will find itself in that predicament. If it doesn't then it's just not competing hard enough.

While we can deal with these occasional sprints to the finish line, sort of like our pilot in an occasional sharp turn, trying to cope in this mode in task after task, project after project can wear any organization down to the point of dysfunction.

Yet that is exactly where we seem to be lately. The need to do more with less, to meet unyielding deadlines, to deal with unprecedented levels of uncertainty and to do it all flawlessly has become the norm, not the exception. We feel constantly drained by the lack of tools with which to handle the complexity and the speed of the global machine of commerce we have built.

None of this should come as a surprise. We have created an ability to move so quickly in today's organizations that the demands have outstripped our ability to deliver—and you know it's only getting worse!

Waxing on philosophically about how we got here is pointless. The plain truth is that we are quickly realizing that the tools we have built are as well equipped to drive these new engines of commerce as a WWI pilot would be to fly an F16.

We need more than tools; we need a new way to approach the very problem of work that travels at the speed of light on a global scale.

This is the essence of Adaptive Case Management (ACM). However, the debate I've often seen on blogs and heard in conversations about ACM typically centers on, "Why call it something new? We have plenty of tools in our organizations to deal with process, task, coordination, and automation."

To those comments I say simply, call it what you will but do not let the attachment to the past prevent you from seeing the promise of the future.

ACM is about changing the very fundamentals of how we view work; how we visualize it, share it, transport it, track it, and ultimately integrate it within a radically new framework of collaboration.

If you are saying, we don't need ACM, what you are really saying is we *didn't* need ACM. As you read through the cases and articles in this book what you will find is that we are closing in on a time when we will no longer be able to recall how we lived without ACM. We will wonder how in the world traditional, rigid command and control models of automation kept pace with the market. Most of all we will marvel at how little we understood about the critically important role of autonomous decision making in unplanned events and uncertain markets.

As Keith Swenson tells us in his chapter;

> The world is moving too fast for centralized control. Decisions need to be made at ever more autonomous points, involving information exchanges and consultations in unforeseen, unplanned, and impromptu ways.

Take heart, however, if all of this sounds a bit too out there on the edge for you; there is a new generation of workers to whom this is second nature. Look at the way your kids collaborate, the way they share their lives and their conversations in real time, 24/7. There is no break in the connection for these kids. While we can argue the merits of this non-stop electronic tether, what we cannot argue is the degree to which it enables them to better deal with the uncertainty of the future. For them uncertainty is an opportunity, and they race towards it rather than cower from it. It may be worth watching how they work to understand how we should work.

My advice to you is simple; rethink what is possible with the ability that ACM provides to live and work in real time. Consider the immense benefits of being able to connect all of the elements of your work and your resources in a way that represents the reality of how you experience the world rather than a representation of how your desktop today presents the world to you, in myriad disconnected pieces; broken chains of conversations, information and process. Imagine instead a connected world where work and all of its parts flow without friction and with complete continuity and reliability.

Do that and you will find that speed is no longer a nemesis, a breaking point, a stressor that takes you away from your objective but instead that it is an inevitable aspect of the way we will work and that is our only option; your only option is to harness and leverage it so that you can focus on what you do best.

Don't buy it? Don't worry, doing business is a lot like flying fighter planes, it's a self-selecting process.

Thomas Koulopoulos

Chairman Delphi Group

Introduction

Nathaniel Palmer, Workflow Management Coalition, USA

During late November of 2009, fittingly coinciding with the centennial anniversary of Peter Drucker's[1] birth, a meeting of minds was held in the town of Maidenhead England. The purpose of this meeting was to address the emerging field of unpredictable work patterns, where processes cannot fully modeled or predefined in advance (if at all) but represent the true nature of knowledge work, as explained eloquently by the writings of Drucker.

It was at this meeting that the concept of "Adaptive Case Management" (ACM) was first identified and defined, to become the definitive term applied to the then-nascent software sector targeted at aiding knowledge workers. In attendance at this meeting would be the authors of the first text explaining ACM, *Mastering the Unpredictable*[2] which would subsequently rise to #2 on the Amazon.com bestseller's list of *Managers Guides to Computing*.

Although never intended as an official tribute or explicitly about Drucker himself, his influence on both that first text and perhaps more vividly on the field of ACM itself is inescapable. In a departure from the focus of optimizing outcomes through increasing certainty, it was Drucker who first focused on the greater wisdom of embracing uncertainty in business strategy and management practices. Achieving mastery of the unpredictable in a way that delivers sustainable business value requires more than a shift in policy or attitude, ACM involves fundamentally rethinking the tools required to support this transformation, the ability to match an organization's most valuable assets to changes in the business environment.

The Journey from Mastery to Taming

The most valuable assets today for most firms are neither physical commodities nor proprietary methods, but the know-how of employees. Viewed through the lens of Drucker's own words, "The most valuable assets of a 20th-century company were its production equipment. The most valuable asset of a 21st-century institution, whether business or non-business, will be its knowledge workers and their productivity."

Where *Mastering the Unpredictable* focused foremost on connecting the dots on why empowering knowledge workers is so critical today, *Taming the Unpredictable* presents a series of case studies and treatises on how this should be done. Although many of the same authors are represented in both texts, what has transpired in little more than a year has been the global coalescence of ideas and activities that has positioned ACM as arguably the most critical bridge across the Business/IT divide.

---

[1] Peter F Drucker is one of the best-known and most widely influential thinkers and writers on the subject of management theory and practice.
http://en.wikipedia.org/wiki/Peter_Drucker

[2] Mastering the Unpredictable: How Adaptive Case Management Will Revolutionize the Way That Knowledge Workers Get Things Done, published by Meghan-Kiffer Press, April 2010

This year alone, following the remarkable success of *Mastering the Unpredictable*, dozens of market-forming events have transpired, from the *Global Excellence in Adaptive Case Management[3]* awards to countless webinars, new product launches, an ACM online conference, and seemingly endless stream of conversations on ACM across social media. Few issues have generated such passionate debate, or presented such compelling promise, as ACM.

The goal of this book is to present a clear and concise understanding of ACM and its potential to transform the knowledge-driven enterprise, that which defines virtually any competitive business or effective government agency today. From *10 Things You Must Know About Case Management* to *Considerations for Implementing Adaptive Case Management,* **Taming the Unpredictable** explains in practical terms what you need to take advantage of ACM in your organization. It should be understood that while ACM itself is a new and emerging category of software, the business drivers behind it are not. Nowhere is this more evident than in the collection of global collection of case studies contained herein. Many are mature projects, yet have evolved to include precisely the same technologies that define the contemporary ACM software landscape. In each you will find the defining characteristics which distinguish adaptability and the dynamic nature of knowledge work from the more predictable patterns common to process automation.

Of course the concept of supporting the knowledge worker through adaptive IT systems is not entirely new, and in fact can be traced back to nearly three decades ago and the first emergence of a field called Computer Supported Collaborative Work or CSCW. This field is where both the genesis of this book and some of the original research on computer-aided workflow management can be found. The idea to support knowledge workers without stifling the process innovation and social nature of collaboration, a challenge referred typically as the "socio-technical gap" was a key theme in those years.

Despite the long history of previous efforts, ACM represents a definitive step forward in both promise and results, leveraging advances made in the related fields of content management, Business Process Management, and social computing. The social thread is woven throughout **Taming the Unpredictable**, from chapters such as *Social + Lean = Agile* to the many practical examples in case studies presented.

Similarly, the notion of agility and how to achieve it is a common thread in ACM and is clearly explained in multiple chapters, including *Advantages of Agile BPM* and *ACM and Business Agility for the Microsoft-aligned Organization,* as well as within case studies ranging from how one of the busiest airports in the world leveraged ACM to dramatically improve the turn-around of airplanes, to how a Dutch insurance firm has transformed its claims processing operations.

Covering industries as a diverse as law enforcement, transportation, insurance, banking, legal services, and healthcare, you will inevitability find instructive examples for how to transform your organization.

Whether or not you have previously read *Mastering the Unpredictable, Taming the Unpredictable* presents the logical starting point for understanding how to take advantage of ACM. This is not a book designed simply for the evangelism of ideas, but for delivering actionable advice for embarking on your own journey of ACM-driven transformation.

---

[3] www.adaptivecasemanagement.org

Overview: *Taming the Unpredictable*

Layna Fischer, Future Strategies Inc., USA

Highly predictable work is easy to support using traditional programming techniques, while *unpredictable* work cannot be accurately scripted in advance, and thus requires the involvement of the knowledge workers themselves. The core element of Adaptive Case Management (ACM) is the support for real-time decision-making by knowledge workers.

Taming the Unpredictable presents the logical starting point for understanding how to take advantage of ACM. This book goes beyond talking about concepts, and delivers actionable advice for embarking on your own journey of ACM-driven transformation.

In award-winning case studies covering industries as a diverse as law enforcement, transportation, insurance, banking, legal services, and healthcare, you will find instructive examples for how to transform your own organization.

This important book follows the ground-breaking publication, *Mastering the Unpredictable*[1] and provides important papers by thought-leaders in this field, together with practical examples, detailed ACM case studies and product reviews.

Contents

In our connected world, there is no tolerance for disconnected approaches to work. This is true as much for the people doing the work, as for the people on whose behalf the work is being done. *Dynamic case management* is emerging as the standard for managing work the way we know it must be done—holistically.

But what *is* dynamic (or adaptive) case management? The principal goal of dynamic case management is to manage *all* of the work needed to handle a given case, regardless of type, such as automated work, manual work done by people, ad hoc work, content-intensive work, etc. The result, if fully embraced, is to create a living, breathing network of work that reflects the dynamism of the environments in which it is performed. By exploring ten common questions about case management, this paper will help you to understand what dynamic case management is, and how you can use it to manage your work more effectively—more holistically.

In this chapter the author covers five essential considerations related to the implementation of Adaptive Case Management:

- Why would we need another way than orthodox BPM to deal with business processes?

---

1 Mastering the Unpredictable: How Adaptive Case Management Will Revolutionize the Way That Knowledge Workers Get Things Done, published by Meghan-Kiffer Press, April 2010

- To gain the benefits of ACM does the business have to change its corporate culture or management style?
- How can an ACM solution gain the all-important adoption rates with business users that will make it ubiquitous?
- How can executives offer user empowerment or knowledge worker support and retain control of strategic objectives?
- What are the future opportunities of ACM that would make it an essential and safe business investment?

USER REQUIREMENTS FOR A NEW GENERATION OF CASE MANAGEMENT SYSTEMS
John T Matthias, National Center for State Courts, United States

As courts continue to update their case management system technology, selecting and implementing a highly-configurable case management allows a court to contemplate managing continuous change in the business environment. Selecting a system depends on judging its configurability capabilities, and developing good user requirements depends on capturing process-oriented requirements to take advantage of those capabilities.

A new generation of case management systems (CMS) emerged in 2007, making it necessary for courts to employ a new approach to identifying requirements when they acquire a new CMS. This has strategic importance for courts in providing service to the public and litigants, and for court managers responsible for wise use and increased productivity of judicial and support resources. The new generation of CMSs brings courts a step closer to the promise of court automation, but it requires an investment in thinking about systems differently and willingness to implement changes, tasks which are never easy.

ADVANTAGES OF AGILE BPM
Keith D. Swenson, Fujitsu America Inc., USA

Agile BPM represents the next generation of business process management—designed to flexibly address all types of processes to support all forms of work. It combines traditional Business Process Management (BPM) style predefined processes, along with Adaptive Case Management (ACM) style dynamic work support. Agile BPM is designed to flexibly address all types of processes used to conduct business: structured, unstructured, and hybrid process types to support all forms of work.

In recent years many organizations have come to the understanding that their business processes are proprietary business assets that can yield competitive differentiation and advantage. This recognition has led to the adoption of first-generation BPM technologies to automate fixed, repetitive processes for efficiency and cost-effectiveness. But the next generation of BPM, Agile BPM, will incorporate product capabilities that extend well beyond the system integration and fixed process automation initiatives that characterized first-generation BPM.

SOCIAL + LEAN = AGILE
Dave Duggal, Consilience International LLC, USA

This chapter provides a foundation for understanding Enterprise Agility. It defines the concept as it relates to Information Systems, identifying modern impediments and highlighting the role of empowered business-users as the agents of change. In conclusion, it outlines a solution based on Social and Lean enablement. Enterprise Agility is the measure of an organization's responsiveness to its environment. The more flexible an organization's systems infrastructure, the more readily it can adapt. Enterprise Agility does not entail a reduction in governance or imply that all things are in flux all the time; rather it's about mitigating structural impediments to variance and change.

ACM AND BUSINESS AGILITY FOR THE MICROSOFT-ALIGNED ORGANIZATION
Dermot McCauley, Singularity, United Kingdom

Is *change* the only constant and *unpredictability* a new norm in your organization? For most organizations, the answer is yes. Simply put, business agility is now one of the most important skills of a successful enterprise, public or private. Adaptive Case Management (ACM) is a new approach that makes business agility achievable. What's more, ACM can release the agility in your organization while leveraging familiar Microsoft products. Agility has been thrust more urgently onto "must do" lists everywhere because the challenges organizations face today are more pressing than any they have previously known.

BPM AND ACM
Nathaniel Palmer, WfMC, USA

In the half-century since Peter Drucker first coined the phrase "knowledge worker," its share of the work force has grown considerably, to as much as half of all workers by some measures. So too have grown investments targeting knowledge worker productivity, with global IT spending reaching $4.35 trillion in 2010, according to Global Technology Index author Dr. Howard A. Rubin.

Yet we are far from realizing the level of improvement seen in manual labor over the course of the last century. Traditionally, IT investments targeting business productivity have focused on one of two areas. The first is automation technologies, such as enterprise resource planning (ERP) or the more contemporary technology of business process management (BPM). Those address repeatable, predictable modes of work and are designed to enforce a command and control management model, where efficiency gains are sought through standardizing how work is performed.

CASE MANAGEMENT: ADDRESSING UNIQUE BPM REQUIREMENTS (PRODUCT REVIEW)
Bruce Silver, Bruce Silver Associates, USA

Over the past several years, Business Process Management Suites (BPMS) have matured into powerful platforms for process automation and performance optimization, many configurable by business-friendly process modeling tools. The benefits of BPMS over a wide range of processes—improvements in cycle time, throughput, resource utilization, standardization and compliance, business integration, and end-to-end performance visibility—are well established. However, an important class of business processes has been unable to enjoy them because of the limitations of conventional BPM Suites: *case management*. This report describes the differences between case management and conventional BPM and shows you what to look for in a BPM solution to truly support case management and describes an ACM product offering.

USING THE *AdaPro Workstream Platform* FOR IMPROVING KNOWLEDGE WORK (PRODUCT REVIEW)
Frank Michael Kraft, AdaPro GmbH, Germany

Kraft's chapter *Improving Knowledge Work* in the book *Mastering the Unpredictable* (Kraft 2010) describes how adaptive case management (ACM) can leverage the abilities of individual knowledge workers. It describes a case study of Leona, who works in the engineering department in a company of about 150 employees and how she uses ACM to manage customer service and subsequent development planning and coordination for the phone systems that her company offers. That chapter was without any reference to an individual tool, but described the holistic approach and how individual knowledge workers can draw immediate benefit from it. This chapter now completes the narrative, by showing how the case can be performed by a tool, the AdaPro Workstream Platform.

Award-Winning ACM Case Studies

The Workflow Management Coalition (WfMC) launched the "Adaptive Case Management Global Excellence Awards" this year to recognize case studies illustrating excellence and best practices in ACM use cases. The final winners were announced at the "ACM Live" Virtual Summit as well as published in KMWorld. Submissions were evaluated by a panel of experts, following a scoring model along various metrics, grouping into the three categories of *Innovation*, *Adaptability* and *Impact* (details on the evaluation criteria and the panel of judges can be found at www.adaptivecasemanagement.org).

Award submissions were received from organizations worldwide, with finalists spanning the Americas, Europe, Africa and Asia. Approximately half came from U.S. based firms, with a mix of local government, courts and legal.

UVIT–FINANCIAL SERVICES, NETHERLANDS
Gold Award: Customer Facing
Nominated by EMC Documentum, United States,

The Univé-VGZ-IZA-Trias group (UVIT) is a Netherlands-based insurance company. During recent years, the people of UVIT have been facing increased challenges from Internet insurance competitors. Because of this, a main objective was to automate outdated processes that were primarily paper-based. To do this, UVIT chose EMC Documentum xCP for the creation of a case management application to process claims. The xCP platform is seamlessly integrated with the UVIT capture platform to digitize all incoming mail, especially the vast quantity of doctor and hospital bills customers forward for payment. The system is used by UVIT service, field, and insurance agents, while in the office, at home, and on the road.

ACHIEVEMENT AWARDS GROUP (PTY) LTD, SOUTH AFRICA
Finalist: Customer Facing
Nominated by Pétanque Consultancy (Pty) Ltd, South Africa

Adaptive Case Management (ACM) is imperative in enterprises where the exception to process becomes the process! ACM, a topic widely discussed and analyzed by academics, professionals and IT specialists, is what is needed whenever processes must react to changing and diverse customer or client needs and interactions to ensure efficient and effective outcomes. This means that defined, rigid processes become responsive to circumstances that require fluid processes in order to address specific requirements. Achievement Awards Group (AAG), based in Cape Town, South Africa, recognized the benefits of adopting ACM as a critical success factor in attaining their strategic goals, and in response to their changing, diverse and unique customer requirements. The focus of AAG is to effectively and efficiently attain what they term "Customer Delight".

GLOBAL BANKING FIRM, USA
Finalist: Customer Facing
Nominated by Virtusa Corporation, USA

A global banking firm required a global Payment Exception processing system for their client support managers operating across the globe. The firm has thousands of named users across the globe who manage dispute related enquiries 24x7 at its Call Centers through varied channels – email, phone, SWIFT message, etc. Each site used their own home-grown case tracking solutions, and few sites which had little or no system support beyond spreadsheets. Virtusa partnered with the client, and completely automated their end-to-end business processes and work flow using BPM/Pega technology. Our solution supports all relevant call center services, ticket tracking and integrated investigation capabilities. The solution covers the investigation and dispute management across various products in Cash, Cards, Securities and Trade businesses.

BAA HEATHROW, UNITED KINGDOM
Gold Award: Innovation
Nominated by Pegasystems Inc., USA

At London's Heathrow airport, a new case is created by a system feed every time an incoming plane is registered by air-traffic control, and closes when the plane is en route to its next destination. This event enabled case-management approach to aircraft turn-around has dramatically improved the overall efficiency of operations at Heathrow. This has also projected increase in retail revenues, by allowing passengers on faster-boarding flights to spend more time in the terminal rather than seated in airplanes awaiting take off. The caseworkers in this scenario are the individuals responsible for the timely and efficient turn-around of airplanes, which includes airline teams, stand planners, air traffic controllers, to cleaning crews, and baggage handlers. With the new system in place these stakeholders were empowered with all of the information they need to make the right decisions (including a real-time visualization of planes on the runways) as well as the ability to initiate the right processes, and ultimately to allocate the right resources.

LAKSHMI KUMARAN & SRIDHARAN, INDIA
Gold Award: Legal and Courts
Nominated by Newgen Software Technologies, India

Lakshmi Kumaran & Sridharan (L&S) is a full service Indian legal firm providing advisory, litigation and compliance review services in the domains of Tax, Intellectual Property Rights, International Trade and Corporate laws. The requirements of the client (L&S) could be stated as 'an integrated document management and workflow management system capable of work allocations, knowledge management and assuring clients timely delivery of their cases with excellence'. Further the system should be capable of generating bills and tracking receivables. The ultimate objective of the system is to improve efficiency in service delivery by enabling legal professionals of L&S to work from anywhere outside the office and anytime of the day. This would provide flexibility in working for the professionals as well as guarantee availability of services to clients from any office. The system should also guarantee confidentiality and security of client information.

PINELLAS COUNTY CLERK OF THE CIRCUIT COURT, USA
Silver Award: Legal and Courts
Nominated by Global 360, Inc., USA

Assuring justice for the nearly one million residents in the most densely populated county in the state of Florida requires both personal dedication and the right technology. For the Pinellas County Clerk of the Circuit Court that meant an adaptive case management solution that could serve the Clerk of the Court office, the courts, and the entire Pinellas County judicial system and its citizenry.

Ken Burke, the Clerk of the Court, was originally inspired to implement their Global 360 case management solution by his vision to "go paperless." The solution has achieved that and more for Pinellas. It positions them for compliance with state legislative mandates on e-filing and access to public records, ensures that all court files and supporting documents are securely available within the judicial system, and provides improved collaboration, court file workflow and audit trails. With case management Pinellas have revolutionized how their work gets done. They have created a team-centric environment with collaborative access to court files, documents, tasks, deadlines, and threaded discussions from within a single virtual case folder, using an interface tailored to each individual's roles and privileges. The result is improved service levels and a reliable platform for future growth.

VELINDRE HOSPITAL INTEGRATED CARE PATHWAY

Gold Award: Medical and Healthcare
Nominated by Cardiff School of Computer Science and Informatics, Cardiff University, UK

Teamwork, collaboration and coordination are key aspects of the patient-centric approach taken by modern healthcare. Although many projects have been and are currently being undertaken to improve support for health care professionals, adequate support for teamwork, communication and coordination has yet to be achieved. The delivery of the healthcare service is very challenging as it involves heterogeneous distributed systems, multi-professionals and dependent tasks among each. In addition, the treatment journey of each patient is unique, as decisions are usually made according to several constraints related to the patient, medical condition, patient's choice, available resources and\or feedback from doctors' consultation.

We believe that, in order to provide the required support, it is necessary to explicitly acknowledge the patients' medical state within their treatment journey. This project proposes the use of a Business Process Management (BPM) system that uses associations between patients, health care professionals, and the Integrated Care Pathway (ICP) to provide improved support for healthcare professionals as individuals and as members of integrated care teams.

LOS ANGELES COUNTY INFORMATION SYSTEMS ADVISORY BODY, USA

Gold Award: Public Sector
Nominated by Global 360, USA

Los Angeles County DNA Offender Tracking System (DOTS)

Los Angeles County is one of the nation's largest counties with 4,084 square miles, an area some 800 square miles larger than the combined area of the states of Delaware and Rhode Island. It has the largest population (10,347,437 as of July 2008) of any county in the nation, and is exceeded by only eight states. Approximately 27 percent of California's residents live in Los Angeles County. There are 88 cities within the County, each with its own city council. All the cities, in varying degrees, contract with the County to provide municipal services; 37 contracts for nearly all of their municipal services.

The Information Systems Advisory Body (ISAB) is a multi-agency, multi-jurisdictional policy sub-committee of the Los Angeles County Countywide Criminal Justice Coordination Committee (CCJCC) established in 1982 to oversee the coordination, planning and development of major justice information systems. In response to the passing of Proposition 69, the "DNA Fingerprint Unsolved Crime and Innocence Protection Act," Los Angeles County ISAB developed a plan to implement a centralized, web-based DNA Offender Tracking System (DOTS) using Global 360's case management solution, Case360, as the application platform.

Case Management 101: 10 Things You Must Know About Case Management

Emily V. Burns, Pegasystems, USA

1. EXECUTIVE SUMMARY

In our connected world, there is no tolerance for disconnected approaches to work. This is true as much for the people doing the work, as for the people on whose behalf the work is being done. *Dynamic case management* is emerging as the standard for managing work the way we know it must be done—holistically.

But what *is* dynamic—referred to as *adaptive* in this book—case management? The principal goal of dynamic case management is to manage *all* of the work needed to handle a given case, regardless of type, such as automated work, manual work done by people, ad hoc work, content-intensive work, etc. The result, if fully embraced, is to create a living, breathing network of work that reflects the dynamism of the environments in which it is performed.

By exploring ten common questions about case management, this paper will help you to understand what dynamic case management is, and how you can use it to manage your work more effectively—more holistically. The ten questions and short answers to each are as follows:

What is a case?	The coordination of multiple tasks—planned and un-planned — for a specific purpose. Almost anything can be treated as a case.
Who works on cases?	Everyone.
How do most people manage cases currently?	The preponderance of organizations currently manage cases using multiple systems or manually.
What makes dynamic case management a better approach to managing work than other software-based approaches?	Because dynamic case management manages all of the work needed to handle a given case.
What is the distinction between a case and a process?	A case is the work that needs to be done (think "noun") A process (or processes) is the path (or paths) it takes as the work is completed (think "verb")
What does "ad hoc" mean?	Ad hoc (adv): for the particular end or case at hand without consideration of wider application. From a work perspective, these are the things that are done to handle the peculiarities of each individual case.
What does "design by doing" mean?	Capturing the model for how to do something by extracting it from what you just did.
What does "dynamic" mean with regard to case management?	Work that changes frequently and a system that can accommodate those changes.
What is an "event," and why does it matter?	An "event" is anything that happens. Events matter because they are often responsible for the changes that need to be made to a case.

If I decide to adopt dynamic case management, do I have to scrap my other applications?	No. A good case management platform will allow you to leverage existing systems though a service-oriented architecture.

2. WHAT IS A CASE?

A *case* is the coordination of multiple tasks—planned and unplanned—for a specific purpose. It contains the data about the case. It includes as artifacts all of the content that is required for its processing and that is generated through its processing.

Any of the following could be managed as a case:

- An insurance claim
- A patient
- An event (such as a conference)
- An identity theft investigation
- A project
- An asset, such as a building
- A customer request
- A customer

Cases can exist within cases. For instance, if I manage my customers as cases, for a single customer case, I might also have several sub cases for each account, and nested within one of those cases, perhaps a case for an identity theft investigation.

3. WHO WORKS ON CASES?

Nearly everyone works on cases, whether they define them as cases or not. A better way to understand case management is to think of it as: [*insert your work here*] management. Different people have different levels of involvement in cases, and the type of case will dictate who is involved and in what capacity.

Systems can also perform work on cases, or store and provide data for those cases. In the example of a customer case, most often, the work done on the case will be performed at the "account" level. Most of that work will be performed through automated work done by systems which process the transactions initiated by the customer. But when the customer calls in, the customer service representative (CSR) will perform work on the case, work that is informed by other work that has been performed by the various systems and any people who have been working on the case (the account or the customer). With regard to an identity theft investigation case, that sub-case might be created automatically by a system based on abnormal buying behavior, but most of the work actually done as part of the investigation would be done by CSRs, and/or identity theft specialists.

4. HOW DO MOST PEOPLE MANAGE CASES CURRENTLY?

The answer to this question really depends on how an organization defines its cases. If "case" is defined as *all* of the work that is needed to process a given case, the answer is that most organizations manage different parts of cases in different systems with many parts managed manually, outside of the "systems of record." Most often, this means via email.

The chart below shows responses to a poll conducted by Pegasystems of IT and line of business directors at Fortune 1000 companies to the question "How are you managing your cases?"

How are You Currently Managing Your Cases?

Multiple apps to manage cases, 41%

Manually, 33%

Purchased app to manage cases, 14%

Developed app to manage cases, 25%

There is an emerging understanding of the importance of managing work at a higher level, at the "case" level. This trend is illustrated by the 41 percent of respondents here who indicated that they are currently managing their cases using multiple applications. They are doing this because they see the imperative for managing work more holistically, and yet with prevailing approaches, no single fit-for-purpose application allows them to do this.

5. WHAT MAKES DYNAMIC CASE MANAGEMENT BETTER FOR MANAGING WORK THAN OTHER SOFTWARE-BASED APPROACHES?

As noted, dynamic case management focuses on managing all of the work needed to handle a given case, regardless of type e.g. **automated work, manual work done by people, ad hoc work, content-intensive work**, etc. Other methods for managing work, for example traditional business process management (BPM) or packaged applications focus at a lower level, either managing an individual process (in the case of traditional BPM), or a specific piece of the case (in the case of packaged case applications). Still other approaches focus on the kind of work, supporting only automated work, only ad hoc work or only content-intensive work.

These traditional case management solutions do not really meet the needs of modern organizations. Organizations are looking for case management that allows them to manage all of the work for a case, no matter how broadly or narrowly they define "case." Each of the approaches listed above manages only *some* of the work needed to handle a case. This is the precise reason why such a large proportion of respondents in the poll above are using multiple applications to manage their cases.

Dynamic case management allows you to manage all of the disparate pieces of work being performed on a case, regardless of where (location or application) it is being performed, or by whom (or what) it is being performed. Dynamic case management allows you to create an interconnected web of work, where a change in one piece of work is registered, and if appropriate, responded to by all of the other pieces of work within that network of work—the case.

By managing work more holistically, dynamic case management allows organizations to significantly improve the outcomes of their work—whether service, revenue or risk mitigation. This is achieved by avoiding duplicative work or contradictory work, greatly improving collaboration to harness the full power of people and fully leveraging existing systems. These are all long-standing goals—dynamic case management makes the most significant strides yet in helping organizations to realize them.

Another way of understanding this distinction between dynamic case management and other approaches to work is to understand what dynamic case management is *not*.

- Dynamic case management is not just automating individual processes— even highly complex ones. Dynamic case management puts those processes in the broader case context—current, past and future. This is true whether that context is relative to the customer for whom many pieces of automated work are being performed, or relative to a piece of work that is being done by a CSR that is mostly ad hoc.
- Dynamic case management is not just about supporting ad hoc work. Support for ad hoc work is a crucial feature of any software platform purporting to support dynamic case management—just as is support for automated processing and many other types of work—but it is only one element of supporting dynamic case management.
- Dynamic case management is not just another way of talking about content management. Again, content is very important to case management, but dynamic case management goes far beyond content management in terms of its requirements for process and in terms of creating an intelligent network of work.

The defining trait of software supporting dynamic case management is its ability to support all of the work being done on the case, creating that living, breathing network of work that is the case. Once that network is created, it can be made visible and actionable to all who should have access.

6. WHAT IS THE DISTINCTION BETWEEN A CASE AND A PROCESS?

To put it in the simplest terms:

- A case is the work that needs to be done
- A process is the path or paths the case takes as it is completed

A case is to a process, as a noun is to a verb. All cases have at least one associated process, even if it is not formalized. This is true even if it is the first time a particular type of case has been encountered—as a person works through it, he or she is tracing a process for how to handle that work.

What is important about these two definitions is that they are just that—*two* distinct definitions. Processes and cases exist independently of one another. This is one of the key differentiators between dynamic case management and traditional BPM, because in traditional BPM, the process almost always *is* the "case" (i.e. the work), and cannot be extricated from it.

This separation of case and process is the principal reason dynamic case management is such a powerful tool for managing work. By keeping these two concepts distinct, a case can be managed as a holistic body of work. This is because a case can have multiple processes executed on its behalf—and frequently in parallel—in addition to having multiple sub-cases, each of which might have multiple processes as well. The context of the case dictates the process or processes that are applied to it. As the context of the case changes, so too must the processes being executed on its behalf, whether that is the adaptation of a running process, the initiation of an additional process or the creation of a new process to handle a new situation. With a more traditional BPM approach, each of these processes would be executed as distinct, disconnected processes. With a dynamic case management approach, all of these processes are tightly associated with the case, and the same is true of its sub-cases and their processes.

Thus, rather than treating work as individual, "atomic" processes, case management allows you to get a complete picture of the work being done on the case. The case/sub-case structure provides a way of organizing the work into meaningful units, as illustrated below.

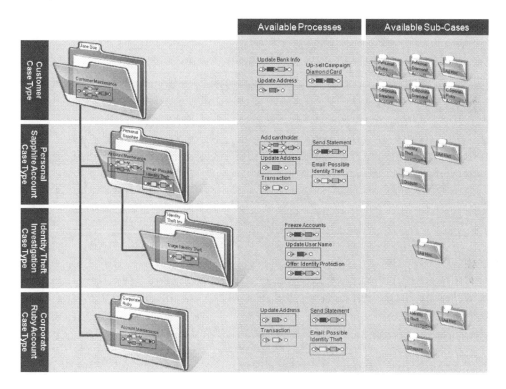

This example shows four open cases that include all of the work associated with this customer, Jane Doe. If there were closed cases, such as closed accounts, these would be part of Jane's case as well. In this example there is the top-level customer case, a sub-case for each of her accounts, another case for an investigation into possible identity theft associated with her personal "sapphire" account. Each of the cases has a process associated with it—two in the case of her personal sapphire account—with the specific step that is being worked on in each process indicated in yellow.

At any time, more processes and more sub-cases might be created, even new ad hoc cases or tasks. The types of processes or sub-cases that might be created for each of these different case types are indicated in the columns showing "Available Processes" and "Available Sub-cases." The processes or sub-cases available will change based on the context of the case, for example, if the identity theft investigation does indicate a breach and require the invocation of the "freeze accounts" process, all of the accounts would be frozen, and many of the available processes and sub-cases for each case type would become unavailable, such as the "transaction" process or any of the "new account" case types.

The power of this approach becomes clear very quickly. A CSR can see all current and prior activity associated with this customer—as well as what will happen in the future based on the current state of the case. With this information, he can reassure Jane that no transactions have occurred, help her to change her user name and password to re-establish security, verify that there have been no attempts to create new accounts or alter existing ones, and offer her additional services that might give her greater piece of mind. Beyond these actions that the CSR can take, this loose network of work makes it possible to create cascading effects, such as locking down all of this customer's accounts or otherwise managing the work for this customer as a cohesive whole.

The compartmentalized nature of the work here—compartmentalized first at the case level, next at the process level, and then at the level of the individual steps within a process—allows for very granular control of who does what work, and who can see what information. While one user might have the ability to see all of these cases, and to initiate any sub-case or process for each, another might have access to only a single sub-case, or perhaps have access to the information about all of the cases, but be able to perform actions on only one of the sub-cases.

This is a marked difference from how work is handled using other approaches. Other approaches will allow the CSR to initiate various processes to alleviate the situation. However, neither he, nor others who might interact with this customer will be able to view that work relative to other work being performed for the customer. This is particularly true when he might want to look at already completed work—invaluable when trying to help the customer to understand what attempted and achieved changes were made to her account.

7. What Does "Ad Hoc" Mean?

Merriam Webster defines "ad hoc" as follows:

Ad hoc (adv): for the particular end or case at hand without consideration of wider application

The term "ad hoc" is tightly associated with case management, because the cases that are referred to by the term "case management" vary significantly from one case to the next. As a result, most will require at least some kind of special treatment "for the particular end or case at hand without consideration of wider application," i.e. ad hoc action.

Ad hoc actions exist along a spectrum. On one end of the spectrum is the ad hoc performance of defined actions, such as starting new sub-cases or processes as discussed in the example above. This type of ad hoc action is typically understood as ad hoc or *dynamic*, case composition. The act of composition could be performed by a person or by a system if rules were defined.

On the other end of the spectrum is the creation of completely new ad hoc work. This is work that has not yet been defined in any way and is created to handle a novel situation (often an exception). Supporting this type of work is one of the key features of dynamic case management software because it is the mandate of case management to support *all* of the work. In the absence of such functionality this type of work gets handled via email, phone calls and meeting—with no record of its performance.

Ad hoc work can be of the "process," or the "case" variety. Support for ad hoc processes means supporting the definition of a new process for an already open case to handle a new situation, or when less is required, simply modifying a running process with an ad hoc change. Users also must be able to create new, ad hoc cases that they can elaborate as the case requires, defining processes on the fly, creating and associating content, assigning tasks to others. In the example above, much of the work done on the "Identity Theft Investigation" case would be this type of work.

8. WHAT DOES "DESIGN BY DOING" MEAN?

"Design by doing" describes the notion of creating the design for something simply by doing it, extracting the model and structure for how to do something based on what was actually done. While the creation of brand new ad hoc work is imperative for case management, the goal of case management is still to standardize as much as possible. Thus, it is important to have a means for migrating ad hoc work from being ad hoc, to being something that can be repeated, evolving greater structure over time. Design by doing is a mechanism for achieving this goal.

No organization wants its people to be in the business of reinventing wheels. A new piece of ad hoc work is only new once. The next time that situation is encountered, whether by the same person or a different one, ideally whatever was learned in the first experience should be applied to the second to ensure consistency and begin building best practices. This is exactly what is facilitated by design by doing.

Design by doing allows end users with permissions to take ad hoc work that they've done and save it as a template that can be re-used in the future, by themselves or by other users. This approach provides a kind of controlled crowdsourcing that allows you to tap into the expertise of your people—and to do so in near real time, with no need to wait for IT to approve of and deploy the changes.

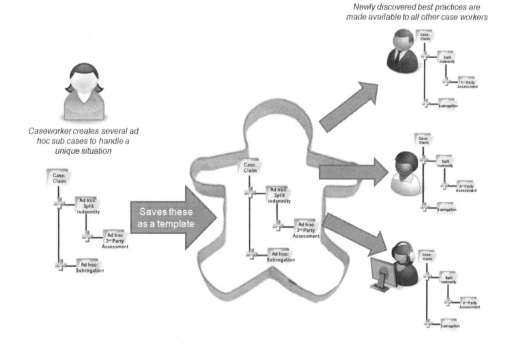

Newly discovered best practices are made available to all other case workers

Caseworker creates several ad hoc sub cases to handle a unique situation

Saves these as a template

With case handling practices constantly evolving, and new exceptions constantly cropping up, this kind of hyper-adaptability is necessary to support case management applications.

9. WHAT DOES "DYNAMIC" MEAN WITH REGARD TO CASE MANAGEMENT?

Dynamic refers both to the kind of work, and the approach being used to handle it.

- With regard to the work, cases are highly dynamic, changing constantly as new information is uncovered, or as new events happen to impact the case. Regardless of the approach for managing cases–manual or software-based–the cases themselves will be dynamic, constantly changing as the case evolves.

With regard to the approach for handling cases, dynamic case management specifically refers to independent software vendors providing software on which to build applications to manage cases. The addition of the word "dynamic" distinguishes this approach from the many point applications that handle specific types of case management (legal case management, benefits case management, claims processing, etc). This new breed of software supporting case management provides cross-industry support to case-management style work wherever it is being done. This is true regardless of whether the people handling the cases refer to them as cases or claims or customers. The functionality is geared toward managing work in a holistic fashion, supporting all of the work necessary to handle a case, whether it is structured, ad hoc or somewhere in between. This software also aims to reflect the dynamic nature of case work. This is true not only for making ad hoc changes, but also for ensuring that where changes impact other work within the case those changes are visible, communicated and the necessary responses carried out—whether by people or by systems. In this way, the dynamic case management approach to work is able to support the dynamic nature of cases.

10. WHAT IS AN EVENT AND WHY DOES IT MATTER?

An "event" is anything that happens. Events matter, because they can impact the way a case is handled. This is true whether you know about the event or not. In the cases where you don't know about an event at the time it occurs, the case handling will still be impacted—it will just be impacted later, requiring re-working or un-doing work.

One of the goals of dynamic case management software is to be able to capture events as they are happening so that case workers or the system can react to them as they occur. The more responsive to events a case management platform can be, the more accurately the work will reflect the real dynamism of the case.

Events can be used to keep people abreast of when something is done on a case by triggering messages to a group of users. Events can provide a means of monitoring and managing a case. For example, when a certain value is reached, such as a cardholder coming within $100 of her credit limit, a notice is sent to her. Within the scenario we have been looking at through the course of this paper, an event that the system might look for is a change to the username or password. If a change has taken place, an email is sent to the customer alerting her of the change and telling her to call if she did not make that change. It might be that if she calls and indicates she did *not* make the change that this event triggers the creation of the identity theft investigation case.

11. IF I DECIDE TO ADOPT DYNAMIC CASE MANAGEMENT, DO I HAVE TO SCRAP MY OTHER APPLICATIONS?

No. The mandate of dynamic case management is to support all of the work needed to manage a case. This includes work that is done by other systems. Dynamic case management allows you to create another layer–a case layer–to help you orchestrate all of the work being done on a case, even if large parts of that work are done or recorded in other systems. Dynamic case management allows you to bring all of the work that is done for a case under one umbrella, to understand it holistically and to handle it as effectively as possible.

It is worth noting that this "case layer" already exists; it exists as armies of people. These people are making truly heroic efforts to try and understand and manage all of the work for their cases. Doing so is a super-human effort. This is why dynamic case management is such a powerful tool—it allows these armies of skilled people to focus on doing the work well, rather than expending inordinate amounts of time trying to understand what the work is and how it relates to other work done for the case.

Considerations for Implementing Adaptive Case Management

Max J. Pucher, ISIS Papyrus, Switzerland

INTRODUCTION

In this chapter I want to cover five essential considerations related to the implementation of Adaptive Case Management:

- Why would we need another way than orthodox BPM to deal with business processes?
- To gain the benefits of ACM does the business have to change its corporate culture or management style?
- How can an ACM solution gain the all-important adoption rates with business users that will make it ubiquitous?
- How can executives offer user empowerment or knowledge worker support and retain control of strategic objectives?
- What are the future opportunities of ACM that would make it an essential and safe business investment?

In my discussions on the subject of process management I frequently refer to scientific evidence as my rationale behind choosing a solution approach for a particular requirement. There are many discoveries and some great research that provide excellent food for thought and decision-making. Many businesses are however not interested in science but only chose solutions that supposedly provide Return-on-Investment or ROI as quickly as possible. I know from experience—and so do you—that a substantial number of those calculations can only be considered illusionary because of the assumptions they are based on. Even if they could be approximately correct they mostly employ a very shortsighted monetary perspective and disregard the long-term effects of 'cost-cutting' with IT and business investments. I see ROI as important but not as all-important for such decisions.

In this chapter I will therefore provide a number of scientific perspectives that provide the school of thought leading to my recommendations for process management. I consider it essential to provide relevant thought and wouldn't dare to make bold and unfounded, all-out claims without proof whatsoever such as providing business agility through a rigidly flowcharted enterprise. I propose further that investments that provide innovation potential and opportunity are more important than cost cutting.

My perspective addresses visionary business managers and executives who are held back by a 'bean counter' mindset in their organizations. While without the promise of immediate ROI the first step into a new process management paradigm could be difficult in terms of finding the right sponsors, the scientific understanding provides enough justification to not miss a substantial opportunity to rid the business from information technology constraints and flowcharting shackles.

I will further add real world examples of globally known businesses where the business concepts I discuss have been successful. Imagine what they could do for your business if you have technology to support them.

WHY WOULD WE NEED ACM FOR BUSINESS PROCESSES?

There is the repeated question why another way to deal with processes than orthodox BPM methodologies might be necessary. While dealing with unpredictability is a valid motivation to use ACM as an additional support system for knowledge workers, ACM offers a much larger benefit for businesses if it is understood and used in the context of Complex Adaptive Systems, social complexity and innovation through emergence.

Understanding Emergence

Beyond 'emergence' being used as a buzzword by some vendors, I propose that we are slowly gaining an understanding of how evolving social complexity drives innovation through emergence, which simplistic methodologies of strategic planning, business and process management fail to take into account. The surprising realization is that social complexity is not an unwanted side effect, but it is actually the only path to achieve continuous innovation. Complexity produces however unease in people who try to exert control. Emergence seems to insult their intelligence when they should understand that emergence created human intelligent capability.

'Strongly emergent properties imply **a global to local causality that is conceptually disturbing** (but allowed!) in the context of conventional science, and is important to how we think about biological and social systems. Emergence is a widely discussed concept in the study of complex systems.

There are two distinct uses of the term. One is used in the form "emergent behavior" to characterize properties of a system that are in some way (possibly in a particular way) not captured by the properties of the parts. The second is a temporal version in which a new kind of system "emerges" at some historical time without in some way being captured in the previously existing systems. *Weak emergence* is considered to be scientifically meaningful as it adheres to the scientific method framework, which describes systems in terms of their parts, whereas *strong emergence* is evoked almost exclusively to suggest that properties of the human mind, specifically "consciousness," may not be understood through science.

The study of emergence is concerned with both physical properties and observations of systems. From an objectivist perspective, it is about how physical properties affect observations. However, because our understanding of systems arises from observations, it is also about how we identify or describe system properties from observations.' (Bar-Yam 2004)

It is the above understanding of emergence that should have profound impact on process management as we clearly observe the social system of a business and try to describe it in various ways—i.e. with process flowcharts. We need to however realize that emergence is a function that can't be causally described or controlled. Let's look at some real-world examples how complexity drives emergence and thus innovation.

The Complexity of Simplicity

While simplification for the user is essential for technology adoption it is the social complexity it enables—mostly through complicated technology—that drives innovation.

For example:

- While information technology builds on the simple binary number system and simple transistor switches the emerging result is one of immense complexity such as the Internet as a whole.
- While I can link up with a large number of individuals using Facebook, it does not mean that I can willingly control the social network that I want to be in and utilize.
- An iPhone is simple to use and it is not a problem that I can't control the necessary technology stack and developer network. We all thrive on the opportunity for innovation it provides.

Technology is however not making our world more complex as many believe, but technology makes the existing complexity visible and usable, while showing us that we can not control it. **A car seems more complicated than a horse**—while a horse is actually complex—but it is easier to control and doesn't require as much care while it is not in use. It is that apparent easier-to-manage 'complicatedness' of a car that executives seek for their businesses. The commonly used coffee making process examples wrongly apply that mechanistic manufacturing mindset to people interactions for simplification and industrialization of processes. To turn people into robots is the grand fallacy of orthodox process management. Even in manufacturing the largest productivity gains are not achieved by automation but by miniaturization and off-shoring to low cost labor locations.

It is thus a substantial misjudgment to see technology as secondary for BPM, because even if you don't use it your competition will, causing a shortening of time scales in the economy, which challenges today's slow strategic planning cycles if you like it or not. It voids the proposition of BPM methodology that process analysis will ensure optimization and innovation in realistic timescales and provide agility through a governance bureaucracy. Rather than relying on analysis, we need to rely on technology empowerment for social business process execution, which is not addressed by today's Social BPM approaches. Real-world social processes emerge and adapt continuously and holistically from all aspects of hierarchy: top-down, bottom-up, inside–out and outside-in.

Complicated versus Complex

What is now the difference between the terms complicated and complex? The English Thesaurus unfortunately treats the terms complex and complicated as synonyms. A system is **complicated** if it is difficult to decompose into constituent parts or if it is difficult to assemble but the function is predictable, i.e. building a car. A system is **complex** if its function emerges from the interaction of its parts but it can't be predicted from their functionality.

Also in mathematics the distinction is not expressed as above. The complexity (or rather complicatedness!) of an entity, defined by Soviet Russian mathematician Andrey Kolmogorov, is a measure of the computational resources needed to specify the object. (Kolmogorov 1963) Also the complicatedness of a business process or work case can be assessed this way by counting, weighting and multiplying the number of interconnected resources, activities and performers. I propose that beyond a certain complexity the analytic approach to process management, using an 'analysis, model, simulate, deploy, monitor, and improve' bureaucracy must fail. Such processes can only be efficiently created and innovated through emergence because they are unpredictable, chaotic and therefore complex.

'Complex Adaptive Systems' (Holland 1980) or CAS describe such structures that cannot be fully decomposed or created by simple assembly. They typically have a chaotic element, meaning that individual outcomes are susceptible to initial conditions. CAS are defined through 'strong emergence' by individually acting entities/agents whose interactions are only loosely coupled. They can be statistically observed but that does not produce data that predict behavior because of the chaotic component. CAS are influenced mostly through the hidden goals of the individual entities and how these entities influence each others behavior without explicitly sharing goals.

While many believe that businesses work best as analyzed and designed structures, I propose that it is the hidden reality of social networks within the organization that actually makes them work and not its reporting lines. And here I see one of the paradoxes of Social BPM. Flowcharts are complicated and social networks are complex adaptive systems. Social networking and BPM automation are at opposite ends of the human interaction spectrum. You can't just link them up and hope they will support each other.

While I tend to rail against bureaucracy I want to point out that hierarchies are a necessity to ensure that the various levels can operate efficiently in their own domain of authority. The highest degree of efficiency comes from division of labor as long as goals and outcomes are aligned by process management rather than top-down, micro-managing activity flows for process owners.

I propose that ACM is an approach that socially empowers business people to perform business process interaction—and not just chats—on well-defined business entities to achieve outcomes, goals, targets and strategic objectives.

DOES A BUSINESS HAVE TO CHANGE ITS STYLE FOR ACM?

Many BPM consultants recommend that a change program and executive sponsorship are essential to deal with the people aspects of process management. Most BPM methodology does not achieve user adoption but requires executive sponsorship to allow people monitoring and process enforcement. It shows a complete lack of understanding of human and workplace psychology by BPM proponents.

I propose that business style trickles down implicitly from the executive and management style and thus it certainly can't be enforced, controlled and not even managed. Style is the uncontrollable outcome of the unpredictable human interactions between the business hierarchies. Employees are like children. When you look they do as you say and when you don't they copy your behavior. So the cheapest and most effective way of changing a business style comes from changing management style. No need to monitor your employees or try to motivate them with monetary rewards.

Obviously a leadership style that thrives through empowered employees, where rules are no more than guidance and where the hierarchy supports autonomy and learning will be able to make the most of ACM or in fact any other software technology. But I propose that there is an unavoidable interaction between business styles and used technology that can help a business to grow without *a priori* changing how a company is managed. Using process monitoring and enforcement sends a clear and loud message about management style to employees that no HR motivation program can undo. Technology can be a change disabler or provide the opportunity for change.

The success and adoption of Internet social networking is simple proof. Or does anyone claim that Facebook change-managed its communities globally?

The Dawn of Social

In 1973 Mark Granovetter started it all with an article in the American Journal of Sociology: 'The Strength of Weak Ties.' (Granovetter 1973) Duncan Watts, Stanley Milgram, and Albert-Laszlo Barabasi created over the next years what is understood today as Social Network Theory. Network Theory has improved our understanding about how revolutions, terrorism, ecology, economics, and organizations work.

Watts found that networks go through a kind of phase transition as they grow outwards and form clusters until they reach a kind of equilibrium of local network communities that are widely linked by people's weak ties. Technology empowerment allows us see them and thus they can grow exponentially. But technology does not change how social networks work, it just makes them broader, more diverse and allows them to evolve faster.

I propose that the same is true for process management and therefore it will have to be technology empowerment and not methodology to bring the benefits of BPM to widespread adoption by people in business. Technology doesn't stop management to employ a BPM mindset, but methodology alone won't improve the execution. Barabasi found that the 'power law' or Pareto principle applies on social interaction, in that only a small percentage of people need to be active and strongly linked for a network to flourish. While most people should belong to the network not all need to be as active. Cities and companies follow the power law as they are social networks. (West 2011)

Influence is Weak and Indirect

Understanding and employing social networking in business is not at all about Enterprise 2.0 in-house Wikis or using Facebook or Twitter for advertising or customer communication. Christakis and Fowler analyzed the impact of social networks in their book *Connected.* (Christakis 2007) The results are counterintuitive because the friends of our friend's friends have through their indirect influence a dramatic effect on our perceptions and perspectives. Now consider how this understanding of social networks should impact business management. The (unknown to you) coworkers of a coworker influence how you do our job more than any management action.

Duncan Watts wrote *Everything is Obvious (Once You Know the Answer)* in which he vividly shows that most of the explanations that we invent to explain something that has happened in social networks are utterly useless. (Watts 2011) He provides a grandstand historic view of why most tries to manipulate human interaction have failed. Watts argues that we do not have usable models of human motivation for individual or collective behavior to predict outcomes of such manipulation. A social network cannot be improved by control or enforcement except for some principal rules. Therefore the BPM control illusion has to be put into the realm of self-fulfilling prophecies. Social Networks can be analyzed once they have formed but they can't be deterministically influenced because they are complex.

The same applies for explanations as to why the stock market moved in a certain direction on any particular day. Why do investors react now to the bad debt in the Eurozone and not several months ago? Why do people riot in London right now and not already years ago? We simply don't know.

Innovation and Change are Natural

In difference to run-of-the-mill consultancy pitch, I propose that the most essential element of process management is **not cost optimization but innovation**. Change is not an afterthought. Many propose that they can control or manage change/innovation through rigid processes. The opposite is the case. Change can only be promoted by offering opportunity and is mostly hindered by controlling it. *People do not resist change or innovation, but they resist the insecurity created by change beyond their influence.* Artificially enforced organizations resist change, because people are insecure in their role in the structure. Social networks grow and change without anyone promoting that in particular.

Take for example product innovation from Apple and its iOS developer community that is driven by highly motivated individuals who thrive on autonomy. There is no change methodology that forces individuals to do anything except for some guiding rules. Their innovation is in principle just gradual improvement like all of Apple's successes. One product may be radically new, but it represents a gradual improvement of the Apple mobile ecosystem **if it finds adoption** with consumers. Even Steve Jobs did not all-out invent a single thing. He just took existing products (PCs, MP3 players, Napster, laptops, phones, tablets, and now even the Cloud) and made them incredibly user-friendly and appealing. Jobs knows simplicity gains adoption and that this needs complex technology. If you want to turn your business into an innovation powerhouse, process creation and innovation must become simple for the business performer. Simplifying (meaning dumbing down) and enforcing process execution will just ruin people motivation.

Change happens naturally and always as long as the environment is friendly. If there is enough social pressure, dramatic changes such as revolutions happen in unfriendly environments too. Even the Arab Spring thrives on mobile and social networks, so why is it that technology is so important and not some top-down methodology?

The Nature of Technology

Economist W. Brian Arthur discusses in his book 'The Nature of Technology' the core principles of technology innovation from an economy perspective. (Arthur 2009) Technological progress is linked to discovering the workings of natural phenomenon and putting them to use in ways that are desirable to people. Beyond the invention of the wheel, virtually all technology is complicated, meaning the functionality is progressively building on previous discoveries. Once we reach a certain level of component inter-dependency the system becomes complex and unpredictable. We are no longer able to even imagine how the numerous discoveries will together form the basis for further innovation. The combinations of technology are not just driven by additive functionality but by applying **intuitive human creativity** to the possible re-combinations. The technological advance as it impacts the social landscape becomes complex and goes through a phase transition of complexity. The system becomes one of individually acting agents and must be considered a complex adaptive system. Geoffrey West (et.al.) discovered that once the growth benefits level off, a new level of innovative opportunity must form or the system (city or business) stagnates and crashes. (West 2011)

Apple could not predict which Apps the now 300.000 developers for the AppStore would develop. They just created the infrastructure for a huge, fairly open social network of developers and customers, only providing the security for money and information. They also made it simple and cool-looking on the surface, while the underlying technology is immensely complicated. But the AppStore ecosystem and rule set **does not prohibit social complexity**. It is now obvious as a hindsight that 300.000 motivated programmers would easily outsmart those rigidly organized Microsoft software labs that don't really listen to consumers. The Appstore was the innovation phase transition that enabled Apple to jump to the next level of growth.

How Can ACM Become Ubiquitous Social Business?

All we have to do now is to follow the above line of thinking and learn to distinguish between businesses that thrive on repeated innovation phase transitions through social complexity or are dominated by bureaucracy and thus destined to fail. (West 2011)

The fallacy of using BPM for human interaction lies in trying to replicate the proven benefits of process automation in manufacturing as defined by Taiichi Ohno and his Toyota Production System. (Ohno 1988) In manufacturing the results of the process are physically visible and simply verifiable because costs can be simply attributed to items and people working on them. Quality and output are not abstract as for human interactive service tasks, where it is defined by human perception and the measurable response (sales figures) of the customer to process changes can be delayed for months.

In difference, the cost and quality aspects of knowledge work and innovation are neither simply measurable nor can't they be predefined. There is little to no opportunity in human interaction and decision making for automation and thus the reduction of cost. Rigidly defining work processes does not free a knowledge worker to perform more important tasks, but it reduces autonomy and the ability to deal with unexpected events. More time spent on an activity may not be waste but essential for effectiveness and not less steps but additional performers may be needed to apply their knowledge for problem resolution. The goals of stakeholders are spread through all business hierarchies. There is also a lot less opportunity for the motivating team aspects in today's distributed organizations.

Tom Davenport (Davenport 2005) proposes four different process types:

- Transactional processes involve routine work; formal rules, procedures and training; and little need for worker discretion or information.
- Integrated processes involve systematic, repeatable work that relies on formal processes, methodologies or standards, and depends on integration across functional boundaries.
- Expert processes involve judgment-oriented work that relies heavily on individual expertise or the experience of "expert performers."
- Collaborative processes involve improvisational work and deep expertise across functions. These processes depend heavily on the fluid deployment of flexible teams exploring multiple opportunities.

I consider these process classifications as interesting but not helpful in defining how to solve process management needs. It does not indicate that four types of systems are required. All work being performed as social interaction can enter and leave any of these quadrants over time or even inhabit more than one at any time. Different process types can be linked together by various goals and events. A business needs **thus a single process collaboration platform** and not several.

A Process AppStore or Repository

Imagine such a single platform to be a 'Process AppStore' (a.k.a. repository) for your business that allows business people to simply create and adapt resources (content), activities, goals, targets, rules and data connectivity from a library of easy-to-use templates that they can more or less recombine at will. If it makes you happy, performers can receive guidance from a Process Center of Excellence coach. It is, however, no *Master Control Program* as in the movie Tron but a support function that gives recommendations.

Let me reiterate that (process) empowerment is not about anarchy but mostly about well-defined authority, goals and means! The ACM platform must foremost support the transparent definition of those three aspects for each performer (group) in the business hierarchy.

If we consider a business and its processes a complex adaptive system, simple (sub-)processes can be designed and more complex, collaborative ones do better emerge. Can we assume that self-organization and emergence will work for even higher process complexity? We can't predict which processes will evolve in which way. One can however apply complexity metrics and monitor which process types evolve by themselves and which stagnate. (Kolmogorov 1963) It is possible to compute complexity metrics by identifying the number and interactions of:

- Goals and milestones
- Gateways, rules, and activities
- Data elements and service interfaces
- Content and content elements
- Involved performers and departments
- Estimated events

All numbers can be intuitively weighted according to their ease-of-change and dependencies and multiplied to produce an overall process complexity value. Over time it will become a helpful indicator as to which processes need to be reconsidered and possibly simplified. It is important to consider how process segments are organized, linked and reused. I propose that this has to be organized and managed by referencing business objectives and process goals to be understandable and usable by performers.

The Language of Process

The enable empowerment and social collaboration a common process language has to be established through a **Business Architecture (BA).** It defines value streams that follow strategic objectives, operational targets, and process goals. A BA doesn't have to be an enterprise-wide effort but can be dedicated to a single end-to-end process. It provides the process framework and ontology (language terms) that the business will speak, but does not nail down rigid processes that assume outcomes. Technology empowerment for adaptive processes by means of a BA reduces thus term confusion, planning depth, late monitoring of outcomes, and time scales. Once a BA focuses on the process language for people interaction and not process standardization it improves people skills and knowledge variety and diversity.

Also Michael zur Mühlen promotes the necessity for the definition of a vocabulary or terminology. It starts with capabilities, leading to resources, which are assigned to activities and performers, translating into objectives, goals, entities, methods, and user roles. (Mühlen 2009)

A great architecture is therefore not bothered by changes in business or in its environment. The architecture enables the performers in a business to act adaptive, but the architecture itself must not be changed all the time as it otherwise fails to provide the stable framework that supports adaptability.

Architecture for a business follows the same principles as that of a building. Architecture is not construction drawings and it doesn't describe how the bricks are being laid or the steel is being welded. These are considered known skills. A well-designed building improves however communication and ensures security and safety. It reduces operating expenditure by being energy efficient. It doesn't describe exactly which work steps people will perform in which room. Here I disagree with zur Mühlen and propose that process flows should not be a part of architecture.

I propose that it is not the process that produces value, but people even if they are guided by a process goal (not a flow) to achieve an outcome. So architecture must not get involved in rigidizing processes, but simply ensure that the architecture models empower management, employees and customers to communicate by means of the architecture entities.

The core elements of Business Architecture:

- **Business Strategy:** strategic objectives that are either linked to programs if new or linked to Business Capabilities. Operational business targets can be linked but they can also provide independent guidance to decision makers, because there is no simple cause/effect chain available. Not every objective produces a directly measurable KPI, because they are conflicting (investment versus cost).
- **Business Capabilities:** describe customer-facing services, supply chain services, core business services, and business management services. They basically can be seen as a grouping of end-to-end processes into so called value streams.
- **Organizational Structure**: defines the relationships among process owners, capabilities and business units. I propose that the business units are empowered to execute processes to goal-fulfilment and targets as they see fit, enabling adaptive innovation and optimization without the need for a central bureaucracy.
- **Business Entities**: for example customer, order, and product data and their relationships. These entities are required in the ontology to define goals, rules, activities and outcomes.
- **Process Goals:** assigns processes to process owners and describes outcomes, as well as authority and means (budgets) to achieve them. Process are defined through goals, roles, resources, rules, but should not contain a flow as part of the architecture as it is too limiting. The Process owner in the business is responsible for flow, activities and tasks. They can change at any time, while goals and outcomes are fairly stable and handle the process handover and completion.
- **Business Content:** 'There is no process without content and content without process is waste.' (Pucher 2001) The inherent link to captured (inbound) and generated (outbound) business content to data and process is still not a subject for general BPM consideration. Even business experts seem to believe that there are only a few special

processes that deal with content and they can be 'simply' done in an ECM system. That is another grand fallacy of BPM.

CAN ACM EMPOWERMENT HELP EXECUTIVES TO ACHIEVE OBJECTIVES?

There are many reasons to consider BPM. Many business executives want to achieve a business transformation that restructures the entire process chain. Process owners who lack the business knowledge look for specific process templates to be implemented quickly and simply. Business management hopes to increase process agility while IT wants to use BPM as the front-end to its SOA-based messaging services to modernize applications. All these desires are understandable but they are misguided by BPM marketing.

Executives who try to use BPM methodology to turn a business into a predictable entity run by bean counters suffer from what economist Tim Harford calls 'The God Complex.' Harford writes for Financial Times the 'Undercover Economist' column. He, too, describes the economy as a complex adaptive system that can't be analyzed and fully understood. He proposes that the economy is far too complex and unpredictable to be controlled by expert opinions and says: "I'd like to see many more complex problems approached with a willingness to experiment." In his latest book *Adapt: Why Success Always Starts With Failure* he suggests that we need to learn to make better mistakes by improvising rather than plan. (Harford 2011)

Business Value through Empowerment

Edward Deming was a firm promoter of iterative and people oriented management and wrote in a letter to Peter Senge: 'Our prevailing system of management has destroyed our people. People are born with intrinsic motivation, self-respect, dignity, curiosity to learn, joy in learning. The forces of destruction begin with toddlers—a prize for the best Halloween costume, grades in school, gold stars—and on up through the university. On the job, people, teams, and divisions are ranked, rewarded for the top, punished for the bottom. Management by Objectives, quotas, incentive pay, business plans, put together separately, division by division, cause further loss, unknown and unknowable.'

Peter Senge, the author of *The Fifth Discipline: The Art and Practice of the Learning Organization*, (Senge 2006) responded as follows: 'I believe that the prevailing system of management is, at its core, dedicated to mediocrity. If forces people to work harder and harder to compensate for failing to tap the spirit and collective intelligence that characterizes working together at its best.' (Larman 2003)

There are however those who claim that a BPM governance bureaucracy represents process maturity and supposedly provides business agility. As discussed before, while one can formalize change processes, one cannot enforce innovation. BPM must be no more than the organizing context on top of the adaptive complexity that the economy and the business represent. Focusing purely on achieving certain numbers or Key-Performance-Indicators reduces the ability to execute as needed. There is no guaranteed causal logic structure that ensures long-term business success. KPIs are late observations that are mostly not causally connected to previous actions in processes.

Empowering people for decision making enables innovation and dynamics. Businesses show the most innovation and dynamics when they are operating at what Stuart Kauffman first called 'the edge of chaos', that phase-transition from an unordered to an ordered structure. (Kauffman 1989) The social dynamics are only productive if they are sufficiently guided by goals. Organize them too strictly by encoding too many processes and too many decisions in flows and rules and you kill the ability to innovate.

Large enterprises try to control their processes because they are wading up to their waists in swamps of unstructured information. Data, content and processes are fragmented across many silos and departments. The business value inherent in those information assets can't be realized unless they are put into business context. Getting the right information consistently to the right people at the right time across the enterprise means to put them into context with business processes. That cannot be done through methodology but only through technology. To achieve their goals, process performers need to be empowered to access these information assets for decision making in a process context. Rigidly planning processes kills decision making.

Planning Creates Risk

Considering the above there are few who realize the true connection between planning and risk. Most people will say without thinking that more planning reduces risk. That is however not correct at all. For non-manufacturing processes **it is the planning that creates the risk.** Risk assessment is not just about reducing an arbitrary risk of the unexpected, but about creating awareness what risks are being created by the plan. The more assumptions a plan makes the more risky it is. The deeper the planning hierarchy is, meaning the level of dependencies of planned outcomes, the riskier a plan is. The more time passes between planning and completion, the more risk the plan creates, mostly because the target context will change whether one plans for it or not.

Like many others, Michael zur Mühlen uses coffee making processes to illustrate flowchart design benefits and likens them to engineering drawings that every engineer understands. (Mühlen 2009) These examples are not only lacking but the success of Nespresso shows that the simplification of (coffee making) processes has to go in hand with user empowerment. Consumers can chose from many types of coffee machines and coffees. It is important to remark, that both Apple and Nespresso are not cheap brands and that there are more people who don't like the products than who do. I for my part like Nespresso and do not consider Starbucks beverages to represent coffee. Both are valid processes. There are **no standard processes that are low-cost and right** for everyone.

One must say that business processes operate in a complex environment and making coffee is not even complicated and that's where the arguments fail. BPM defined processes are no more than 'repeatable plans' that make the risky assumption to guarantee outcomes. The process analysis uses however ambiguous 'terms' to describe the plan, carrying over the risk of term confusion. Complex rule sets create the risk of missed event/context mismatches and poor term linkage. New data remains unconsidered. Process monitoring uses a measurement assumption the increases the risk of self-fulfilling prophecies. Each rigidly defined process increases the risk of business execution not producing intended outcomes. Each task- or sequence-enforcing process flowchart hinders the evolution of innovation from where the knowledge resides: at the performer and customer.

Bursts of Innovation

While Charles Darwin surmised that evolution was slow and gradual, he did, however, not propose that the pace of change was constant, as he could not find related fossil evidence. In 1972, evolutionary scientists Stephen Jay Gould and Niles Eldredge proposed a *punctuated equilibrium*, meaning that long phases of genetic stability were interspersed by rapid bursts of change that resulted in new species. (Gould 1972)

In 1995 Jeff Sutherland and Ken Schwaber presented a formalized Scrum process for the first time to the public. (Sutherland 1995) According to Sutherland, Scrum builds on the theory of Complex Adaptive Systems, 'to deal with physical reality where things are often not linear, not simple, and not predictable. Scrum—by virtue of its iterative and incremental nature—mimics the biological instinct to survive through constant adaptation.'

Sutherland says, 'When enough mutations occur in multiple parts of an organism, the system shifts to a higher plateau of functionality.'

ACM supports a Scrum-like Business Management Approach

While the use of ACM does not require a change in management style it is worthwhile to consider what benefits and opportunities it can provide for bringing management style into the 21st century.

Steve Denning is a bestselling author and thought leader in leadership and innovation. In *The Leader's Guide to Radical Management* (Denning 2010), he shows that the future of management needs five fundamental shifts in terms of the firm's goal, the role of managers, the way work is coordinated, and turning from cost to values and from command to conversation. Denning says: 'Traditional management has failed. To deal with a radically different marketplace and workplace, today the whole organization must be focused on creating a stream of additional value to customers through continuous innovation. This reinvention of management reflects an application of Agile/Scrum thinking to the whole organization.'

Scrum was originally defined as a project management approach for very skilled people who don't excel under strict guidance and are unable to utilize their creative abilities. What is interesting is that Scrum principles are virtually identical to the requirements of empowerment: authority, goals and means!

- Define work goals clearly by the intended outcome for the user.
- The team interacts and discusses results with the user not management.
- Teams are autonomous in work estimation, assignment and measurement.
- Management doesn't interrupt the team during a work cycle.
- Management provides means and removes obstacles.

Nothing in the above definition indicates that this will only work for software development or engineering projects.

THE FUTURE OPPORTUNITIES OF ACM

Although BPM methodology can supposedly improve processes without software tools, most organizations leverage a substantial amount of technology in support of it:

- Business process analysis (BPA)
- Automated business process discovery (ABPD)

- Business activity monitoring (BAM)
- Business Intelligence (BI)
- Business rule management systems
- Complex-event processing
- Process optimization/simulation
- BPM suites (BPMSs)
- Application integration
- Service-oriented architecture (SOA)
- Business content creation and capture
- Collaboration tools
- Case management
- Enterprise 2.0 Social Networking

While it seems plausible that several software products offer best-of-breed special functionality that are then integrated, I propose that the cost and limitations of software integration and change management severely impact the achievable dynamics and adaptive nature of processes. The needed IT involvement dramatically reduces the adoption of such capabilities by business users, which in turn limits the achievable social dynamics for innovation.

Therefore I propose that ACM is not just another technology stack to be added to the software portfolio. ACM will only provide the change dynamics beyond knowledge work if it is the main platform that business uses to execute all of their processes. That makes it more difficult to sell as especially IT resists software that seems to duplicate existing functionality. ACM is therefore driven by business needs and not IT-department software portfolio planning.

The Definition of ACM

In 2009 at a WfMC (Workflow Management Coalition) meeting, the attendees decided to name such a Scrum-like approach to process management *Adaptive Case Management*. (Pucher 2009) As I am not a friend of three-letter-acronyms I often refer to it as **Adaptive Process** especially when used for more than support of knowledge work. While ACM is about business process management it follows the concepts of Agile and Scrum versus the Tayloristic control illusion of orthodox BPM. ACM is naturally AGILE process management without the need for a change management bureaucracy. The difference is not just product functionality but in management concepts and therefore fundamental.

ACM empowers the executive to bring out the best in his/her organization without enforcing processes or changes in company culture! By clearly defining and verifying objectives, process goals and outcomes, ACM creates opportunity and potential for change and innovation that then can be utilized by any management approach. ACM will be immensely beneficial to knowledge workers regardless. If ACM is used with orthodox top-down management concepts the full potential benefits won't be realized, but at least it will reduce the amount of bureaucracy needed to make BPM work.

It pays to follow Edward Deming's advice: **'Don't optimize, synthesize!'**

I see the following capabilities as essential to enable the future opportunities for an ACM platform.

- Provide an ecosystem that enables structured (business data) and unstructured (content) information to members of structured (business) and unstructured (social) organizations to securely execute – with knowledge INTERACTIVELY gathered in previous processes – structured (process) and unstructured (case) work in a transparent and auditable manner (Pucher 2009).

- Provide a modelling repository that allows the explicit definition of the aforementioned Business Architecture ontology.
- Allow the instantiation of business entities from the ontology with (SOA or similar) data links to backend silos.
- Empower business users to create and adapt processes from repository components as they perform the process.
- Organize processes and their resources and tasks around process goals and store those as templates.
- Enable the definition of natural language rules by business users based on the ontology in the repository.
- Enable the creation of business resources (content and data) from the repository by the business user.
- Enable the capture, classification and data extraction of incoming business content from any channel.
- Allow execution-time delegation of tasks to authorized performers from a skill database.
- A real-time trained pattern matching capability for complex events and their business context based on the ontology.
- Offer a real-time view of all processes as either task lists or graphs that can be manipulated by authorized users.
- Provide the ability to store runtime created processes as templates for future use to fulfil defined process goals and customer outcomes.

Human Decision-Making uses Patterns

One key element of ACM deserves detailed discussion. The support for real-time decision-making has to be seamlessly linked into any process as needed and thus can't be realized using separate software products but needs a homogenous process platform with a common architecture repository.

Real-time decision-making could use data from business intelligence that operates on statistics but that information is needed in a process context. Only through a repository it can link the data with current process and transactional data that are then used by expert performers to influence process execution. **The proposal that process relevant decision-making could be automated in standalone rule systems ought to be seriously doubted.**

Real-time decision-making requires a snapshot of relevant information at a certain point in time related to the current business context. That time is usually marked through some event that happens in a particular context. Statistical business intelligence data are quite useless as they lack the timing information and they come too late.

How do then humans come to decisions? Apart from the emotional, intuitive aspect, it is accepted science that the human brain doesn't use Boolean logic, but utilizes pattern recognition. Large recognition clusters in the brain link up sensory information to produce correlating patterns of perception. These patterns are not created but are trained through the repeating observation of similar patterns. These patterns are considered relevant when they appear in context to a particular event trigger, which is also identified by a pattern. I propose that the same approach is desirable for identifying business patterns and have developed software to achieve that. (Pucher 2006)

One of the main issues of applying simplistic rules to such events in the hope of using them to identify such patterns is the misunderstanding that correlation is causation. Just because data points correlate in some manner does not mean that they are causally related. It is already difficult to identify correlation from business intelligence because the time slices may be nowhere enough synchronized to allow the assumption of correlation. But even if data points actually correlate it is not easy to decide on which causes which or if they have a common cause and what that could be.

Only pattern matching mechanisms that function in real-time environments stand even a chance to discover relevant data patterns. They just ought to trigger users to judge any recommendations before they act rather then assuming causation and trigger actions blindly.

I thus propose that real-time pattern matching mechanisms will be essential to provide additional guidance to business users where rigid flows can't be used to control process execution.

Gartner Group: Intelligent Business Operations

As a final element of consideration I want to point at an interesting overlap with my definition of ACM and recent Gartner Group research. It is not just about the expansion of BPM into dynamic or adaptive capabilities but the focus is on real-time process creation and adaptation.

In *The Trend towards Intelligent Business Operations* Gartner analysts propose that businesses are starting to build more intelligent facilities for supporting business operations. (Gartner 2011)

Gartner says 'that while most intelligent business operations (IBO) running today are relatively simple and localized to a few processes they are being expanded to provide holistic situation awareness for decision support by correlating event data from multiple internal or external sources. A rule engine or statistical analytic tool may be incorporated to complement the BAM or event-processing platform, or the process orchestration or workflow engine.'

This follows Gartner's most recently updated definition of BPM that emphasizes process visibility, accountability and adaptability as new measures of operational excellence. They propose that the leading tools make the visible process model executable and adaptable. The graphical model metadata are interpreted and execute the process. I propose that in ACM there is no distinct design time, but all models can be adapted by authorized users at any time during execution or reused from previously executed processes.

Gartner also says that 'some leading-edge vendors have *recently* added event-processing platforms, where capabilities are integrated and share a common meta model so that all roles—business and IT—involved in the process improvement life cycle use consistent composition and development tools, metadata repositories and administration facilities.' I fully agree while I just don't see it as a 'recent' development. (Pucher 2006)

Businesses could implement intelligent business operations by mix and match of products using a general-purpose SOA and application integration infrastructure. The technological effort will seriously hinder adaptive capability. The question is if such a technology can provide the frontend for business users that will facilitate adoption and thus the social complexity for innovation. From my perspective IBO is just another name for ACM.

CONCLUSION

I propose that it is important for executives to consider the scientific evidence of Complex Adaptive Systems, the benefits of Systems Thinking, the heuristics of human decision-making, as well as workplace psychology in terms of people motivation for process innovation rather than purely financial motives.

Asking for simple out-of-the-box technology to analyze standardized, repeatable flowcharts is exactly the wrong thing to do. It kills the innovation capability inherent in your business because it disables social complexity.

Like Michael zur Mühlen, (Mühlen 2009) I came to the conclusion that process modeling requires more a business (organizational) perspective than a BPMN-flow perspective, while we disagree on the detail of process planning. In difference, I propose to use GOALS as the main structuring concept of a process or case. It does not only structure the process dependencies, but it also directly defines the WHY and measures completion. It is right there in the process, visible for everyone.

Let me quickly summarize:

- Autonomous goal fulfilment ensures outcomes and motivates users in difference to mindless flow-enforcement.
- Reusable, goal-organized sub-processes and resources enable social complexity and thus foster continuous innovation where the knowledge resides – by the performers during execution.
- Rather than end-of-flow handoffs, I propose (sub-)goals to keep the process paths asynchronous through events. They can also be simply used across process/case boundaries.
- There is no longer a happy path, but simply fulfilled or unfulfilled goals, with the opportunity of alternative goals defining the happy path on the fly.
- All real world processes are event-driven and not flows and therefore an event should never throw an exception, but be simply dealt with through a new (sub-)goal.
- Process patterns linked to events are used to select the best execution and not complex rule sets that are difficult to analyze and maintain.
- Rules are used primarily as so-called boundary rules to ensure compliancy where necessary. Each unnecessary rule produces according to Systems Thinking a rule-beating effect by users that increases execution cost.
- Customers (internal and external) should be included in the process execution to immediately rate perceived outcome and define success.
- All performers and stakeholders can rate the process resources as to ease-of-use and how well they fulfill or achieve their interests.

By means of the above capabilities, the process technology of an ACM platform must offer end-user process simplicity for all hierarchy levels that provides the rate of adoption needed for social complexity.

While 'simple for the business user' means to provide understandable, reliable, predictable, repeatable, inter-connectable and low-unit-cost process resources it is wrong to assume that therefore all end-to-end processes must be optimized for lowest cost and rigidly encoded to fulfill the above criteria. A platform such as ACM provides the infrastructure that ensures simple, reliable and predictable use of process resources. It empowers people to embrace socially emerging complexity by creating and using process building blocks that they can assemble at will. The key to success is however user guidance, process transparency and performer ratings which allow the selection and reuse of goal-achieving activities. It is more effective to simply let business execute processes at will and then guide it by adding process goals and targets as organizing principles.

ABOUT ISIS PAPYRUS

ISIS Papyrus Software was founded in 1988 and was first to introduce in 2001 a consolidated process/case management platform with embedded business content capture and creation. More than 2000 businesses use ISIS Papyrus solutions and 250 the Papyrus Process and Content Platform. While Papyrus supports BPMN since 2009 as an alternative way to create, view and adapt processes, its core process model is real-time adaptable and subject-driven through state-event controlled business entities.

The Papyrus Platform provides the most complete ACM framework of the marketplace that can be used to implement socially empowered processes in a very short time. It provides embedded natural language business rules, user-trained pattern matching for complex business events, goal-oriented process/case design for the non-technical business user. The Papyrus EYE user interface enables freely-definable interaction for each user role in the browser and for mobile technology. Inbound and outbound content management are tightly integrated and managed through the same deployment model from the repository.

The Papyrus UTA User-Trained Agent is a patented pattern matching capability that monitors user activity related to business event patterns and recommends goal-fulfilling processes and activities to business users.

REFERENCES

(Arthur 2009) W. Brian Arthur, *The Nature of Technology: What it is and how it evolves.* Free Press (August 11, 2009)

(Bar-Yam 2004) *A Mathematical Theory of Strong Emergence Using Multiscale Variety* by Y. Bar-Yam – 2004 Wiley Periodicals, Inc.

(Christakis 2009) Nicholas A. Christakis and James H. Fowler, *Connected, The Surprising Power of Our Social Networks and How They Shape Our Lives* Little, Brown and Company (September 28, 2009)

(Davenport 2005) Thomas H. Davenport, *Thinking for a Living: How to Get Better Performances and Results from Knowledge Workers*, Boston: Harvard Business School Publishing, 2005.

(Denning 2010) Stephen Denning, *The Leader's Guide to Radical Management*, Josey-Bass 2010

(Gartner 2011) W. Roy Schulte, Janelle B. Hill, Nigel Rayner, *The Trend towards Intelligent Business Operations* - June 24th, 2011, ID:G00213721

(Gould 1972) Stephen Jay Gould, *Punctuated Equilibrium*, Harvard University Press, 2007

(Granovetter 1973) Mark Granovetter, *The Strength of Weak Ties* in American Journal of Sociology, 1973

(Harford 2011) Tim Harford, *Adapt: Why Success Always Starts With Failure,* Little, Brown (2 Jun 2011)

(Holland 1995) *Hidden Order: How Adaptation Builds Complexity.* New York: Helix Books (Addison Wesley) 1995

(Lansing 1980) J. Stephen Lansing, *Complex Adaptive Systems*, Annual Review of Anthropology, 2003.

(Kauffman 1989) S. Kauffman, *Principles of adaptation in complex systems* in Lectures in the Sciences of Complexity (E.Stein, ed). Addison-Wesley

(Kolmogorov 1963) A. N. Kolmogorov, *On tables of random numbers*, The Indian Journal of Statistics, Series A, Vol. 25, Part 4 (1963)

(Larman 2003) Larman, Craig and Basili, Vic, *Iterative and Incremental Development: A Brief History.* IEEE Computer, June 2003, pp. 47-56

(Milner 1989) Robin Milner, Joachim Parrow and David Walker, *Calculus of Mobile Processes,* 1989

(Mühlen 2009) http://www.slideshare.net/mzurmuehlen/primitives-and-design-patterns-for-topdown-soa-implementations

(Mühlen 2010) http://www.slideshare.net/mzurmuehlen/making-things-simpler-how-primitives-help-integrate-bpm-and-enterprise-architecture

(Ohno 1988) Taichi Ohno, *Toyota Production System: Beyond Large-Scale Production.* Productivity Press; 1st Edition (March 1, 1988)

(Pucher 2001) Max J. Pucher, http://isismjpucher.wordpress.com/quotes/

(Pucher 2006) Max J. Pucher, US Patent Application 20080114710 - Method For Training A System To Specifically React On A Specific Input http://www.patentstorm.us/applications/20080114710/description.html

(Pucher 2009) Max J. Pucher, http://isismjpucher.wordpress.com/2009/12/04/adaptive-process-defined/

(Senge 2006) Senge, P. M., The Fifth Discipline: The Art and Practice of the Learning Organization, Revised Edition. New York, Doubleday.

(Sutherland 1995) J. Sutherland, A. Viktorov, and J. Blount, *Adaptive Engineering of Large Software Projects with Distributed/Outsourced Teams*, in International Conference on Complex Systems, Boston, MA, USA, 2006.

(Watts 2011) Duncan Watts, *Everything is Obvious (Once You Know the Answer)*, Crown Business (March 29, 2011)

(West 2011) Geoffrey West, The surprising math of cities and corporations. http://www.ted.com/talks/geoffrey_west_the_surprising_math_of_cities_and_corporations.html

User Requirements for a New Generation of Case Management Systems

John T Matthias, National Center for State Courts, United States

As courts continue to update their case management system technology, selecting and implementing a highly-configurable case management allows a court to contemplate managing continuous change in the business environment. Selecting a system depends on judging its configurability capabilities, and developing good user requirements depends on capturing process-oriented requirements to take advantage of those capabilities.

THE VALUE OF AN ADAPTIVE CASE MANAGEMENT SYSTEM

A new generation of case management systems (CMS) emerged in 2007, making it necessary for courts to employ a new approach to identifying requirements when they acquire a new CMS. This has strategic importance for courts in providing service to the public and litigants, and for court managers responsible for wise use and increased productivity of judicial and support resources.

Software technology since its invention has been searching for the "holy grail": methods to develop systems for judicial and support staff that (1) fulfill the mission of judges and support staff for the courts; and (2) evolve using skills of business analysts (rather than IT professionals) to adapt to the continuous changes in the business environment. The new generation of CMSs brings courts a step closer to the promise of court automation, but it requires an investment in thinking about systems differently and willingness to implement changes, tasks which are never easy.

Customization of systems is replaced by configuration of systems. A configurable framework enables flexible setup and modification of data entry and update screens and corresponding database elements, and processes. Configuration of the system, now a framework rather than a customized code base, provides flexibility in setting the system up to match the needs of the court, rather than forcing the court to bend to the computational needs of the system. This requires heavy involvement by court staff and judges to figure out what they want.

A court's ability to improve case handling effectively from the bottom up is strategic. The ability to provide an enabling environment for judges and support staff is strategic in capturing the best ideas of employees as they find better ways to perform their jobs in a changing internal environment, and respond to legal mandates from the external environment.

Primary use of electronic documents takes advantage of system capabilities and automated work methods. One of the goals of court automation is to eliminate paper from operations, making paper available on demand for specific, limited purposes.

Gathering complete and useful software requirements calls for a different method with the new generation of systems. Case management requirements are often incomplete because (1) they are difficult to discover from judges and support staff, and (2) shortcuts due to time and budget constraints reduce the quality of the requirements and of the implementation. Conventional approaches to software development do not capture the kinds of interaction needed between judges and support staff and IT professionals to achieve this goal.

A system that tracks tasks in work queues can help measure and manage user performance. Currently only limited worker performance measurement is available in most case management systems, limited to counting activities at a coarse level. A system that tracks duration of finer tasks, and how long it takes before a user performs them, will improve management's ability to analyze overall work and make ongoing improvements.

FUNCTIONAL REQUIREMENTS ARE NOT ENOUGH

The perennial challenge of software engineering (and software development in general) is the development, operation, and maintenance of software for users that is adaptive, resilient, and "good enough" for its intended purpose. In 1998 the court community, both court people and court CMS vendors, responded to a call to develop CMS requirements through a standards process.

Beginning in 2001, the National Consortium for State Court Automation Standards issued Case Management System Functional Standards, for case types of civil, domestic, criminal, juvenile and traffic, followed in 2005 by the Consolidated Case Management System Functional Standards. The premise of functional standards is that they identify what the CMS should perform, leaving the question of how the system should accomplish those functions to the designer because such questions are design issues. This is a sound approach, but issues remain, as court customers continue to use some variant of these functional requirements in their requests for proposals in acquiring new case management systems. CMS vendors respond to functional requirements during procurement, generally saying that their systems meet most of the requirements, at least partially.

Despite best efforts at clarity, many functional requirements are worded ambiguously and are capable of being interpreted in subjective ways, and they have to be translated to a configuration setup. Functional requirements alone are not enough to adequately specify a court CMS (even including "non-functional" system requirements involving security and performance issues). Though they serve some useful purpose, no generally accepted alternative approach to functional requirements has been developed.

Due to the inherent vagaries of requirement gathering and software development, and despite the efforts of software tool manufacturers and industry pundits to establish and declare "standard" methods, there are still as many techniques for requirement gathering and software development as there are managers responsible for developing and acquiring systems. The effects of this are realized through continuing rates of partial or incomplete software development and COTS implementation projects.

One alternative to primary reliance on functional requirements is to aim at the heart of the new generation of systems: their configurability.

JUDGING SYSTEM CONFIGURABILITY DURING CMS ACQUISITION

Beyond the basic hardware and database requirements for a court's computing environment, the main consideration during system acquisition is judging how flexible a system is through configuration, without customization of the source code. To the extent that a court can modify elements of the system (e.g., screen arrangement and content; add data fields to the database and reports; modify workflow, business rules, ticklers, and alerts), the fewer workarounds clerks and judges will be forced to create to do their jobs more efficiently.

TYPES OF SYSTEM CONFIGURABILITY

Table 1 sets forth some kinds of configuration capabilities and examples of how configuration affects the user experience by keeping information in the system that would otherwise be solely in the user's mind or in an adjunct manual and automated systems (e.g., checklists, spreadsheets, Access databases).

Table 1: Types of CMS Configuration

Configuration Capability	Example of Configuration
Set up multiple judges and courts/ agencies as jurisdictions, each with separate or shared event logs, schedules, assignments, multiple kinds of cases, and public and private notes	♦ Trial court, problem-solving court(s), administrative docket, probation department, marshals department, collection unit
Set up user interface appropriate to user function and scope of authority	♦ Place data fields on screen for all entry and update screens ♦ Select search criteria per case type ♦ Select alerts to appear when case or person results are displayed
Set up business rules appropriate to business processes as set by court policy	♦ Pretrial conferences are set 30 days out ♦ Each side is allowed one change of judge assignment without cause ♦ Private attorneys are assigned to indigents on rotation from a list
Set up work workflow and task queues appropriate to user function in different divisions of the organization	♦ When a defendant pleads guilty, bond is transferred to pay fine and costs ♦ When a warrant is issued, it is sent to the marshals for service ♦ When a defendant is sentenced to probation, that department is notified
Set up ticklers that are triggered when a condition is met, and alerts (person-level and case-level) that appear at the top of the screen when person or case information is displayed	♦ Ticklers: time period has elapsed ♦ Person status alerts: Outstanding warrant, On probation, Monetary balance owing, Non-public/confidential information, Need interpreter ♦ Case status alerts: Case sealed, Case inactive for bankruptcy
Set up data validations and prompts for data entry	♦ Birth date is within a certain range ♦ Officer badge number is on a list
Set up user performance criteria for work queues, triggered by a condition of a case or person, and measuring latency before the user takes action or how long it takes to perform an action	♦ Failures to appear at a traffic arraignment should be acted upon within four hours after the court session by generating a warrant (or a warning letter, depending on court policy); if the time is exceeded, notify a supervisor

One of the primary realities of public and private sector business is constant change in the external environment and internal business objectives and policies. Configurability is valuable because court business analysts can change configuration settings (through a governance process) without involvement of IT professionals. A solution not able to keep up with changes will force users to cope any way they can (i.e., develop system workarounds and a variety of subsidiary manual and computer-supported mechanisms) to help them automate their work or perform it more efficiently.

EVALUATING CONFIGURABILITY THROUGH USER SCENARIOS

Judges, clerks and court administrators know what their jobs require, and can identify scenarios associated with case types and with non-case functions. They know what work they need to perform, and can provide lists of features and functional requirements. The list may include hundreds or thousands of items; it is difficult to prioritize such a list. As a supplement to configurability evaluation, scenarios identify requirements at a higher level during system selection. A few examples of user scenarios are set forth in **Table 2** below:

Table 2: User Court CMS Scenario Examples

Configure an alert for fine payment past-due, driven by a flag automatically set based on date a payment was due

Clerk generate warrant, send to a judge for review and electronic signature, return to clerk for sending to law enforcement, and automatically docket issuance of the warrant

When scheduling a case, for a given case type and event type, see next available date, displaying time slot/session limits on the online calendar view for greater detail about the scheduled events for that session

Receipt a payment on a case, including type of payment, payee, cashier identifier, amount tendered, payment amount, change given, time of payment, location (e.g., mail, counter, internet)

Reassign several cases with the same court event setting from one judicial officer to another and generate a docket entry and notice for each one.

When CMS vendors identified as finalists demonstrate dozens of scenarios, court people will show how easy or difficult the system will be to configure, and how closely it can be adapted to the court's way of doing business.

IMPLEMENTING A CONFIGURABLE CMS

Once a system is selected, the process begins of loading and configuring it with the kinds of information used to operate the court.[1] The advent of highly-configurable systems introduces a new task: configuring events and the sequence of actions the system takes automatically when a given event is triggered. This requires a new way of thinking about the everyday work of a court, and requires articulating the court's business policies and the rules that implement them, how tasks flow from person to person, and time goals and constraints involved.

---

[1] Operational information that must be configured includes the following: statute table; court holidays; calendar structures; courtroom configurations; organization charts from the courts; names, titles and contact information for all persons in the courts and justice agencies; event types; search fields and results screens; case types and subtypes; case status types; hearing types; statistics for reporting; document types; information on interfaces; general ledger payment distribution codes; information associated with court programs.

This section provides advice on how to develop good CMS requirements for configurable electronic document-oriented, workflow systems.

AUTOMATING EVENT-DRIVEN ACTIVITIES

Caseflow adapts to events as they actually occur, so the court itself must be able to tell the implementer what events occur, and what action the court takes in response to them (because it's risky to depend on a third-party implementer to know or analyze this information). Analysis of court business processes has two layers. Experience indicates that flowcharts are easily handled by court support staff at two levels:

(1) At a higher level of abstraction, the upper layer of processes is a more summary view;

(2) At a lower, more detailed level, the processes each represent a chunk of work for the user and the system to perform.

An event is triggered by (1) an action of a participant in the case, or (2) an internally-set trigger that is activated because a condition is met. Events may have a source external to the CMS, or arise from a rule configured in the CMS, examples of which are in **Table 3** below:

Table 3: Examples of Case Events

Source of Event	Example Events and Subsequent Actions
External	◆ Case participant files a document, as a party to a case or providing information to the court, and a clerk records it
	◆ Judge announces/ issues a ruling or order, a clerk records it and notifies case parties
	◆ Change in custody status of criminal defendant (released)
Internal	◆ Tickler reminds user of an action to take
	◆ Trigger identifies obligation as overdue, and a clerk (or the system) takes action according to court policy

An event triggers a process which contains actions taken by the user or the system. Taking advantage of system workflow capabilities requires identifying all of the events that flow from a triggering event, and the court policies that underlie business rules in a particular situation.

A process hand-off diagram in **Figure 1** is a high-level view of multiple event processes—hand-offs from one job role to another, with participants in swim lanes. The example below is Bench Warrant/ Summons Process Hand-offs and includes four sub-processes and hand-offs between a clerk and a judge:

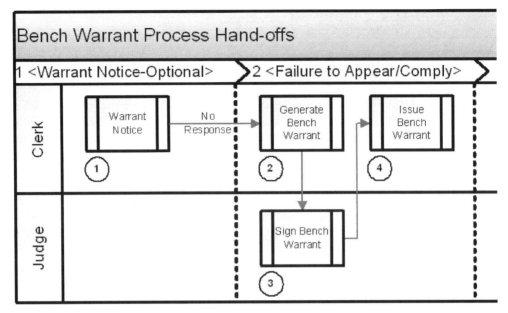

Figure 1: Bench Warrant Hand-off Diagram

A high-level process view highlights a court's policy choices, such as the following choices about issuing a bench warrant for a failure to appear (FTA) vis-à-vis failure to comply (FTC):

Table 4: Policy Choices in Configuring a Bench Warrant Process in Figure 1

Process	*Policy Choice*
1. Warrant Notice	◆ How long after FTA/FTC should warrant notice be sent? ◆ Treat FTA differently from FTC (e.g., send notice on first FTC, but issue warrant on every FTA)? ◆ Issue warrant notice if this is the first FTA/FTC in the case, or issue warrant for every FTA/FTC in the case?
2. Generate Warrant	◆ If a date for hearing is set, how many days out should the date be set in warrant notice?
3. Sign Bench Warrant	◆ How much time should be allowed for the judge to review and sign before notifying of the lag?
4. Issue Bench Warrant	◆ Assess a warrant fee? ◆ How communicate warrant to Law Enforcement?—paper or electronically?

Business rules containing such policy choices must be configured into the processes.

An event process diagram in **Figure 2**, process number 4 in Figure 1, shows the actions taken by the clerk or system in response to an event trigger of a judge signing a warrant:

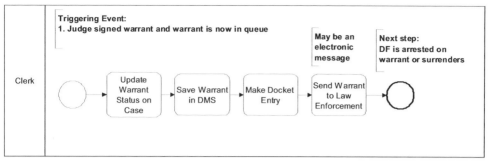

Figure 2: Issue Warrant Queue Process Diagram

All four steps after the warrant has been signed can be configured as automated workflow steps, not requiring the clerk's involvement. The power of highly-configurable systems multiplies the savings of effort and eliminates the risk of neglecting process steps or time standards.

Automating event-driven processes also enables monitoring of performance. Time standards are configured into processes, so the system facilitates central monitoring of work in process and reallocation of tasks to other workers, reflecting priorities and balancing of user workloads.

NEED FOR ITERATIVE REQUIREMENT DISCOVERY/ CONFIGURATION/ DEPLOYMENT PROCESS

CMS requirements will be more effective, and more likely result in a successful system, through an iterative requirement discovery/ configuration/ deployment process. Judges and support staff must be involved in discovering requirements, and in deciding that the requirements are met during configuration and deployment.

For each configurable element—setting up a search screen, setting up a data entry screen, setting up a workflow process—multiple sessions will be necessary for court people to see how it looks and works, and for the implementer to make changes requested. Managing this dynamic process requires attention to know what is "good enough for now" with the knowledge that, within practical limits, any element can be revisited later. A quest for perfection can harm the process.

It's commonly said that court people are anecdotal, not conceptual, and this plays out in the following ways:

- People don't analyze what they do and can't tell how they do it
- People base what they want on what's wrong with what they have
- People know what they *don't* want when they see it in prototype form
- People don't know what they want until they see it in prototype form, and then it takes time for reflection before they can think critically about it—and they may agree to every step of the process but refuse to accept the final product

THE QUESTION OF "WHEN ARE WE DONE?"

Implementation of any system—whether custom developed or a configurable framework—can be abandoned or fail to meet objectives if the system provider and customer cannot agree on when a requirement is met. The customer cannot endlessly change its mind about what it wants, and the system provider must make a good faith effort to meet requirements established at the beginning. Good contract sanctions and project management are necessary to reach a point of completion that was mutually agreed to. Implementation is likely to be a discovery process for vendor and customer alike, because "one size fits all" does not apply.

That's the blessing and the curse of case management.

Resources

(Matthias 2010)"User Requirements for a New Generation of Case Management Systems," *Future Trends in State Courts 2010,* 174. http://contentdm.ncsconline.org/cgi-bin/showfile.exe?CISOROOT=/ctadmin&CISOPTR=1605.

Consolidated Case Management System Functional Standards V0.20. www.ncsc.org/Services-and-Experts/Technology-tools/Court-specific-standards.aspx

(Swenson 2010) Keith D. Swenson. Mastering The Unpredictable: How Adaptive Case Management Will Revolutionize The Way that Knowledge Workers Get Things Done. Meghan-Kiffer Press, 2010.

(Wolfe 2005) Gary Wolfe and Vince Kasten, "Bringing Courts into the Future—The Agility Imperative," by 20:2 *Court Manager,* 8.

Advantages of Agile BPM

Keith D. Swenson, Fujitsu America Inc., USA

Agile BPM represents the next generation of business process management—designed to flexibly address all types of processes to support all forms of work. It combines traditional Business Process Management (BPM) style predefined processes, along with Adaptive Case Management (ACM) style dynamic work support.

INTRODUCTION

Agile BPM is designed to flexibly address all types of processes used to conduct business: structured, unstructured, and hybrid process types to support all forms of work.

In recent years many organizations have come to the understanding that their business processes are proprietary business assets that can yield competitive differentiation and advantage. This recognition has led to the adoption of first-generation BPM technologies to automate fixed, repetitive processes for efficiency and cost-effectiveness.

But the next generation of BPM, Agile BPM, will incorporate product capabilities that extend well beyond the system integration and fixed process automation initiatives that characterized first-generation BPM.

Three essential areas constitute Agile BPM:
- Continuous Process Optimization
- Collaboration and Social Networking
- Extending Enterprise Ecosystems

CONTINUOUS PROCESS OPTIMIZATION

An issue that lies at the heart of process automation is the lack of agility in many BPM implementations and technologies, putting process automation initiatives and technologies out of synch with the dynamically changing business conditions they are supposed to reflect and support. There exists a critical need for continuous process visibility and analysis to ensure that key business processes are performing effectively to support the business as its practices and requirements evolve.

But process discovery and visualization are challenging for most organizations. In fact, industry research has stated that in the conventional BPM cycle of Discover-Model-Simulate-Automate-Optimize, the Discovery phase consumes over 40 percent of the time and effort to implement BPM. This is because discovery of existing processes is largely a manual, time-consuming exercise conducted through meetings and human interactions. Most workers lack a holistic view of processes, even processes they are involved in. Typically they know the immediate previous and subsequent step of any process in which they are participants. As a result, identifying and modeling existing processes is, at best, anecdotal and inefficient, and at worst, highly inaccurate. The consequence of this is that most organizations that have automated business processes do not perform continuous visualization, analysis, and optimization of existing key business processes that may be out-of-date.

What is needed is evidence-based process detection and verification that provides insight to both IT and the business side of how well or poorly existing business processes are delivering efficiency and business advantage. Process Mining, also known as Automated Process Discovery (APD), performs off-production analysis of existing business processes—uncovering typical flows, repetitions, and loopbacks to highlight process inefficiencies and bottlenecks where they exist and identifying the right processes for improvement and continuous optimization.

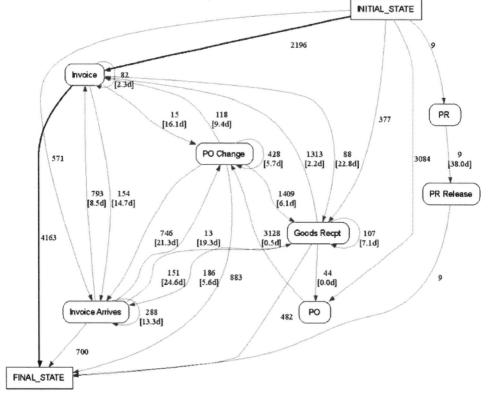

Figure 1: Automated Process Discovery visualizes actual process paths, identifying the most critical processes for improvement.

With system-based evidence on the true "as it really is" state of existing business processes, IT and business management can collaboratively identify and prioritize the key processes for improvement. Armed with actionable process insight, processes can then be optimized and automated. Where too many or overlapping processes exist, APD can help rationalize them and create lean process profiles.

APD highlights the most commonly traversed process paths, the least common paths, repeated steps, loopbacks, and the cost of each process. By identifying the most common business process patterns, it provides end users with the opportunity to standardize on existing common processes that are effective.

This process mining works in combination with traditional BPM to identify the critical process intersections and stages that affect business performance. Once identified, the traditional BPM can use analytics techniques to set performance thresholds and monitor these Key Performance Indicators

(KPIs) for any potential deviations in process that could degrade business performance.

Process owners and business executives require this management view on process latencies or redundancies. The system can monitors process performance and issues alerts corresponding to business conditions requiring corrective action. This delivers real-time business intelligence for continuous process performance and optimization.

Figure 2: sets performance thresholds and monitors Key Performance Indicators for any potential deviations.

COLLABORATIVE AND SOCIAL

The next capability of Agile BPM is accommodating and managing semi- and completely unpredictable business processes that involve collaboration among teams.

The first generation of BPM technologies has been traditionally applied to manage routine, repeatable business processes within a company. These processes—such as invoicing or order processing—typically follow exact steps that are normally repeated without exception. But there is another area of work—*knowledge work*—that is conducted in nearly all forms of business. This type of work involves judgment, can involve team collaboration, and almost never follows predictable, identical, repeated patterns.

Knowledge work and collaborative work represents the most valuable and differentiated work performed in an organization and as such, it tends to involve the highest value business initiatives and most expensive and highly trained workers in the company. Yet this work is not immune from inefficiency. The challenge has been how to provide system automation to track, measure, monitor, and manage processes and steps that cannot be defined in advance.

Agile BPM includes capabilities to address these ad hoc process flows necessary for knowledge-work, allowing process participants to punch out of structured processes and to task others for additional insight, input and approvals. Or they can instantiate a process outside of a defined process model, one whose course will proceed along dynamic, unpredictable steps to completion. Interstage BPM provides dynamic routing, workload balancing, and creation of processes on the fly. And it addresses the hybrid process scenarios where a structured process can spawn the need for collaboration or where a dynamic process can invoke structured process fragments.

When using Agile BPM, users can easily veer from previously defined, structured processes to respond to business change by extending existing processes dynamically with new tasks or by creating new processes from scratch to address these situations. Business users create completely new processes by simply creating a list of activities—a process outline—and Interstage automatically converts it into a sequence of tasks. In this way, business team members implicitly participate together in defining processes based on actual work.

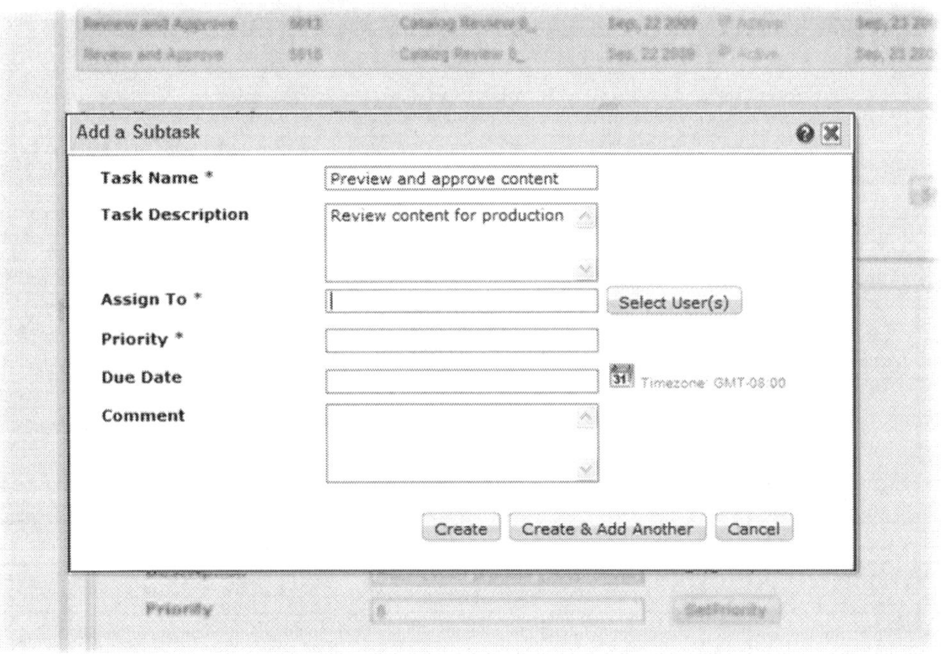

Figure 3: dynamic tasking lets users address and manage all forms of work, including ad hoc tasks and activities.

In this way, one can support collaborative, unstructured, and dynamic business processes needed for knowledge work. This is also known as case management in specific industries such as legal, healthcare, and insurance. Addressing individual business situations and work types that are unique, case management is now a relevant and commonly occurring work pattern in numerous other pursuits including mergers and acquisitions, financial portfolio management, and customer exception handling scenarios.

Dynamic process support allows users to model and manage a process where the starting point is known but the end point is not. It also lets users modify processes at runtime to accommodate necessary changes in process to support the work objective. It even lets people retroactively start processes for the case that work got started before the case manager realized that a process would be needed.

Collaborative work models and social media are teaching us that self-direction for teams and individuals are superior to the old "command and control" work models in nearly all situations involving knowledge work. Controls are moving downward in organizations. The world is moving too fast for centralized control. Decisions need to be made at ever more autonomous points, involving information exchanges and consultations in unforeseen, unplanned, and impromptu ways.

Increasingly, social interaction is figuring prominently in the development of a participatory culture for collaboratively producing work. The concepts of online communities where team members can contribute ideas, share information, and obtain information are central to next-generation Agile BPM. It includes social, collaborative capabilities for decentralized communication and immediate information updates to keep broad-based teams current and in possession of all of the facts related to a process-based work initiative.

Business processes involve numerous people, tasks, and decisions. Users need to be able to collaborate with each other via instant messaging, exchange knowledge through wikis to help complete tasks, and even sign up for RSS feeds so that they remain up-to-date on the status of tasks.

Users need a workplace that forms a dynamic, Web-based community framework for collaboration. They need tools for organizing people and information assets involved in work projects and provides information about the status of Workplace members and their tasks. And users should be able to leverage the process wikis and outlining capabilities to enable better collaboration and sharing of process knowledge.

EXTENDING ENTERPRISE ECOSYSTEMS

Today's business processes are not exclusively native to one entity. Now they span corporate boundaries to connect multiple, different audiences including customers, suppliers, partners, and other constituent parties. These extended corporate ecosystems increasingly involve shared business processes and as such need the capability to streamline, monitor, measure, and manage workflows that cross individual company and organizational boundaries.

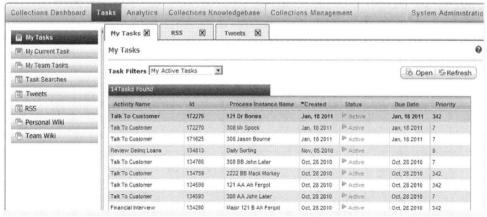

Figure 4: supporting social interactions – sharing knowledge, insight, and best practices to accomplish work more effectively.

An Agile BPM approach is ideal for linking process participants across these boundaries. Because it is Web-based, deployments can easily link to any process participants, regardless of where they are situated. The benefits of this approach include reduced capital costs, the ability to design and run processes from anywhere, and the capacity to easily extend processes to and among varied constituent parties.

CONCLUSION

A fact that is sometimes overlooked is that the point of Business Process Management is to improve the way that people perform and complete their work. Users demand capabilities to make it easy to have a pulse on business or project-based work performance. Unified dashboards present real-time access and detail of all tasks, processes, reports, KPIs, and alerts. Team leaders can quickly drill down into the specifics of an issue, compare team members' performances, identify the right person to assign to a task based on past performance, and even examine potential workload scenarios for particular team members before reshuffling assignments to get work done optimally. Empowered to quickly and flexibly sub-task work to different team members in response to dynamic conditions, managers are able to optimize all forms of process—structured, unstructured, hybrid—in support of accomplishing work and overall business performance.

Next-generation Agile BPM is designed to address all of the requirements of managing work in today's enterprise: from streamlining routine, repeated business processes to managing dynamically evolving business cases involving teamwork, collaboration, and judgment across and among diverse sets of process participants.

ABOUT FUJITSU AMERICA

Fujitsu America, Inc. is a leading ICT solutions provider for organizations in the U.S., Canada and the Caribbean. Fujitsu enables clients to meet their business objectives through integrated offerings including consulting, systems integration, managed services and outsourcing for enterprise applications, data center and field services operations, based on server, software, storage and mobile technologies. Interstage BPM is Fujitsu's leading edge product that presents powerful Agile BPM capabilities, combining both traditional BPM and ACM capabilities into a single unified approach. Fujitsu provides industry-oriented solutions for manufacturing, retail, healthcare, government, education, financial services and communications sectors.

For more information, please visit: http://solutions.us.fujitsu.com/

Social + Lean = Agile

Dave Duggal, Consilience International LLC, USA

ABSTRACT:

This chapter provides a foundation for understanding Enterprise Agility. It defines the concept as it relates to Information Systems, identifying modern impediments and highlighting the role of empowered business-users as the agents of change. In conclusion, it outlines a solution based on Social and Lean enablement.

Enterprise Agility is the measure of an organization's responsiveness to its environment. The more flexible an organization's systems infrastructure, the more readily it can adapt. Enterprise Agility does not entail a reduction in governance or imply that all things are in flux all the time; rather it's about mitigating structural impediments to variance and change.

While the definition is straightforward, it suggests a fundamental rethink of information architecture.

The last forty years of mainstream business computing brought tremendous efficiencies through standardization, but this was predicated on relatively static models of processes, data, and capabilities.

For all the investments in technology, change itself is still a largely manual process conducted offline. The modern systems infrastructure simply wasn't designed to be responsive. Fixed models mean fixed conditions, precluding interaction context by definition.

This is evidenced by process 'exceptions' and by expensive corporate change management programs [1]. The problem with this approach is that approved change is delivered long after the request, if at all, resulting in lost initiative and lost business value.

Moreover, studies have shown that process improvement programs tend to stagnate [2], giving rise to shadow systems that compound the Agility problem.

Ironically, change management programs have become an inefficient rate-limiter, the chokepoint for Enterprise Agility.

While controls are important, gratuitous controls stifle problem solving and innovation. Tremendous value can be released by simply empowering people with greater discretion to meet business objectives [1, 5, 6, 9, 10] where it does not directly impact compliance requirements. Where circumstances dictate specific procedures, technology can support 'release valves' to allow in-flight approvals for variance and change so neither time nor value is lost.

It's important to note that the modern Enterprise is really a complex and distributed System of Systems [3]. Enterprise Agility necessitates a holistic approach; it has to work with existing ERP and Service Oriented Architectures. This suggests a flexible collaboration layer that enables dynamic interoperability between people and data, capabilities and policies.

A Mandate for Change

At the boundaries of the enterprise, where interactions between customers, partners and co-workers take place, the environment is increasingly frenetic.

Global competition is driving a new customer-centric era. Organizations must find ways to efficiently satisfy individual requirements [4]. This represents a phase change from the age of standardization to the age of specialization.

While some areas of the economy are more dynamic than others, no industry escapes the mandate for Enterprise Agility. The "Topple Rate" [5] of Fortune 500 companies is now only 15 years and curving downwards.

The Enterprise needs a new form of Collaboration Architecture to engage people [6] with the latitude to improvise, while providing for transparency, governance and audit.

THE NETWORK IS THE PEOPLE

Rigid operations are anti-social! They are emblematic of non-responsive bureaucracies best captured by the Dilbert comic series[1].

Fixed procedures alienate people from their work, squandering human ingenuity. According to Deloitte's Center for the Edge [5], 80 percent of workers are unengaged at work!

Following a linear process regardless of circumstances is nonsensical. We can't anticipate all scenarios; an unrelated chain of events can impact best laid plans.

Rather than focusing on standard procedures, people need the authority to flexibly meet corporate objectives. People need to be able to respond to the environment, to adjust plans to keep goals in sight.

The scale of unleveraged human capital reveals a tremendous opportunity to tap the enterprise cognitive surplus [7]. After all, businesses are socio-technical systems. Technology may connect, automate, and report, but people are the agents of change. The Network *is* the People!

IMPEDIMENTS TO CHANGE: YOU CAN'T GET THERE FROM HERE

Business sustainability requires agility; however rigid systems infrastructure is a straitjacket on the Enterprise.

The 20th century automation technologies that enabled tremendous efficiencies [8] now inhibit the effectiveness of 21st century networked collaboration. The standardization of business processes removed human discretion, problem solving, and innovation.

Businesses have to overcome this structural barrier; systems need to support a looser form of organization that accommodates variance and change. Enterprise Agility requires a shift from standardized transactions to dynamic interactions.

---

[1] © Reproduced with permission Dilbert.com

Social needs to be integrated into the process itself, it has to be able to direct flow otherwise it is simply chatter that is ultimately still dependant on conventional change management schemes. Processes need to become two-way conversations.

SOCIAL + LEAN = AGILE

Enterprise Agility is not about liberation, it's about optimization [9]. It's about giving people joint-custody of their activities so they can co-author processes on-the-fly, using authorized discretion to best meet business goals in a transparent and auditable fashion.

In this view, process participants co-author processes with both the business owners that define default requirements, *and* IT, which develops capabilities and maintains underlying systems. This is a new form of social collaboration that supports real-time alignment of all stakeholders.

The foundation of this model is Social Collaboration, but it is also fundamentally Lean Integration as system resource utilization can be fit for purpose. While standardization leads to the 'Goldilocks dilemma,' where generic methods are 'too hot' or 'too cold', a Social and Lean approach to Enterprise Agility enables people to reconcile requirements to get it 'just right.'

Technologically, it must support loosely-coupled processes where structure is a variable that is negotiable based on context [10]. The absence of fixed structures allows the system to evolve in a controlled fashion through use. In this open environment, people mediate technology.

For its part, technology connects process participants, provides capabilities and augments situational-awareness. An interaction-driven architecture is capable of supporting informed decision-making with targeted real-time feedback. Business intelligence can be dynamically injected into tasks to customize content and guide next steps, closing the loop between data and process.

Practical Impact

- A holistic application architecture for collaboration and integration that dramatically lowers the cost of managing variance and change.
- Loosely defined processes; uncoupling tasks from rigid flowcharts - with no fixed process definitions there is nothing to break.
- Empower people to drive processes and enable change to be managed in-flight.
- Enable enterprise context-awareness to deliver just-the-right mix of data, capabilities and policies for every interaction
- Provide flexibility while supporting governance, transparency and audit history.

While the Web introduced the notion of self-directed navigation of linked content, popular social sites facilitate distributed collaboration, and consumer apps have introduced the notion of context-awareness, there hasn't been a unified approach to Enterprise Agility. It's time for change.

ABOUT CONSILIENCE INTERNATIONAL, LLC

Consilience is the developer of the Ideate Framework™; a real-time application-integration platform based on web-style architecture. It links people, information, capabilities and policies in virtual interoperability layer, an EnterpriseWeb™.

The EnterpriseWeb™ provides a native graph data model for navigating information free from the constraints that traditional business silos and systems pose. It is the ideal environment for mashing-up information. Rather than winding-around complex and 'expensive' joins between disparate systems, Ideate uses simple link traversal to efficiently correlate information.

Resources are connected to each other by direct relationships and degrees of separation – like 'friends' and 'friends of a friend', but Ideate applies it universally to all information (business entities, reference data; documents; rules; functions; Services; etc.). Resource relationships are 'social'; they evolve dynamically based on real-time activity. In this way, end-users participate in continually co-developing the EnterpriseWeb of relationships. This facilitates flexible perspectives, unanticipated uses, and change management; critical business capabilities sorely missing from conventional system designs.

In Ideate, applications co-evolve with their Resources making them more resilient to change. In addition, all changes to a Resource, including its relationships, are recorded for version control in a wiki-like fashion. This provides developers with a native method of source control and business users with a detailed audit history.

While the World Wide Web is primarily for navigating content; Ideate has made the web functional. It has leveraged the scalability, link-ability and interactivity of the Web to provide a practical and scalable solution for Enterprise Agility.

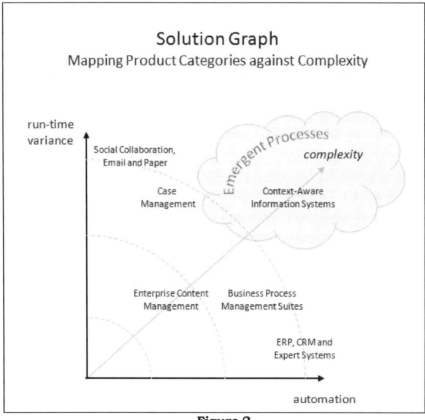

Figure 2

Ideate Framework apps support a range between structured processes (e.g. BPMS; ERP; Expert Systems; etc.) and unstructured actions (e.g. Enterprise Content Management; Case Management; Social Collaboration; Email; Paper; etc.) within one system.

REFERENCES

1. Sameer Patel, July 7, 2011, "Why Exception Handling Should be the Rule," Blog.
2. Satya S. Chakravorty, Wall Street Journal, January 25, 2010, "Where Process-Improvement Projects Go Wrong," Article.
3. Stafford Beer, 1972, "Brain of the Firm," Book.
4. The Corporate Executive Board Company, 2010, "The Future of Corporate IT," Report.
5. John Hagel III, John Seely Brown, Duleesha Kulasooriya, Dan Elbert, Deloitte's Center for the Edge Deloitte Development LLC, 2010, "The Shift Index," Report.
6. Geoffrey Moore, TCG Advisors, AIIM, 2011, "Systems of Engagement and The Future of Enterprise IT," Report.
7. Frederick W. Taylor, 1911, "The Principles of Scientific Management," Book.
8. Clay Shirky, 2010, "Cognitive Surplus," Book.
9. Tom Davenport, Harvard Business Review, November 8, 2010, "Want Value From Social? Add Structure," Blog.
10. Jim Sinur, Gartner, Inc., July 21, 2011, "What Kind of Gear is Needed for Social BPM?" Blog.

ACM and Business Agility for the Microsoft-aligned Organization

Dermot McCauley, Singularity, United Kingdom

Is *change* the only constant and *unpredictability* a new norm in your organization? For most organizations, the answer is yes. Simply put, business agility is now one of the most important skills of a successful enterprise, public or private. Adaptive Case Management (ACM) is a new approach that makes business agility achievable. What's more, ACM can release the agility in your organization while leveraging familiar Microsoft products.

WHY AGILITY MATTERS

Agility has been thrust more urgently onto "must do" lists everywhere because the challenges organizations face today are more pressing than any they have previously known.

Among the most significant of these challenges is the ever more widespread impact of globalization. Competitors can, and do, appear from anywhere. Old barriers that slowed or stopped new competitors from entering a market—such as geographic distance, the quality of communications connections, legislative constraint, or supply-chain frictions—have rapidly disintegrated. The move to a "friction-free" global economy is now well underway. To survive and prosper, all organizations must adapt faster today than ever before.

Compounding the globalization effect into a "double whammy" has been the global recession that impacted every organization at the end of the first decade of the 21st century. The necessity to become more efficient, more responsive, more attentive, more cost conscious, and to work faster than in the past has become more urgent as a result.

The "better, faster, cheaper" mantra sounds today in every organization. Companies are now more open to global sourcing of raw materials and services and to supplying new markets. Public agencies are increasingly choosing radical options to cut costs while maintaining citizen services. All organizations continually consider the outsourcing of many front, middle and back office services.

Contexts in technology, legislation, knowledge, and innovation are all moving quickly. Mobile working, social software and cloud computing are among the recent drivers of change, providing opportunity for the innovative and threat for the inertia-bound organization.

These dynamics contribute to an ever more rapid pace of change in the way organizations operate. Fast change externally must be matched by fast change internally. Only agility enables organizations to respond quickly and positively to today's more demanding environment.

WHAT IS AGILITY?

An agile organization is like a successful sports team. Consider the excellent basketball player and his winning team. He is continually able to **sense** what is happening, **prioritize** his best next actions, and then **act** effectively. And he does this within a team and in a highly constrained time frame. A professional basketball team has twenty-eight seconds to make its play and score. Every player must sense, prioritize, and act quickly for the team to win.

An agile organization is one that can sense opportunity or threat, prioritize its potential responses, and act efficiently and effectively.

Sense

An agile organization excels at recognizing opportunities and threats. It is aware not merely of its own organization, but also of its operating environment. It understands its customers' demands and how these change; its competitors' capabilities and how these change; and the macroeconomic environment and how this affects its operation and those of its customers and competitors. Its own performance capability is transparent within the organization, enabling it to respond to changing external realities.

Prioritize

An agile organization has a clear purpose, which is clearly articulated and widely and deeply understood by its people. The organization's destination is known. It ensures that the organization's entire population is aware of corporate priorities at the enterprise, department, function, and individual levels. It has a set of goals that are coherent and connected, and the achievement of these goals is pursued in a joined-up fashion across the business. The joined-up goals of the organization are used by its people to choose the best action in any circumstance.

Act

Agility culminates in people taking appropriate, timely action. In an agile organization, people execute existing business processes exceptionally well, and crucially, they also adapt those processes quickly as business needs change.

Few organizations excel at sensing, prioritizing or acting. Even fewer excel at all three at the same time. Those that do are the successful agile organizations. Take a few moments to answer the following two simple questions and write your answers in Table XX-1.

- How agile is your organization today?
- How agile must your organization be in twelve months' time?

TABLE 1:
Agility Assessment and 12-Month Agility Goal for Your Organization

	AGILITY TODAY	AGILITY NEEDED ONE YEAR FROM TODAY
	(SCALE: 1-10)	(SCALE: 1-10)
Sensing	4?	7?
Prioritizing	6?	8?
Acting	5?	9?

Do you have a plan and the right tools in place to ensure that your organization will achieve the 12-month agility goal you set for it in Table XX-1? Let's discuss the relevance of Case Management to agility and then consider the Case Management platform your organization will require for its agile journey.

AGILITY AND CASE MANAGEMENT

I hope you are not working in an organization where statements such as "we can't do it that way" and "it would be too hard to change our process to allow for that" are commonplace. Unfortunately, such statements are in fact very common. Indeed, many organizations operate as though in straight-jackets, even if these "not possible here" kind of statements are not uttered.

The truth is that many organizations find it difficult to deal with non-routine work. They cannot accommodate the unpredictable as part of everyday practice. Agility is not part of the organizational DNA. These organizations cannot deal well with unanticipated customer needs, with changing markets, with new policy or regulation. They cannot recognize and exploit opportunities for improvement. It is eventually the customer who suffers. Indeed the customer is often the first casualty.

Agile organizations, on the other hand, are as adept at handling the unpredictable as they are at executing routine work. Innovation and continual improvement are second nature in the agile organization. Agile organizations are masters of the unpredictable.

Case Management is a common term used in relation to unpredictable work. To understand how Adaptive Case Management relates to agility and unpredictability, consider Fig. XX.1 'The Process Spectrum'.

In Case Management, such as in the legal industry, each case is different even if there are some common groundrules, constraints or norms in operation. The people involved in Case Management are often called knowledge workers and their judgement and discretion are critical to the effective progress of the case—in effect it is very often the human who decides what happens next.

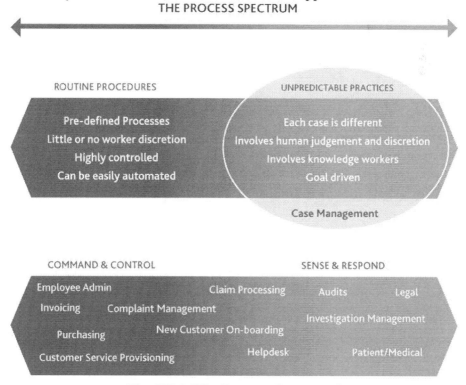

Fig. XX.1 'The Process Spectrum'

Knowledge work is goal-driven, rather than driven primarily by predefined procedure. For example, when a citizen makes a request for information from a government entity under the Freedom of Information laws that now operate in many countries, only the delivery date is known. All work is driven by the need to deliver the requested information to the citizen by the required date. But the work to be done is not predefined or known at the outset—it is largely unpredictable—the knowledge workers decide what to do.

I'll explore the key characteristics of Case Management further below, but provide meanwhile the following definition:

> *Case management is the management of long-lived collaborative processes that require coordination of knowledge, content, correspondence, and resources to achieve an objective or goal. The path of execution cannot be predefined. Human judgment is required in determining how to proceed, and the state of a case can be affected by external events.*

In Case Management the organization operates in a "sense and respond" mode; akin to the sense, prioritize, act mode we recognized above as the DNA of the agile organization. At the other end of the Process Spectrum, where workers execute routine procedures, the organization operates in a "command and control" mode.

Of course, most organizations spend time every day performing routine work in "command and control" mode. It is the agile organization which is equally able to deal with unpredictable work in "sense and respond" fashion. And Case Management is the approach these organizations use to master the unpredictable and to operate with agility.

I have cited the Legal industry and Freedom on Information requests in the Government sector as contexts where Case Management is relevant. In fact, knowledge work and hence Case Management is widespread as the table below shows. Take a moment to identify some examples of knowledge work in your industry and organization.

TABLE 2: Knowledge Work by Organization Type

ORGANIZATION TYPE	KNOWLEDGE WORK
Law Enforcement	♦ Firearms licensing
	♦ Investigations
	♦ Forensics management
Government	♦ Social welfare benefits applications
	♦ Licensing and permits management
	♦ Freedom of Information Act requests
	♦ Planning applications
	♦ Industrial health and safety enforcement
	♦ Immigration applications
	♦ Regulatory monitoring
Financial Services	♦ Corporate customer onboarding
	♦ Regulatory compliance management
	♦ Insurance claim processing

	♦ Trade settlement exception management
Telecommunications	♦ Customer provisioning
	♦ Fault reporting and resolution
	♦ Billing issue resolution
	♦ Order processing

The agile organization is one that, like the excellent basketball team, senses what to do, prioritizes its options, and then acts appropriately, player by player. The organization might be pursuing a new sales opportunity, bringing a new client onboard, responding to a customer complaint, or processing an insurance claim. Whatever the particular situation, organizations that are agile and use Case Management in their knowledge work win more new deals, keep more customers happy, operate less wastefully, and spot more opportunities for improvement.

CHARACTERISTICS OF CASE MANAGEMENT

Knowledge work may appear to vary substantially across organizations. In practice, however, case-handling practices are usually very similar. Knowledge workers need to manage a complex set of steps from the start of a case through to its completion. This usually involves interaction with others in their organization or external agencies, and it requires the generation of and complex interaction with correspondence, documents, and records. The key characteristics common to most case management processes include the following:

Goal Driven—Every case is pursued for a purpose. Without a purpose, the effort would be groundless, directionless, and impossible to deem a success on conclusion.

Knowledge Intensive—Typically, processes require the intervention of skilled and knowledgeable personnel. Staff acquire their knowledge through their experience of working on similar cases and through collaboration with more experienced colleagues, becoming thoroughly familiar with the tacit and explicit rules governing how cases should be managed.

Highly Variable Processes—While a particular type of case will share a general structure (e.g., handling benefits applications), it is not possible to predict the path that a particular case will take. A case can change in unpredictable, dynamic, and ad hoc ways. Basic procedures may be fixed, but there can be considerable variation in how steps are executed according to circumstances.

Long Running—Cases can run for months or years—much longer than the short interaction cycles handled by standard Customer Relationship Management (CRM) systems, for example. Because a case is long running, it changes hands over time, different people work on different aspects, and often, no single individual has a persistent view of the case all the time.

Information Complexity—Knowledge work involves the collection and presentation of a diverse set of documents and records. Emails, meeting notes, case documents, and correspondence related to a case must be easily accessible. This can be difficult for knowledge workers to organize and manage efficiently, with the risk that an important record, note, or file will be unavailable, lost, or overlooked when it is needed. Retrieving the correct information required at a particular decision point may depend on the knowledge of the case worker and the effective linking of electronic and physical filing/storage systems.

Highly Collaborative—Knowledge workers usually need to coordinate interviews and meetings among interested parties (e.g., the applicant, colleagues, legal representatives). Many cases require a team-based approach, with different specialists working on different aspects of a case or acting as consultants to their colleagues. Team members need to access case information and discuss this. And people outside the organization, such as clients, third party experts, loosely interested parties, and others must be part of the case community. Increasingly, with the advent of social networking and other community-enabling technologies, the community of parties that a case can engage is expanding.

Multiple Participants and Fluid Roles—Case Management must cater for the fact that organizations are not stable and that people often change position or role. Yet, try calling your insurance company today; it is unlikely that you'll be able to speak to the same person you spoke to last time you called, even though you'll be speaking to a person in the same role, perhaps about a claim you filed 4 months ago. Staff members leave or case workers' roles may change in the course of a case. Multiple parties are likely to be involved directly or indirectly, and they may play different roles in the case at different times.

Inter-related Cases—The outcomes of separate cases may have an impact on each other. For example, an application for citizenship by an individual may be affected by the success or failure of an application by a spouse or immediate relative. Cases can be explicitly linked, or they may need to be linked by inference and conducted with this inferred link in mind.

Juggling Fixed and Flexible Timescales—While cases may vary in how they are conducted, they may be subject to the same inflexible requirements for case completion such as legislation or service level agreements (SLAs). For example, if you've taken longer than you should have to get to a certain point in an insurance claim process then you must speed up in the (flexible) remaining time so that a (fixed) claim deadline can be met.

Sensitivity to External Events—External events and intervention can change the state of a running case (e.g., a phone call from a lawyer, the unscheduled arrival of compliance documentation, or the enactment of new governing policies while a case is in progress).

Cross-Organizational Visibility—It can be difficult for supervisors to monitor progress or for case workers to do so after handing cases to colleagues in other departments or organizations to undertake specific steps. For example, when onboarding a new client, the client onboarding manager may lose sight of the case when it goes to the legal or KYC (Know Your Customer)/compliance department.

History—Every action performed, every decision taken, and every piece of correspondence received has to be tracked, not just for audit purposes, but also to provide guidance for future similar cases. Workers need access to this history when making decisions, while auditors and compliance officials need the history to ensure policies are adhered to. The case history is the organization's defense mechanism and a key learning tool.

Demanding Security Requirements—Strict control is necessary to protect access to sensitive information. The scope of this security challenge is unusually wide in case management processes, enveloping many pieces of information/data, many documents and other artifacts, a wide range of case participants in multiple roles and organizations, and many related information systems.

Isolated Pockets of Automation—The knowledge worker plays an essential role but requires automation to assist in coordinating and orchestrating isolated pockets of automation relevant to the case. Legacy software applications, paper documentation, physical folders, and multiple electronic artifacts (e.g., original signature copies of legal agreements) need to be readily available to the knowledge worker. Case Management requires that these pockets of automation seamlessly work together so that "application switching" doesn't undermine the knowledge worker's agility.

So, can you create an Adaptive Case Management (ACM) platform that will enable the agile practices that your organization needs?

ACM FOR THE MICROSOFT-ALIGNED ORGANIZATION

Microsoft products are the most pervasive software in the modern organization. Many other software products are also in use, but the most familiar software to you, your colleagues, your organization and others is likely to be Microsoft software. It may be Microsoft Explorer, used to surf the Web; Microsoft Outlook, used for email, calendars and tasks; Microsoft SharePoint for team collaboration and document/content management; Microsoft CRM, used for customer data management; Microsoft Lync, used for Instant Messaging, Video Calling and Presence-awareness. In many varied combinations, organizations use familiar Microsoft technology to get work done, including knowledge work.

If your organization is Microsoft-aligned, by which I mean simply that your organization uses some combination of Microsoft products, you can assemble an Adaptive Case Management platform that releases agility in your organization, supports your knowledge workers and wrings yet more value from your Microsoft assets.

In the Microsoft-aligned organization this means that the ACM platform must have the capability of leveraging the strengths of SharePoint for content and collaboration, Dynamics CRM for entity management, Lync for unified communications and Outlook for email, calendar and contact management. For ease of adoption and to reduce training requirements the ACM platform should also allow the knowledge worker to access and adapt their case workflows from their preferred Microsoft interface.

The ACM platform extends the capabilities of the Microsoft suite to deliver a holistic solution that supports goal management, empowerment of case participants, adaptability in execution, effective availability of information and enables continuous improvements.

Some organizations try to support Case Management by extending the capabilities of technology platforms not designed for the purpose. For example, some Commercial-Off-The-Shelf (COTS) software solutions meet a departmental need today but cannot extend effectively or affordably beyond that initial need. COTS solutions are deceptively attractive on account of ready-built features that appear to quickly meet, for example, a specific Complaints Management need. But inherent inflexibility is the Achilles heel of COTS solutions.

An Adaptive Case Management (ACM) platform that leverages familiar Microsoft products, augmented with Microsoft-based Case Management technology, provides agility that COTS solutions cannot while leveraging individual Microsoft products to gain greater ROI.

Fig. XX.2 'ACM for the Microsoft-aligned Organization' illustrates how familiar Microsoft products, augmented in this example with Singularity's TotalAgility software product, deliver on the key characteristics of Case Management discussed above.

Fig. XX.2 'ACM for the Microsoft-aligned Organization'

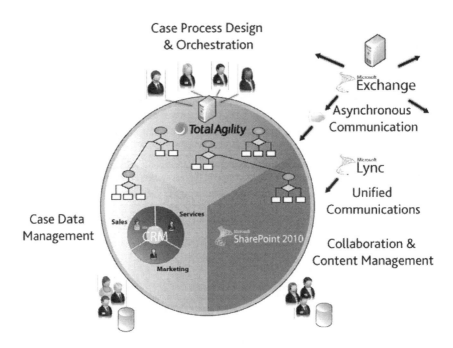

You may use a different combination of Microsoft products in your ACM platform, but let's walk briefly through the configuration above to highlight how the essential characteristics of Case Management are supported.

Case Data Management: Microsoft Dynamics CRM manages data about your customer relationship, ranging from basic identification data to information about any case involving that customer. Dynamics CRM may be the familiar interface used by your sales, marketing or service team. In this example, those knowledge workers have access not only to basic customer data but also to information about current and historic cases, such as ongoing or prior insurance claims. Information, documentation and case performance information can be surfaced in the familiar Dynamics CRM interface if your ACM platform properly integrates the other components shown.

Collaboration and Content Management: Microsoft SharePoint is widely used to support collaborative working. Teams create "sites" for the purpose of getting a given project done or simply as a means for their regular team working. Many organizations also use SharePoint as a store for documents and other types of content. SharePoint may be the familiar interface for middle or back office workers, who are engaged perhaps in an insurance claim adjudication but are not users of Dynamics CRM. Those workers in a correct ACM platform configuration will also have access to case information that may have originated in or be maintained in Dynamics CRM or elsewhere.

Unified Communications: Microsoft Lync, previously known as Office Communications Server, enables knowledge workers to interact "right now" with colleagues. In technical jargon, this is sometimes called "synchronous" communication. Essentially, Lync allows you to know who is available "right now"; allows you to send messages instantly and get instant responses from those people; and allows you to initiate voice and/or video calls with available colleagues or third parties. For the knowledge worker dealing with urgent cases, such as accidents or other incidents, a well-configured Microsoft-based ACM platform will make the capabilities of Lync available in a familiar context. In fact, the "presence awareness" of Lync also allows non-urgent Case Management to move ahead rapidly. The simple ability to talk immediately to a colleague can remove much of the common delays in everyday knowledge work, eliminating latency and accelerating achievement of case goals.

Asynchronous Communications: Microsoft Exchange, most familiar through its Outlook interface for email, is frequently used by knowledge workers. Outlook's "asynchronous" communication allows Case Management to include the issue and receipt of email to colleagues, customers and third parties involved in a case. Those communications are **not** dependent on the immediate availability of the other party. For an ACM platform to work well, however, it must have a means of tying all email communication back into the case. Rather than "fire and forget" email, your ACM platform must include a listening and monitoring capability that recognizes when email has arrived, has been answered or has a required document attached. Indeed, when an asynchronous communication should result in an action your ACM platform should automatically move the case forward toward conclusion—for example, when a road accident photograph is enclosed in an email, your ACM platform should recognize it and move the processing of the case forward.

Case Process Design and Orchestration: Singularity's TotalAgility product is built on Microsoft technology and integrates out-of-the-box with all the Microsoft products discussed above (and more). To your Microsoft-aligned ACM platform, the TotalAgility product adds the capability to graphically design and adapt Case Management processes. Surfaced in Dynamics CRM, SharePoint or other familiar interface, this equips your knowledge workers not only with easy-to-understand status information on how a case is progressing, it also allows them to alter the course of the case using a simple graphical interface. A case worker, working in Dynamics CRM or SharePoint or other familiar interface, can "step back" to redo previously performed steps or "jump forward" if they determine that a given case should be dealt with in that way. Ad-hoc next steps can be created by the knowledge worker, responding in agile fashion to the unpredictable circumstances that often occur in Case Management. The TotalAgility product also provides seamless "orchestration"; that is, it ensures that without expensive IT projects or coding all the Microsoft products work together to get Case Management done.

In practice this means, for example: ensuring that insurance claim progress information and documents are available to the service desk employee in his/her Dynamics CRM interface, even though they have been created or changed elsewhere; allowing the completion of work by a back office worker in, for example, SharePoint to result in the creation of front office work surfaced in Dynamics CRM; or, embedding Lync presence awareness intelligently in context, so that an emergency worker is automatically given the short list of present colleagues who have the skills and experience to help in the current case.

I have not dwelt in this example on other Microsoft-aligned ACM platform components, such as document production via Microsoft Office. Whichever Microsoft components you incorporate into your ACM platform, the keypoint is that they must be integrated in an agile fashion so that your knowledge workers can act flexibly, handling the unpredictable as it arises.

CHALLENGES IN ADAPTIVE CASE MANAGEMENT (ACM)

I am sometimes asked by organizations exploring how best to do Adaptive Case Management, "Can I do ACM with the technology I already have?" Occasionally the question is, "Surely Dynamics CRM [or SharePoint] is sufficient for my Case Management needs?"

My first response is always to ask for more specifics of what type of work the questioner is trying to get done; how do they want Case Management to work in their organization? Listed briefly below is a selection of the most common ACM challenges that stretch an organization's existing technologies, including their Microsoft products, beyond their capabilities. If these challenges are relevant to your organization, consider augmenting your current software products to create an ACM platform that can handle these challenges efficiently and flexibly.

Case Handling and Guidance

- Skill-, Competency-, Availability- or Priority-based Work Allocation (e.g. "urgent, allocate to an available person", "this is a complex case, allocate to a specially skilled person", "Platinum customers first", etc)
- Case Worker Guidance, provided in context (e.g. easy access to policy documents, wikis, etc., visibility of who else is participating in the case, in which roles, who are *relevant* experts, etc)
- Choice by the Case Worker of which process fragments to execute next
- Creation of Ad-hoc tasks, that can be tracked as part of overall Case Management
- Case Alerts and Notifications
- Pre-emptive Escalation Management

Workflow Design and Execution

- Graphical and Standards-based Case Modelling (BPMN, XPDL)
- Milestone-driven Processes
- In-flight flexibility to Jump back, Skip forward, Re-Do
- Advanced workflow rules (e.g. "Initiator/requestor cannot approve")
- Version management, including upgrading of in-flight cases to new versions of procedure
- Support for multiple case states, including 'wait' state
- Ability to change your Case Management process in-flight

Case Performance Management

- Multiple, independent processes managed in a single case context
- Time, effort, cost, milestone, state, etc tracking and reporting (e.g. in a "Case Health Monitor")
- Comprehensive Case History and Audit Trail
- Enterprise Case Performance Management (i.e. across multiple cases, case types, organizations, etc.)

Policy and Rule Management

- Expose policy and rule flex-points to non-technical staff
- Rule definition, execution and enforcement
- Autonomous rule-sets, independently configurable

Content Generation and Handling

- Multi-repository content and document management (e.g. where more than one document storage system is needed in the course of Case Management)

- Process-driven correspondence and content tracking
- Document- and folder-level content management

People Resource Management
- Allow people to fulfil multiple or changing roles in a case's lifetime
- Define, configure and manage your human resource base in terms of skill, competence and availability (e.g. to intelligently manage work and holiday calendars, experience levels, etc so that cases are always dealt with by the right people at the right time)

Simulation and Optimization
- Walkthrough of case processes
- "What if?" analysis of process improvement ideas
- Use of historic case data in "What if?" simulations
- Continuous improvement of Case Management processes

Choreography of Human and System Resources
- .NET and Web Services-based open integration, to reduce or eliminate the need for expensive software projects and coding so that the multiple components of your ACM platform can be assembled cost-effectively
- Built-in, Wizard-driven Database Integration, so that your ACM platform is easily configurable to provide knowledge workers with relevant data from multiple databases in context of the case they are handling

ACM PLATFORMS SUPPORT GREATER AGILITY

I began with a discussion of the agility imperative—the urgent need to increase every organization's ability to sense, prioritize and act. I drew a contrast between the inertia that impairs so many organizations and the agility that enables a top basketball team to win the league title. And we have seen in this discussion that much of the day-to-day operation of organizations of all types involves knowledge work, to which agility is crucial.

Whether knowledge workers are dealing with a social security claim, the onboarding of a new customer, the pursuit of litigation proceedings, or the arbitration of a customer complaint, their approach to Case Management shares many common characteristics we have identified. An agile approach to Case Management, supported by an Adaptive Case Management platform, equips your knowledge workers to become a winning team.

For many organizations the pervasive Microsoft products provide some of the essential components of an Adaptive Case Management (ACM) platform. Incorporating the familiar interfaces of Microsoft will make an ACM platform easily adoptable by employees and third parties—so you can become a better team more quickly. That said, we have seen that some of the common challenges organizations face in Case Management may not be adequately supported by the Microsoft software products alone. So it is wise to clarify your Case Management needs early and assemble an ACM platform that meets them.

An agile organization is one that when managing cases, like the excellent basketball team, senses what to do, prioritizes among options, and then acts appropriately, person by person. Organizations that increase their agility by embracing the right ACM platform will win more new deals, keep more customers happy, operate less wastefully, and capitalize better on opportunities for improvement.

BPM and ACM
Nathaniel Palmer, WfMC, USA

Nathaniel Palmer, WfMC, USA

INTRODUCTION

In the half-century since Peter Drucker first identified and coined the phrase "knowledge worker," the share of the work force represented by this group has grown considerably, to as much as half of all workers by some measures. So, too, have grown investments targeting knowledge worker productivity, with global IT spending reaching $4.35 trillion in 2010, according to Global Technology Index author Dr. Howard A. Rubin.

Yet we are far from realizing the level of improvement seen in manual labor over the course of the last century. Traditionally, IT investments targeting business productivity have focused on one of two areas. The first is automation technologies, such as enterprise resource planning (ERP) or the more contemporary technology of business process management (BPM). Those address repeatable, predictable modes of work and are designed to enforce a command and control management model, where efficiency gains are sought through standardizing how work is performed.

Yet scripting work processes in advance, as is presented through work automation, offers little benefit for increasing knowledge worker productivity, without the ability to adapt to changes in the business environment. Much of the knowledge worker's daily activities cannot be accurately defined in advance, at least not with the precision necessary to code into IT applications, and therefore they most often take place outside the realm of ERP and BPM. Where it does occur, it is in the other common target area of IT investments—the tools and infrastructure that enable communication and information sharing, such as networking, e-mail, content management and increasingly social media.

As IT investments have advanced their footprint in the workplace, a gap has emerged. It can be found between e-mail and ad hoc communication tools, which, while used in one form or another by all knowledge workers, offer little with regard to task management, and the ERP/BPM realm, premised on predictable work patterns defined in advance. What has emerged to fill this void is Adaptive Case Management (ACM).

WHAT IS KNOWLEDGE WORK?

Knowledge work as a concept was really introduced just in the last 50 years; ancient in IT years, yet relatively new in the history of mankind. In "Management Challenges for the 21st Century," Drucker posits that during the 20th century the greatest contribution for management was the fifty-fold increase on productivity of manual work or the manual worker, particularly in manufacturing. That had been the goal from the beginning of the industrial revolution, and even before, with Adam Smith's allegorical pin factory onto Frederick Taylor's Scientific Method. Throughout the 20th century what could have been thought of as "knowledge work" was most often limited to coordination of manual workers. While there were doctors, lawyers, bankers and other knowledge-based professionals, they represented a relative small percent of the workforce. It was not until the 21st century that the shift had begun, to the point where today so much more of what we do is inarguably knowledge work. So much more is about leveraging our know-how in intellectual capital. As Drucker writes, "in the 21st century the absolute imperative for management is productivity of the knowledge worker."

Recently we took a survey of two hundred organizations and asked about the hurdles and pain points that knowledge workers face relative to productivity. What keeps them from being productive? Curiously, it is not the knowledge-intensive activities, it is not the stuff that really requires their know-how, such as determining what steps to take, or who to collaborate with or getting together a team of collaborators. Ultimately, the greatest productivity traps are found in the more mundane activities, simply tracking who's doing what, where they have dependencies on co-workers. Where are they in the course of their work, what's the state of their work? How are they managing the documentation that they need, the information and documents that they need to support a given task? These are the things that knowledge workers find the most challenging.

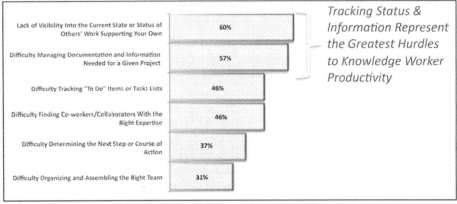

Source: 2011 ACM Survey

Common Productivity Hurdles Faced by Knowledge Workers

Looking at the how knowledge workers spend their day, the same group reported overwhelmingly that it's in unstructured and most often unpredictable work patterns. As shown above, only a third of their time is spent structured work that can be most easily can be or already has been automated. In most organizations, low hanging fruits have already been plucked, leaving few remaining opportunities. Yet for specific structured-but-not-automated processes that remain, they nonetheless add up to comparatively little of any given workers day and thus not an ideal target.

Where knowledge workers do spend most of their time is either in the purely ad-hoc space where nothing ever happens the same way twice, or otherwise within *barely repeatable processes*. The latter is involves specifically defined goals and milestones, but inevitably the sequence to realize these changes from day-to-day.

Barely repeatable processes are often those where the pathways are relatively complex with different variations and different decision points. Often with these types of processes it is possible to define and apply policies and specific business logic around how that work is performed (read "business rules") as well as high level patterns of how the process is going to flow (read "milestones") yet still be impossible to determine in advance the exact sequence of tasks and activities. For example, such a process may involve an electronic form or something that is launched by the BPM system, otherwise achieving the same milestone may instead involve a purely human task occurring entirely outside of this system. In each case, a series of activities is involved, as well as predefined outcomes required, yet that exact combination and sequence of activities is determined by the unique circumstances of a given case.

This pattern (described above) fits well with ACM, but not BPM. With BPM, all the possible paths and permutations are defined in advance, and as each activity occurs, the state of the process changes. As the state changes and is transferred from one activity to the next, control flows similarly from one activity to the next. So the business process map shows the flow of control or specifically who has management of the process at any given time.

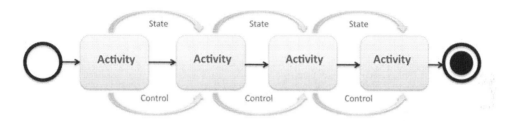

BPM Involves the Flow of Control and the Sequencing of State Changes

Contrast this with ACM, which really focuses on events and outcomes. An event occurs, a case file is opened, and then the end point is known. The circumstances, which define how and when the case is completed is known, but the means to reach that is not predetermined. A series of activities will occur, information will be created and added to the case, as that information and the context around it is added to the case, that's what determines the state of the case ultimately. And it's only when that goal is reached that the case is completed. There may be any number of processes that are kicked off during that time, but the sequence for those activities, the activities themselves may be predetermined but the sequence, how the work is performed and how it flows, that can't be determined in advance.

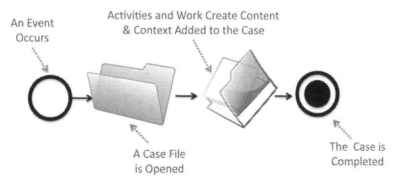

ACM is Event-Driven, Content- and Context-Aware

Comparing BPM and ACM exposes the difference between deterministic and non-deterministic processes. Deterministic processes are determined in advance. The actual pathways may be very complex, yet the decision points, the business logic, the business rules—all the attributes that determine how a process can flow are predefined. State is determined by whatever activity just occurred and how that relates to the process going forward.

ACM, in contrast, is inherently non-deterministic, where the end point is known but the pathway for reaching the outcome is determined by each stage, each milestone in the management of that case. The state of the case is not determined by where it fits on a particular flow chart or process map, but by the content and the context within the case.

Considered a basic process where an event occurs, here's a simplistic example; a customer reports a problem, a case is opened and then what happens next is the movement toward realizing and resolving the goal, but exactly *what* happens is not determined in advance. In this case an issue is investigated, could be that potential solutions are tried, maybe successfully, maybe un-successfully. No doubt there is correspondence with the customer, whether that is an external customer or an internal customer, where it's supplied unsuccessfully, alternatives are going to be researched. It may be something that takes months to resolve, it may be something that takes hours to resolve.

Yet unlike a BPM process where sequence is predetermined, with ACM all that is known is what the goal is, what the end state is defined as, and the policies, the rules, the resources, the players that are involved in that case, but not exactly how it's going to transpire. For that reason, because ACM is goal driven, it is also inherently nonlinear. A case evolves over time, toward achieving that goal, but often in unpredictable directions. It requires the ability to jump ahead, jump back, to go to any point based on the circumstances of that case. It is not a sequence that can be determined in advance.

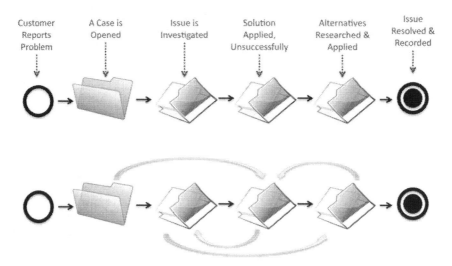

With ACM Goals Are Predetermined, Sequence and Pathways Are Not

With a BPM process, at any given point you are launching a process that has to run its course and be completed and that maybe that there are several processes that are involved. For example, managing the lifecycle of a relationship of a customer, using ACM you're managing that from beginning to end, without predetermining when that relationship is going to end. Rather, over the course of that relationship you will be advancing toward specific goals, such as on-boarding steps and product or services provisioning, as well as other specific milestones which in all likelihood do follow a managed or even automated process, yet the specific sequencing of these are predetermined. In all reality, all organizations have patterns of work that fall into the categories consistent with both traditional BPM and ACM. It is not an "either/or" proposition of "BPM vs ACM" exclusively, but rather a matter of when to apply which approach.

ACM PATTERNS: TAMING THE UNPREDICTABLE

We asked organizations about the type of work patterns that are consistent with ACM but that apply to their organization, whether or not they feel that today that they are doing ACM. Certainly there are ones that have a very mature notion of ACM, in the process or work pattern as it is managed today. A great example of this is adjudication or investigative case management. In these work patterns, it is not about the process per se, it is about the case– i.e., achieving the outcome and capturing how it was realized, rather than automating that process in a predefined way.

Here the notion of long-lived may indeed apply, as an investigative process, such as a background check or a criminal investigation that needs to live until that goal is reached, until the case is resolved. With background checks performed by government agencies, for example, backlogs of in-process and thus incomplete investigations are widespread. The role of ACM is to streamline these expediting that process, which requires improvement of both the quality of the information that is being captured as well as efficient as possible. Because the information capture in this process must be of evidentiary quality (something that can be proven in court if it's ever challenged) it is processes involved cannot be fully automated, but require considerable oversight by the professionals involved (e.g., knowledge workers.).

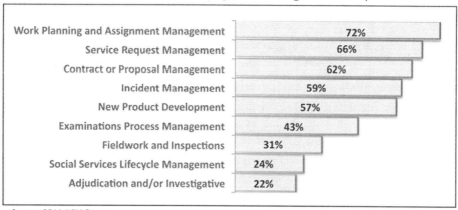

Source: 2011 ACM Survey

ACM Patterns Applicable to Surveyed Firms

Another example common to government agencies is "Social Services Lifecycle Management" involving the end-to-end interaction between the services provider (be it a government agency or non-profit organization) and their relationship with the beneficiary of those services. That cycle might last a single individual's lifetime, or it may be short-lived. In either case it will follow the lifecycle of the relationship, not any particular task or process or single activity. This is probably the most commonly understood pattern of case management.

"Work Planning and Assignment Management" was cited as being applicable to 72 percent of survey respondents. This pattern involves circumstances of managing and tracking who performs work, what their assignments are, and the interplay between projects and resources, not specifically managing the work itself. This presents a compelling example of the benefits of ACM as it can be either short-or long-lived with little opportunity to define this at the outset. It's something that very often will run over the relationship with a particular employee which may go on for decades, or in some cases, it may be a matter of weeks or months.

In contrast, "Service Request Management" presents a use case or work pattern where by its definition, the process should not be long-lived. The service incident, whether via an internal help desk or external customer, originates with an event or issue where the goal inevitably to be resolved as expeditiously as possible. The pathway realizing this will likely follow standard procedures, including predefined processes at various points, yet will also involve some degree of unpredictability. There will be investigation, things that are tried; you can't determine in advance exactly how that's going to unfold. What is required is to capture all the interaction, while also providing the tools to guide those involved to resolve the issue as quickly as possible. This is an ideal application of ACM—capturing context, guiding knowledge workers, but aiding rather than automating that which requires human intervention.

RETHINKING KNOWLEDGE WORK

In a recent McKinsey Quarterly article entitled "Rethinking Knowledge Work," Tom Davenport defines case management (going forward referred to as "ACM") as a combination of workflow, content management, business rules, portal and collaboration tools, which collectively allow for the completion of an entire "case" or unit of work. In other words, it is the orchestration of those tools together that support the entire lifecycle of a case, from end-to-end. ACM ties together the tools that support knowledge work, as single application and environment, whether virtually or physically, with a single point of access. That involves the integration of external tools and social media (think "mashups") to facilitate communication and assist with data visualization, with various information sources or repositories.

ACM differs from tools such as BPM and ECM because it is not simply a parallel silo, but rather a superset or master system of record, capturing both the "what" (data, files, records or most often links to the physical sources of those) and the "how" (metadata, audit trail, as well as the context of decisions and actions). As a result, adaptive ACM facilitates better data and records management through the ability to identify and organize content distinctly from other cases—whether shared or unique, it is connected to the specific business context in which it was used.

In this way, an ACM system, the case folder and the case itself is a system of record. This is in contrast with BPM; even though it is connected with ECM or other information management abilities, the function of BPM is to provide a transactional thread across multiple systems of record.

Case management, by its definition, is a system of record of what happened. It captures the context as well as links the information as the case evolves. It can include email, voice mail, traditional documents, GIS documents and video. All the content and the related context are edited around that which is required to have a 360-degree understanding of what has happened with that case. The files of that media may reside outside and, in fact, may be used by multiple cases but the ACM system pulls it all together in a virtual folder to have one version of the truth, ultimately providing the permanent record of that case.

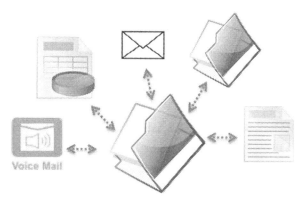

Virtual or Physical, ACM is System of Record For All Forms of Content

Davenport writes, "[ACM] can create value whenever some degree of structure or process can be imposed on information-intensive work. Until recently, structured provision approaches have been applied mostly to lower-level information tasks that are repetitive, predictable and thus easier to automate." ACM offers the chance to improve the productivity of knowledge work by allowing knowledge workers to make smart choices and apply best practices, not to simply automate decisions for them.

Productivity improvements, measured in both financial and non-financial terms, come from reduced re-work, as well as improved customer and employee satisfaction. In part, that results from greater visibility into areas of work previously "under the radar" when performed in purely ad hoc environments, offering the ability to prioritize activities across multiple cases, balancing workloads, as well as monitoring quality, timeliness and speed.

BUSINESS IS DRIVEN BY GOALS

Supporting the dynamic nature of today's business environments and the self-directed, non-repetitive nature of knowledge worker processes requires the ability to assemble structured and unstructured processes from basic predefined business entities, content, social interactions and business rules. It requires capturing actionable information and supporting decisions without having to model or reengineer processes in advance, but instead based on patterns defined by business users. Unlike traditional BPM systems, where the focus is the process route along which the item of work or case information follows a predefined path, with ACM the case itself that is the focus.

Drucker has labeled this orientation or management practice as "management by objectives" or MBO. With this approach, knowledge workers and management establish specific goals or objectives within the organization so that the outcome is mutually understood, but the specific course of action and the decision-making are left to the knowledge worker. ACM provides guidance and measurement of outcomes, as well as the long-term maintenance of data surrounding the process to demonstrate how objectives were realized and decisions were made.

Highly predictable work is easy to support using traditional programming techniques, while unpredictable work cannot be accurately scripted in advance, and so requires the involvement of the workers themselves. Aiding knowledge workers, enabling real productivity gains, would logically come from both automating repetitive work where possible, while facilitating the less predictable, more dynamic work modes requiring the flexibility to be defined according the circumstances and context of a given moment in time.

Consistent with this, in our recent survey respondents reported that knowledge workers spent two-thirds of any given day in activities which did not follow a predetermined path and were unpredictable in nature, but much of this also involved specific goals. In other words, most of a knowledge worker's day is spent working toward an identified outcome, yet the means for achieving this cannot be predetermined.

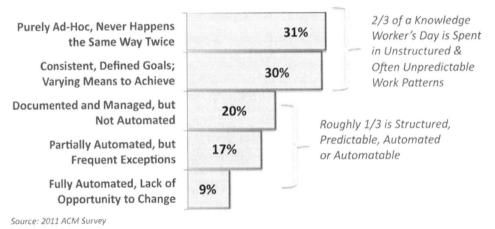

Source: 2011 ACM Survey

Percent of Day Spent in Different Work Modes

ACM assists the knowledge worker to apply know-how and make decisions. ACM addresses those issues in the productivity hurdles, the mundane activities and transaction costs involved in managing work such as having visibility into the state of affairs and current activities, managing and capturing information in context—as well as having business rules and analytics to be able to apply to that.

Providing guidance in the form of help in knowledge management functions and to be able to provide that in context; that's where the notion of adaptability applies—adapting to circumstances of the case as it evolves rather than simply predetermining at any given time what is supposed to be occurring. It has to occur, it has to adapt based on where that state is, where that case is. State is determined based on the information in the case.

Adaptive, Not Ad Hoc

The use of "adaptive" in *Adaptive* Case Management refers to the need for knowledge worker support systems that are not explicated, programmed or hand-coded by specialists as they have been in the past, but instead can be dynamically modified by ordinary users in the course of their work.

This orientation frames the definition of ACM systems that are not simply ad hoc and devoid of any manageability, but are able to support decision-making and data capture, while allowing the freedom for knowledge workers to apply their own understanding and subject matter expertise to respond to unique or changing circumstances within the business environment.

One core quality of ACM is support for goal-seeking and goal-driven processes, where goals can be modified "in flight" by the knowledge worker. Similarly, knowledge captured during the performance of the case can support the identification and creation of new processes or case rules, without requiring IT/developer involvement.

Ultimately, adaptability is defined as more than simply the ability to change, but how the change is facilitated. It can be measured through a reduced need for training and change management of knowledge workers, as a result of guidance provided by the system. With ACM, this is based on the current context of the work and what needs to be done, including the ability to identify and initiate collaboration with specific subject matter experts. If this is starting to sound like knowledge management, it should. Although not designed as a repository for codifying implicit knowledge in the traditional spirit of knowledge management, it should provide an effective means for identifying know-how by capturing the context in which knowledge work is performed.

Other examples of adaptability in ACM include providing access to reusable templates for initiating new cases, including the use of completed cases as templates. That allows knowledge workers to take advantage of automated tasks, while controlling if and when they are invoked, for example, having the ability to create standard correspondence (letters, e-mails, etc.) at any point in the case, with the system automatically capturing context of interaction and responses.

BUILDING RESPONSIVE SYSTEMS

In many ways, emergence of ACM represents the shift from adapting business practices to the design of IT systems, to building systems that reflect how work is actually performed. The latter is the way all IT projects should be approached, yet the former spotlights the traditional gap between business and IT understanding. Accurately assessing the business impact of IT is often difficult because the introduction of software changes the way people work, as well as the way they are organized.

In this way, the case may live on in perpetuity, retaining this last state until another event occurs to launch it or it may be specifically or officially put into a suspense state, able to be restarted at any time. But it can also be used to launch another case.

So the case itself can be a template for a new case instance. For example, with a costumer resolution scenario, it may be that a particular customer issue now has become a best practice for unrelated issues, related issues, or other occurrences of that issue and that case can then be the template for how that's is going to be solved going forward.

Enabling Knowledge Workers to Work The Way They Work Best

ACM enables better records and data management by connecting context and outcomes with the actual information. The ability to identify cases, to be able to access that information based on the case, based on the context of what occurred, as well as to manage that separately so the different files can be cross referenced and linked between cases, ultimately this allows for capturing and managing the context and the know how-from what has occurred in the course of the performance of that case.

ACM is ultimately about allowing knowledge workers to work the way that they work the best. To provide them the tools and information they need to do their job in the way that they want to work. Increasingly, this means having access to social media and outside information sources. There is a significant amount of work currently conducted through LinkedIn, Twitter and other social sources as well as resources selected by individual workers that create input and contextual information that's a critical part of the case record, but is not part of any centrally managed IT infrastructure. ACM provides the ability not only to pull that in as part of the case record, but also to be a platform for enabling mash-ups and to work in the chosen environment.

Similarly, extending the transactional management of traditional BPM with the adaptable goal driven benefits of ACM, provides the ability for delivering work and managing where and the way the work is done today. Rather than creating yet another island of automation, ACM allows us to work the way we work best.

The direction for ACM allows the work to follow the worker, providing the cohesiveness of a single point of access. ACM does not impose whether this work is virtual or physical but pulls all the end points, information, environments and provides that long-term record of how work is done, as well as the guidance, rules, visibility and input that enable knowledge workers to be more productive.

Case Management: Addressing Unique BPM Requirements[1]

Bruce Silver, Bruce Silver Associates, USA

Over the past several years, Business Process Management Suites (BPMS) have matured into powerful platforms for process automation and performance optimization, many configurable by business-friendly process modeling tools. The benefits of BPMS over a wide range of processes—improvements in cycle time, throughput, resource utilization, standardization and compliance, business integration, and end-to-end performance visibility—are well established. However, an important class of business processes has been unable to enjoy them because of the limitations of conventional BPM Suites: *case management*. This report describes the differences between case management and conventional BPM and shows you what to look for in a BPM solution to truly support case management.

WHAT IS CASE MANAGEMENT?

One problem with case management is that no single definition for it exists. It has been variously described as a segment or style of document management, knowledge management, or customer relationship management. Certainly, document content, collaborative decision-making, and customer interactions are important elements of case management, but they are important in conventional BPM as well.

The essential distinguishing characteristic of case management is the "unstructured" progression of a case from initiation to its final state. In conventional BPM, by definition, a process instance progresses through a sequence of steps you can describe explicitly as paths in a diagram, leading from a single start point to one or more end points. The path logic for any particular instance might be determined by human judgment, external events, and business rules, but the steps, branching logic, and exception paths are all definable in advance.

In case management, by contrast, the flow logic cannot be expressed in such a diagram defined in advance. In case management, human judgment, external events, and business rules don't just determine paths through a predefined diagram. Instead those factors determine at runtime *which* activities need to be performed and whether additional steps are required, either picked from a predefined menu or conceived on the fly. While this flexibility is an essential ingredient of many types of real-world processes, conventional BPM Suites demand a process model—however complex—that can be completely defined in advance.

Moreover, a case is rarely a single process in the conventional BPM sense. It is a *collection* of processes and isolated tasks, the number and identity of which cannot be fixed by a predefined template or rules. While case templates provide a convenient starting point for cases of a particular type, the actual steps and information required to complete each case are determined by a combination of human judgment, rules, and events occurring at runtime. Conventional BPM can sometimes manage individually the various processes involved in a case, but it has difficulty managing progress of the case as a whole.

---

[1] © Reproduced with permission of BPMS Watch by Bruce Silver.

In case management, the case folder provides overall coordination of the case as a whole, partially defined in advance by the case template, but with the flexibility to change at runtime as each case proceeds.

Despite its semi-structured nature, case processes suffer from the same problems as conventional structured processes.

- They take too long to complete.
- Resources are not used efficiently. Information is misplaced or not retained.
- No standardization across the organization.
- Difficulty of enforcing compliance with policies, regulations, and best practices.
- Lack of visibility into key performance indicators, either at the individual case level in real time or historical trends in the aggregate.

BPM Suites bring relief for all of these issues with conventional processes. Case management processes need the same capabilities... but this requires a different type of BPM platform.

PROFILES OF CASE MANAGEMENT PROCESSES

Case management processes are a common occurrence in many industry segments, including government, insurance, banking and credit, legal, and healthcare.

DISPUTE RESOLUTION

A good example of dispute resolution concerns billing and credit card disputes. Processing payments is a conventional structured process, but when a customer disputes a charge or demands a refund, case management is usually required.

Even if the credit card issuer provides a standard form for initiating the case, the activities required to resolve each case depend on a myriad of factors. What is the reason for the dispute? Were the goods delivered or services provided? Were they defective? Was the defect the fault of the manufacturer, the shipper, the customer, or some other party? Does the dispute concern the amount of the charge? And so forth.

Resolution of the dispute could depend on any or all of these factors, each of which typically involves production and review of documents. The credit card company may require information from the customer; the manufacturer, retailer, or service provider; the shipper; possibly legal counsel, attorneys, or even law enforcement. The rules involved could depend on the customer's location. As the facts unfold, new tasks and documents may be added to the case.

In the end, there is no way to define in advance the credit card company's dispute resolution "process" as an explicit flow from case initiation to resolution. But many of the same factors that motivate conventional BPM—timely resolution, efficient utilization of resources, compliance, and end-to-end performance visibility—are still important.

Other examples of dispute resolution case management include healthcare claims and grievance procedures, HR termination, and civil litigation and mediation.

BENEFITS ADMINISTRATION

Case management is well established in many segments of benefits administration, particularly in the public sector. Examples include disability, veterans' benefits, welfare assistance, student financial aid, and grants programs. Within a single case there are issues of eligibility, disbursement of funds or services, changing circumstances of the beneficiary, reporting and compliance.

UNDERWRITING

In various segments of financial services, including commercial lending, life and disability insurance, and securities, the underwriting process is really case management. The activities and documents required depend on the circumstances of each case. While the components of "standard" cases may be predictable, there are many exceptions, requiring additional input from lawyers, accountants, regulators, and investigators.

PROJECT MANAGEMENT

An application area that could benefit from case management BPM, but has received little attention to date, falls under the heading of project management. Examples include launch of a new product or service, a major IT system upgrade, or mergers and acquisitions. There may be relatively few instances of a particular type of case, but each may represent high value and high risk. As with the other examples, the significant attribute is the fact that unanticipated tasks and processes may be added once the project is underway. Project management software typically provides just planning and tracking; case management adds the BPM dimensions of automated workflow, enforcement of business rules, and application integration.

Differences from Conventional BPM

TECHNICAL REQUIREMENTS FOR CASE MANAGEMENT

These examples share a number of common factors. Some of them are absent entirely in conventional BPM, while others simply play a different role in case management.

Case Information Managed as Documents

A large fraction of case-related information is received and managed in the form of *business documents* rather than structured data. Where conventional BPM applies automated logic to data, case logic more often applies human judgment to information contained in documents. Thus a case management platform must include a complete document management system, a comprehensive facility for creating, capturing, indexing, storing, finding, viewing, sharing, editing, versioning, and retaining a wide variety of document types. Simple document attachments and a viewer, as provided by conventional BPM, are not enough. Case-oriented BPM should be able to apply rules to document events—check-in of a new version, for example—for automation and case status tracking. Just as you cannot predefine all the tasks needed to complete the case, you cannot specify in advance all of the documents required. While common ones can be required by the case template; others may be added ad-hoc at runtime.

Case Activities Added at Runtime

Some tasks and processes needed to complete the case may be defined in advance through the case template, but *ad hoc tasks*—whether selected from a predefined menu or defined from scratch—are a critical distinguishing element of case management. Often, those tasks are related to creating, obtaining, reviewing, and approving documents. Some of those tasks could represent conventional processes involving multiple participants. Managing a case as a single unit composed of independent tasks and processes—some added at runtime—is simply beyond the scope of conventional BPMS.

Case Advancement through Events

In BPM, an *event* means "something that happened." Conventional BPM often *initiates* processes based on some event, such as receipt of a document, but from there the instance progresses like a train moving down a track. Subsequent events might switch the train to another track at specified points in the flow, but for the most part the process advances by itself. Completion of one task is what triggers the next one down the line.

Case management does not normally work by routing the case folder to the next task sequentially down the line. Instead it advances through events, both external and internal:

- *External events* include receipt of a phone call, letter, fax, or email related to the case. The contents of that message are added to the case folder, and new tasks or processes may be created.
- *Internal events* include assignments and business rules. Case workers assign tasks and initiate processes as they deem necessary as they work on the case. Business rules within the case may automatically create and assign tasks—or perform fully automated actions—based on either external events, completion of other case tasks, or expiration of task deadlines.

Thus, instead of a train moving down a track from task to task, the conceptual model of a case is a collection of independent parallel tasks interacting via events. Those tasks define the case context and are visible, along with case documents, from the shared case folder. The state of the case as a whole is determined by the combined state of all its tasks and documents.

Case Context through Shared Case Folder

Human judgment about advancement or resolution of the case frequently depends on not a single document in isolation, but the document collection as a whole. Thus, all case information—subject to specific security and access control rules—is typically available to users working on the case in the form of a *shared case folder*. The assumption that case workers know where to look for the case information they require represents the *knowledge dimension* of case management. In addition to case data and documents, the case folder provides shared access to case tasks and deadlines.

CHALLENGES: WHY CASE MANAGEMENT IS HARD FOR CONVENTIONAL BPMS

As awareness of the case management gap in BPM has increased, BPMS vendors are beginning to add one or two features to their standard offering and declare it suitable for case management. But even with these isolated enhancements, conventional BPMS has a hard time addressing case management for several reasons:

The process engine. The key feature of a BPMS is its central orchestration engine, which automates the flow of a process instance according to a predefined process model. Some BPMSs have added the ability to insert ad-hoc tasks from another task in the model. But such tasks are not independent, running in parallel, with their own rules or possibility of spawning other steps from within them. They are simply grafted into the sequential flow for that instance. The fallacy here is that a case is not a single process. It is a collection of tasks and processes interlinked by events, rules, and business judgment. Conventional BPMS cannot manage such a collection as a single complex "thing."

Content-awareness. Most BPMSs are designed to operate with data, not business documents. They treat documents as attachments, available for viewing, but they rarely support creating, editing, versioning, organizing, or finding the specific document types required by the case, or storing documents in large volume, or responding to content events, or retaining documents for years after the case is complete. Good content management systems can do those things, but they need to be deeply integrated with the BPM component to meet the needs of case. BPM Suites from content management vendors do this part reasonably well, but they tend to fall down on the next requirement.

The Case Folder. As the central feature of a case management system, one would think that an out-of-the-box case folder would be part of any purported case management feature in a BPMS. Not so. BPMS vendors are far more likely to propose that the tools used to configure the conventional process portal environment can be used create something like a case folder. Outside of the hassle involved, particularly in integrating the tasks, documents, rules, and events involved in the case, this approach misses the core idea of case management: a case is not just a collection of isolated things, like processes and documents, but *a single thing* that is progressing toward completion. That is what the case folder represents. If you cannot understand the status of the case as a whole through simple inspection of the case folder, you can't really do case management very well.

CASE360: A CASE MANAGEMENT BPM PLATFORM

The first BPMS that really meets the needs of case management is a product you may not have heard of: Case360 from Global 360. Case360 is a special-purpose BPMS dedicated to case management. It provides all of the technical requirements described above and overcomes the three challenges. While its primary focus is case management, Case360 can support conventional processes as well, either standalone or as aspects of a case folder.

The heart of the system (Figure 1) is the case folder. Underneath are a complete set of supporting services, including process modeling and automation, document management, business rules, collaboration, and performance analytics.

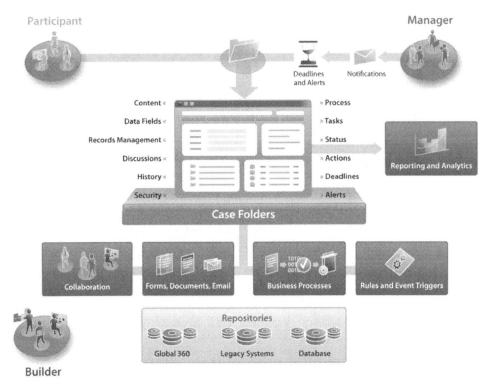

Figure 1: Case360 Case Management Capabilities. Source: Global 360

THE CASE FOLDER

Figure 2 illustrates a typical case folder. All case folders contain the same set of information panels—Data (form), Contents, Tasks, History, and Discussions—but are offered in a wide variety of prebuilt configurable layouts that can be easily modified. While a case owner can be assigned, the case folder itself is a shared resource, typically not locked to one user. This is critical for true case management in order to allow multiple activities to happen in parallel.

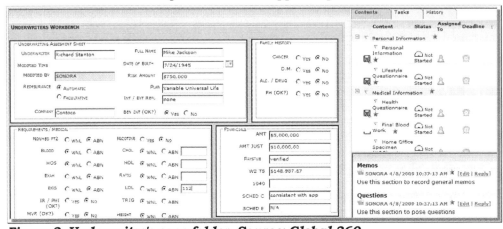

Figure 2. Underwriter's case folder. Source: Global 360

Case360 separates the case folder's business logic from its presentation, which can vary based on the user, stage of the case, or virtually any other case information. This allows task-specific views of a case, simplifying user interaction. The History panel provides a complete audit trail of task, content, and data state changes for the case, and can be configured to include even read-only actions to comply with regulatory demands. The Discussions panel provides collaboration via threaded discussions and offers an alternative to hand-written "sticky notes" typically found within paper case folders.

Figure 3. Tasks panel showing case status at a glance. Source: Global 360

TASKS

Given the nature of case management business processes, task management is a critical capability. The Tasks panel (Figure 3) lists all of the tasks for the case, their assignee (by name or role), deadline, completion status, and deadline. A task can be standalone or represent a complete BPM process. (Case360 provides a Visio-based process modeler and associated execution engine, just like a conventional BPMS.) Users are automatically notified when they are assigned tasks, and access the task user interface either via the case folder as a whole or a task form. Case360 includes a full graphical, scriptable form builder for this purpose.

Tasks that are always expected to be part of a case can be predefined in the case template, but others may be added at runtime from the Actions menu, either from a list of predefined tasks or defined on the fly (Figure 4).

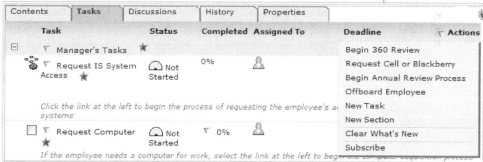

Figure 4. Add ad-hoc tasks from a drop-down. Source: Global 360

DOCUMENTS

A strength of Case360 is support for documents, both as part of the case folder and as standalone entities. Unlike most other case management solutions or BPM Suites, Case360 includes a complete document repository (Figure 5), supporting check-in/check-out, versioning, storage migration, and retention management. Documents are defined through the use of templates, much like with case folders. These templates define specific document types, including formats and metadata.

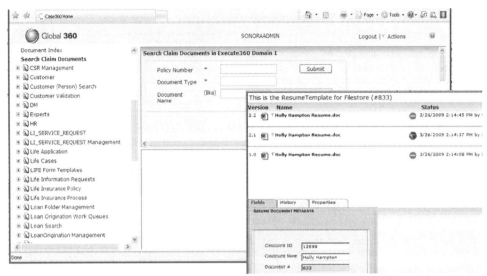

Figure 5. Case360 Content is managed in a true ECM repository. Source: Global 360

Content	Status	Assigned To	Deadline
▽ Application Pages			
▽ Personal Information	Completed	Matt Mulcahey (nba)	7/28/2009 4:33:32 PM
▽ Traditional and Universal Life Policy Details	Completed	Matt Mulcahey (nba)	7/28/2009 4:33:28 PM
▽ Life Financial Information	Completed	Matt Mulcahey (nba)	Must be filled 1 business hour(s) after th "Life Financial Information" is in progress.
▽ Fraud Notice	Completed	Matt Mulcahey (nba)	Must be filled 1 business hour(s) after th "Fraud Notice" is in progress.
▽ Authorization	Completed	Life Manager	Must be filled 1 business hour(s) after th "LI_Traditional_Universal Life Application" is in p
▽ Agreement	Completed	Lorne Stein	Must be filled 1 business hour(s) after th "Personal Information" is in progress
▽ Agent's Statement	Completed	Bella Winston (Agent Service Associate)	Must be filled 1 business hour(s) after th "Personal Information" is in progress.
▽ Conditional Receipt	Deferred		
▽ Applicant Questionnaires			
▽ Lifestyle Questionnaire	In Progress	Jack Montague	7/28/2009 1:00:00 PM
▽ Health Questionnaire	Not Started	Life Analyst	7/28/2009 1:00:00 PM

Figure 6. Case folder Contents panel shows documents and placeholders for missing documents. Source: Global360

The Contents panel (Figure 6) lists documents attached to the case as well as *placeholders* for documents required by the case. As with tasks, a base set of documents and placeholders is typically specified by the case template, but others can be added ad-hoc from the Actions menu. A placeholder represents a document that is expected to be included as part of the case, and may have an assignee, completion status, and deadline.

Of critical importance is the fact that a single document may be included in multiple cases. In addition to Global 360's own content repositories, Case360 can access documents in third party repositories such as Documentum, FileNet, Sharepoint, and others.

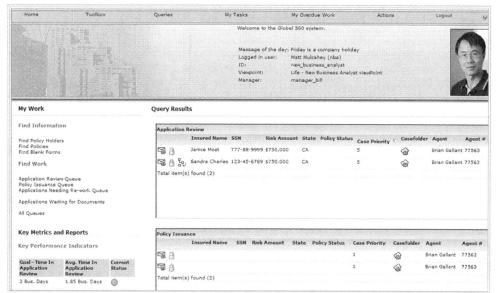

Figure 7. Case360 home page allows users to access assigned work and documents. Source: Global360

PROCESS MANAGEMENT AND EVENTS

While case workers may be prompted by a task notification or external event to access a particular case folder, they can also access Case360 as a conventional BPM process portal (Figure 7) to see all of their assigned tasks, search for documents, view performance metrics, etc. Each user's home page can be set up with predefined queries for work or documents, and supports additional queries from the portal.

In addition to manual interaction with the case folder and portal, the case template definition tool provides a scripting environment supporting event-triggered automation of case processing. State changes of case tasks, content, and data trigger scripts that can assign new tasks or placeholders, update case data, or execute a web service. Scripting has access to the entire Case360 API, so it can do about anything you want. Event-triggered automation is a key element of case management. Also, Case360 supports Corticon's business-friendly decision table designer and rule engine, allowing automated decisions to be triggered by case tasks and events.

PERFORMANCE AND TRACKING

While analytics are an afterthought in other case management solutions, Case360 includes performance visibility and optimization tools. Task and content events are aggregated and tracked by an analytics engine that can provide dashboards of KPI charts, tables, and alerts. Supervisors can monitor the productivity of case workers and teams, and adjust QC/audit and priority review thresholds as current performance conditions warrant (Figure 8). Such features are just as important in case management as in conventional BPM for many types of processes.

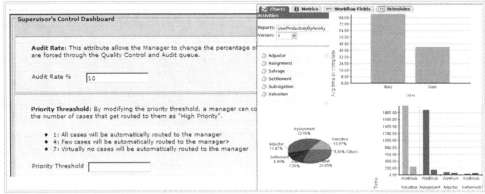

Figure 8. Monitor performance of case management and traditional process work. Source: Global 360

CASE360 CUSTOMER EXAMPLES

Dispute Resolution

Merchant services providers enable businesses to accept payments from their customers through credit cards, debit cards or stored value gift cards and checks. Retrievals, chargebacks and customer service requests are a daily occurrence in which the handoffs and information involved is determined by human judgment as the case is progressing. Case360 promotes compliance with regulations and best practices without constraining users to a static path of "first A then B then C". Having a complete case history is critical for understanding the root cause of the problem, speeding them to a solution.

Paperless Judicial System

In courtrooms around the country, judges, attorneys and clerks are engaged in the complex process we call the judicial system. Whether related to Traffic, Probate, Misdemeanor or Felony offenses, the volume of information required to complete a case is staggering. Motions, filings, judgments, receipts, and correspondence must all be tracked. Hearings need to be scheduled and re-scheduled, all within statutory timeliness limits. Case360's paperless approach allows rapid access to all information pertinent to a specific case, ad-hoc reassignment of tasks, and other capabilities missing in conventional BPMS.

Medical Claims Appeals

The normal process for handling medical claims is structured enough to be handled by conventional BPMS. However, when a claim is denied, the Appeals and Grievances process is not. A patient's appeal of a denied claim kicks off a thorough review of the claim and all supporting information. This involves sending copies of a patient's records to various interested parties, including third party physicians and lawyers. The order in which activities occur is not fixed in advance, and enforcing timeliness of reviews is a challenge. Case360 coordinates the Appeal and tracks all documents and tasks to ensure that all parties complete their tasks in the allotted time, which can often stretch in some cases to years.

THE BOTTOM LINE: WHAT TO LOOK FOR IN A CASE MANAGEMENT PLATFORM

I expect to see a growing list of BPMS vendors declare their offerings case management platforms, based on some facility for dealing with documents and ad-hoc activities. To meet the needs of real-world case management processes, however, you need more than that. Here's what to look for:

Case folder out-of-the-box. It should provide a central access point for all of the tasks, processes, documents, data, and other artifacts related to the case, in a presentation that lets you understand the overall case status at a glance. BPMS vendors' portal and mashup builder tools have gotten pretty good, but you don't want something that just looks like a case folder. It has to actually be a case folder. The difference is integration under the hood between the tasks, processes, documents, data elements, and discussion threads that comprise each case. You want that integration to be prebuilt.

Case templates. A case template is a model for a particular type of case, specifying a list of tasks and documents typically required. Of course, in any instance you can elect to omit some or add new ones, but the case template provides the starting point. The case management platform should include a rich case template design tool that supports event-triggered automation in addition to interactive tasks.

Ad-hoc tasks and documents. A key distinction between case management and conventional BPM is the ad-hoc element. At any point in a case you need to be able to add new tasks and document placeholders, either selected from a menu or defined on the fly.

Support for conventional processes. You shouldn't have to give up conventional BPM to handle a case. Real-world cases often contain multiple conventional processes, and these should be supported with conventional BPMS functionality: workflow automation, application integration, business rule support, etc. The point is a case is not a single process. It contains multiple processes, including those added at runtime. The processes need to be managed as processes in addition to managing the case as a whole. Ideally, you want a single platform for both the case management and conventional BPM support.

Document-awareness. Documents play a critical role in case management. A single document may be referenced by multiple cases, and its lifetime is independent of the cases that use it. You need a true enterprise content repository for case management, providing foldering, search, versioning, access control, and retention management. There are many ECM repositories out there, and many conventional BPMSs can integrate with them without too much difficulty. But case management really wants tight integration, so that when a document is added or updated or approved, the case is made aware of that event and can take action on it automatically.

Event-triggered automation. Cases progress by means of events, both internal and external. Because there is no "map" for progressing through the case, all the component tasks and documents announce their status changes through events. External events—a phone call, email, or letter—also move the case along. The case management platform should be able to define rules that automatically trigger actions when particular events occur. This not only ensures efficiency but standardization and compliance.

Performance visibility. Business activity monitoring (BAM) and analytics are an important feature of conventional BPMS, and the need is no less in case management. Managers and supervisors need dashboards key performance indicators and alerts at both the case instance and aggregate level.

Clearly, the technical challenge is great for case management BPM vendors. The platform needs to provide everything a conventional BPMS provides, and add case management on top. That explains why BPMS vendors typically promote case management "features" rather than a true case management BPM platform.

Case360 shows that it can be done. If you've been wondering why conventional BPMS doesn't seem to be flexible enough for your business problems, you perhaps should think about a case management platform.

Using the *AdaPro Workstream Platform* for improving Knowledge Work

Frank Michael Kraft, AdaPro GmbH, Germany

My chapter *Improving Knowledge Work* in the book *Mastering the Unpredictable* (Kraft 2010) describes how adaptive case management (ACM) can leverage the abilities of individual knowledge workers. It describes a case study of Leona, who works in the engineering department in a company of about one hundred and fifty employees and how she uses ACM to manage customer service and subsequent development planning and coordination for the phone systems that her company offers. That chapter was without any reference to an individual tool, but described the holistic approach and how individual knowledge workers can draw immediate benefit from it.

This chapter now completes the narrative, by showing how the case can be performed by a tool, the AdaPro Workstream Platform.

As you know from (Kraft 2010) Leona's regular job is to design new functionality for the telephone system they sell. This includes requirements for hardware components ordered from a supplier and software components developed by their software development team. This week, it's her turn to provide second-level support: she takes customer calls that cannot be solved by first-level support to ensure that the more difficult cases are solved.

In (Kraft 2010) it is described, how Leona performs some steps with the help of the ACM system. These steps are now shown in this chapter together with some additional functionality.

- Creating a Case in a Workstream
- Using past Knowledge Work Results
- Detailed Process Planning
- Managing Responsibilities
- Sprints and Burndown
- Working with Templates

CREATING A CASE IN A WORKSTREAM

When the telephone rings and a customer is on the line describing a problem with dropped calls under certain conditions, Leona asks some questions about when the problem occurs, what the circumstances are, and whether it is reproducible. Her knowledge of the design of the system guides this line of questioning.

Leona has the *AdaPro Workstream Platform* system available and she wants to create a case—or as it is named in the *AdaPro Workstream Platform* a *workitem*.

A workitem is always part of a *workstream*. What is a workstream? A workstream is a group of knowledge workers that work towards a common purpose, the workitems and documents, that are needed for it, and milestones (or *sprints*) that are defined to manage the timeline. Also it is a search unit and a unit for analytics.

One workstream can have many members (user accounts) and one knowledge worker having one user account can be member of many workstreams. Workstream members can be added and removed from workstreams as needed, also while the workstream is ongoing.

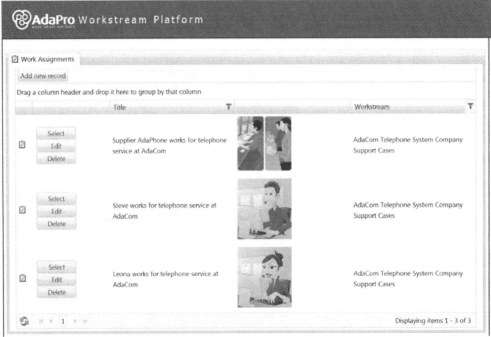

Figure 1: Assignments of Knowledge Workers to a Workstream

In Figure 1 we can see the workstream for *AdaCom Telephone System Support Cases* and the assigned members, which are Leona, Steve and one user account for the hardware supplier AdaPhone. AdaCom is Leona's company that offers the phone systems, while AdaPhone is the hardware supplier. AdaPhone has only one user account in this example. Of course each individual knowledge worker of AdaPhone could have an account.

Here we also can see why it is important, that the *AdaPro Workstream Platform* is software in the cloud. Workstreams can be cross company or cross organization in general. They may include some knowledge workers from the own organization and some from others. However they work together in a network—depending on the actual workstream. Which organization will host the workstream platform in this case? This is not always clear. However hosting the workstream platform in the cloud makes it possible to participate in many workstreams across many organizations and still have one central place to manage knowledge work including search over all own workstreams (which will be explained later).

Figure 2: Workstreams of Leona

If Leona logs in, she can see that she is part of the *AdaCom Telephone System Support Cases Workstream* and that she has a personal workstream for her own workitems. Her personal workstream content is not visible to anybody except herself. All content of other workstreams is visible to those members of the other workstream—depending on the knowledge worker assignments. It is an advantage of the *AdaPro Workstream Platform* that Leona has all workstreams at one glance with only one user account. She does not have to log out and log in again to a different workstream, if she wants to see different content. Still the visibility of the individual workstream content to others is different.

Now Leona chooses the menu item *workitems* under the menu section *AdaCom Telephone System Support Cases Workstream*. By this she makes sure that she enters the new workitem into the right workstream. She would create a Workitem, take notes about the symptoms, and try to estimate for the customer how long it will take to close the case.

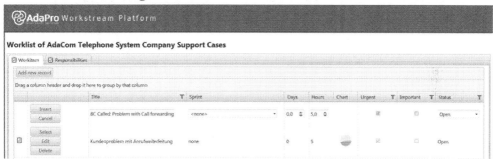

Figure 3: *Creating the Workitem*

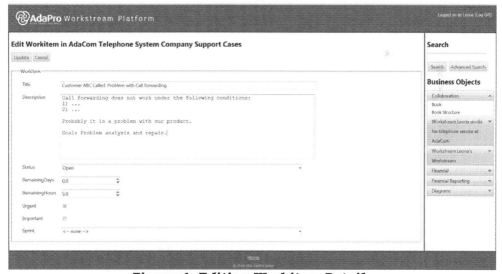

Figure 4: *Editing Workitem Details*

USING PAST KNOWLEDGE WORK RESULTS

Leona remembers that some weeks ago there was another similar case where she attached some documentation. So she searches the *AdaPro Workstream Platform* for that past case and she gets the link to the documentation.

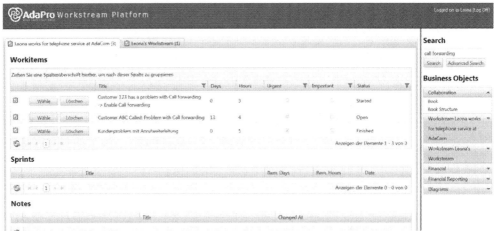

Figure 5: Search Results from different Workstreams

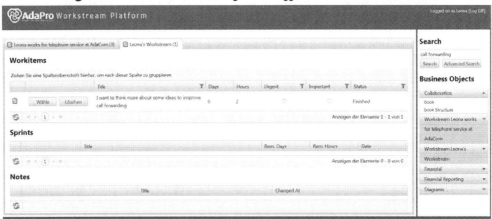

Figure 6: Search Results from personal Workstream

Workitem [Customer YXZ has a problem with Call forwarding] in AdaCom Telephone System Company Support Cases

Figure 7: Attached Documentation in old Workstream

A search in the *AdaPro Workstream Platform* is a global search in all workstreams of the user account. In this case, Leona finds three entries in the workstream for telephone support, that she shares with other co-workers (see Figure 5) and one entry in her personal workstream (see Figure 6). Her colleague, Steve, would find three entries as well in the workstream for telephone support but probably none in his personal workstream. The global search is an advantage, because in this case it is not necessary to log in to different user accounts to search. It is easier to find the entry, if you do not exactly remember in which workstream you had the entry you are looking for.

After reading the documentation, Leona decides, that it is a different problem that must be analyzed in more detail. This will take much longer because the problem cause must be analyzed and mitigated. In the next step Leona prepares a plan—she defines a process for this.

DETAILED PROCESS PLANNING

To plan the details of the problem analysis and mitigation Leona needs to involve different parties. Because of the nature of the problem, she is quite sure that some software checks and hardware checks are needed. The software check can be done by own personnel, but the hardware check needs to be done by the supplier of the module. So, as next steps, Leona creates all these sub-workitems she can tell for now—drawing from her knowledge and experience. Figure 8 shows the diagram from (Kraft 2010), Figure 9 and Figure 10 show some of the steps that Leona performs in the *AdaPro Workstream Platform*. In Figure 11 we can see how the resulting structure looks like in the workstream platform. This is a tree where Leona can drag and drop sub-trees—if necessary.

Of course, she cannot be sure at this point in time, that the goal *Find the Problem Cause* is reached, if all sub-workitems including all planned checks have been executed. Therefore she describes the goal of the workitem *Find the Problem Cause* as text in the detailed description as well. This is important, because this is a difference to classical process modeling and also classical project management. In classical process modeling a super-task is completed, if the sub-tasks are completed—or if the defined sub-process has reached a defined end—and only then. In adaptive case management this does not fit. The super-workitem may be completed earlier than planned—if the problem cause is found earlier than planned. It may also not be completed, even if all sub-workitems have successfully been finished. Even then, maybe, the problem cause has not been found yet.

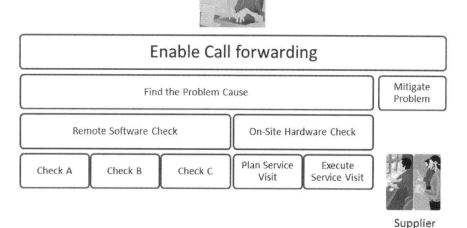

Figure 8: The plan that Leona has in her mind

Workitem [Find the Problem Cause] in AdaCom Telephone System Company Support Cases

Figure 9: Maintaining Sub-Workitems

Workitem [Remote Software Check] in AdaCom Telephone System Company Support Cases

Figure 10: Maintaining detailed Checks

Figure 11: Resulting Structure of Workitems

Leona has always estimated the effort for the detailed workitems. This effort can be aggregated by pressing the button *Aggregate* for one level aggregation and *Aggregate All* for aggregation of all levels below, so that the resulting overall effort can be seen (see Figure 12).

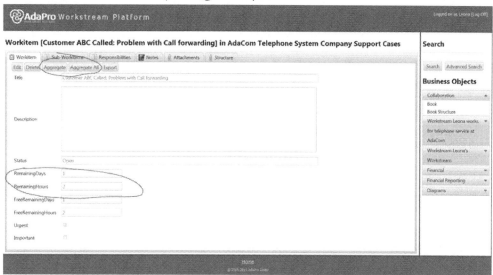

Figure 12: Aggregating the Remaining Effort

There is no definite sequence in the planned activities, only one she can think of: The problem can only be mitigated if the problem cause has been found. Often, in process modeling and project planning many dependencies are modeled. This makes processes and plans inflexible. Sometimes it makes sense, as sequencing the problem analysis and the problem mitigation. Very often too many dependencies are modeled. We can even discuss what the advantages to model this dependency are. Most knowledge workers of the case know the dependency anyway. They would not prematurely start to solve the problem. They even do not know what to do. If they want to start problem mitigation, even before problem analysis is completely finished, then it often has a reason. For example there may be two problems, while one is already analyzed and the other ones analysis is still in progress. So it is fine to start mitigation of the first problem already, even if the problem analysis is not yet fully completed. I do not speak absolutely against sequencing constraints. The workstream platform will offer them as well later, after the research about them has finished. But I want to emphasize, that oftentimes they are less decisive than people tend to think. Sometimes they are even part of the problem, not of the solution, because they create inflexibility. I have met many people who have started to manage their knowledge work with project plans and they have given up, because it just was annoying. This has a reason: Too many dependencies. So—if dependencies are used— then they should be different than in the past. That's why there is an ongoing research project about them.

However the *AdaPro Workstream Platform* offers a hierarchical structure of the workitems—which is already a dependency—and which is more than a flat worklist. We know this also from project planning solutions. But the typical project planning solution is not a multi-user online application for day-to-day knowledge work. In the following sections we will see more advantages compared to project planning solutions—for example the template library or analytics to mention two.

In my opinion, the most important ingredients of a knowledge worker process is a clear definition of the goals and sub-goals (workitems), a clear status, a clear responsibility, priorities and analytics about remaining effort versus the timeline.

Later, as it turns out for Leona, the problem was not identified after all steps have been completed. The status is updated and a new Workitem is planned, a conference between the supplier AdaPhone, the customer and some Ada-Com employees. Therefore Leona creates a new workitem as described in (Kraft 2010). You can imagine how this looks like in the workstream platform. However it is important to mention, that the status of the workitems can not only be *Open, Started, Completed* or *Error*—as in many workflow applications—but also other statuses are possible like *Postponed, Withdrawn, In Approval, Approved, Rejected*. The status values in classical workflow applications are very technical. The status values in the *AdaPro Workstream Platform* have more meaning for the knowledge worker.

MANAGING RESPONSIBILITIES

During the conference call, Leona and the team determined that it is a combined hardware-software problem. This allows the problem mitigation to be planned.

In this example, it turned out that the hardware must be changed, which breaks down as shown in Figure 13.

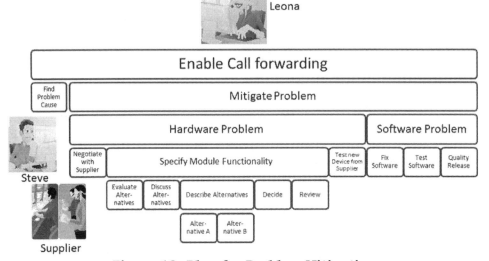

Figure 13: Plan for Problem Mitigation

It is necessary to negotiate with the supplier, create a specification for the new functionality, and test the new device that the supplier delivers. The software problem must be fixed by her development team. Since it is Leona's area of expertise, she takes over the software problem but she delegates management of the hardware problem to Steve—however, she remains the overall case manager. Steve will detail the hardware part of the case, while she details the software part of the case.

Of course it is necessary to assign clear responsibilities. So workitems on all levels can be assigned to the members of the workstream (Figure 14). Each user can see his own workitems (see Figure 15 till Figure 17). It is possible to filter by status, for example, exclude finished workitems.

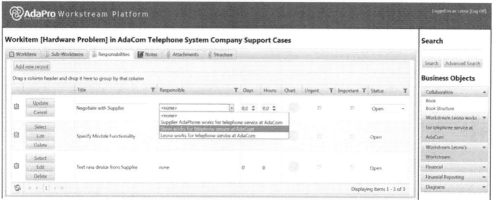

Figure 14: Assigning Responsibilities

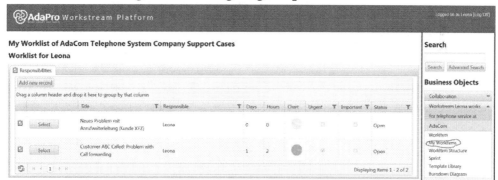

Figure 15: Worklist of Leona

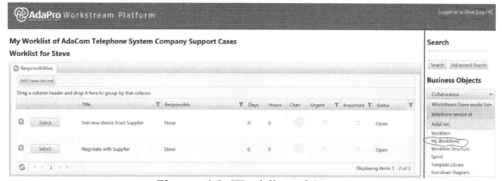

Figure 16: Worklist of Steve

Workflow engines additionally filter by tasks that are not yet active, because their predecessors are not completed. This makes sense, if there are workflows that are executed very many times. In knowledge work it is questionable if this makes sense. It is often good to know, what the pipeline of work is. This helps to prepare or even start already, to plan the effort, even if it only starts later and to actively make sure, that preconditions will be fulfilled in time. Again I am not completely condemning predecessor relationships. I only want to say, that they also cause problems—especially in knowledge work. As soon as the *AdaPro Workstream Platform* will offer predecessor relationships, after the research project has been finished, it will also support filtering workitems by that.

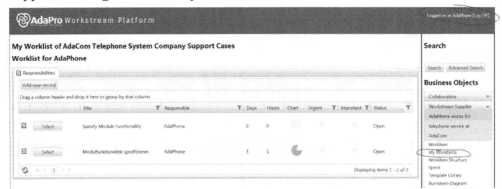

Figure 17: Worklist of AdaPhone Hardware Supplier

SPRINTS AND BURNDOWN

Leona has to manage the remaining effort versus the timeline. For this she creates some milestones or *sprints* (see Figure 18). Now individual workitems can be assigned to sprints (see Figure 19) by Leona. After that it is possible to aggregate the remaining effort for the sprints (see Figure 20). It is also possible to see all workitems that have been assigned to each sprint (see Figure 21).

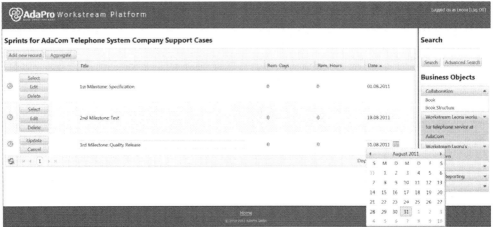

Figure 18: Defining Sprints

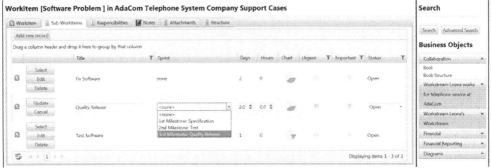

Figure 19: Assigning Workitems to Sprints

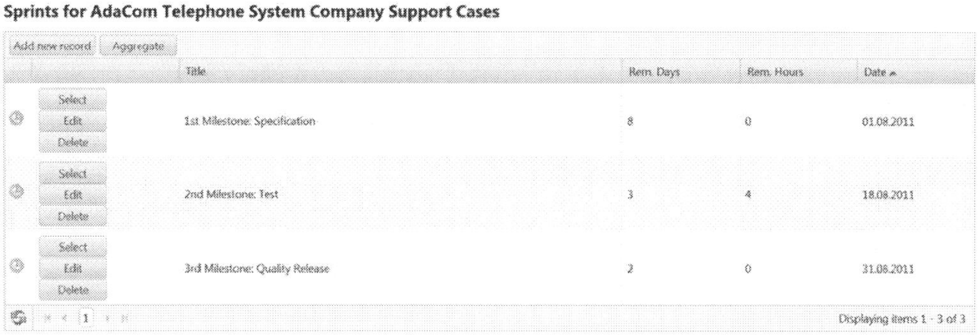

Sprints for AdaCom Telephone System Company Support Cases

Add new record | Aggregate

	Title	Rem. Days	Rem. Hours	Date
Select Edit Delete	1st Milestone: Specification	8	0	01.08.2011
Select Edit Delete	2nd Milestone: Test	3	4	18.08.2011
Select Edit Delete	3rd Milestone: Quality Release	2	0	31.08.2011

Displaying items 1 - 3 of 3

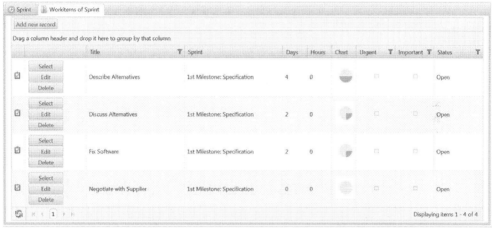

Figure 20: Aggregating Remaining Effort for Sprints

Sprint [1st Milestone: Specification] in AdaCom Telephone System Company Support Cases

Sprint | Workitems of Sprint

Add new record

Drag a column header and drop it here to group by that column

	Title	Sprint	Days	Hours	Chart	Urgent	Important	Status
Select Edit Delete	Describe Alternatives	1st Milestone: Specification	4	0				Open
Select Edit Delete	Discuss Alternatives	1st Milestone: Specification	2	0				Open
Select Edit Delete	Fix Software	1st Milestone: Specification	2	0				Open
Select Edit Delete	Negotiate with Supplier	1st Milestone: Specification	0	0				Open

Displaying items 1 - 4 of 4

Figure 21: Listing Workitems that have been assigned to a Sprint

If Leona regularly performs the sprint aggregation, she can take advantage of the *burndown diagram.*

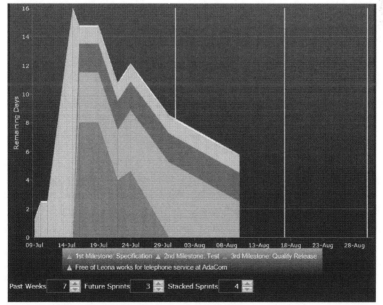

Figure 22: Sprint Burndown of Telephone Service Workstream

The burndown diagram shows the remaining effort history. So when Leona looks at the burndown diagram for the telephone support workstream (Figure 22) she can see that the effort in the beginning was relatively low. That was, when she thought, the problem is relatively easy to solve. Then, after the problem analysis and after the full planning for the problem mitigation the remaining effort was much higher. However it was not yet assigned to individual sprints. One day later Leona had assigned the remaining effort to individual sprints. That is visible by the different colors in the curves. The sprint dates are marked as vertical lines in the diagram. By this it is always possible to see, if the remaining efforts decrease is fast enough to reach zero at the sprint in question. If not, some countermeasures can be taken ahead of time – re-planning, delegating work, postponing work, and withdrawing work. This helps Leona to keep the timeline under control.

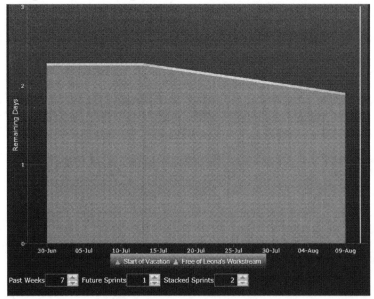

Figure 23: Sprint Burndown of Leonas personal Workstream

Each individual workstream has an individual burndown diagram. Leona's personal burndown diagram can be seen in Figure 23. In the personal workstream Leona has different sprints; here she has planned to complete some problem with her company car until her vacation starts; which she did not completely achieve—as the diagram shows.

However having different workstreams, it is important to have an overall overview. Figure 24 shows a combined burndown diagram for all of Leona's workstreams. It contains the combined efforts as well as the combined sprints. Here she can see that she might have a problem with her vacation and the remaining work. She has to make sure to delegate the work before her vacation starts. Of course the overall burndown diagram would look different for Steve, even if the burndown of his telephone service workstream is the same as for Leona. But he also has other workstreams.

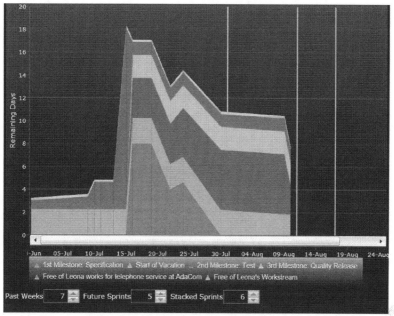

Figure 24: Overall Sprint Burndown of Leonas Workstreams

Working with Templates

As I have written in (Kraft 2010) in adaptive case management case instances emerge as they are necessary. This means the knowledge worker can start the work without any templates: just with the empty ACM system. A knowledge worker enters the first case, just as the working day requires from them. If they want, they can work in that way forever adding case by case. In the beginning, one case looks different than all the others. As work becomes repeated, the individual knowledge worker identifies snippets of cases that he might want to convert into a template and reuse.

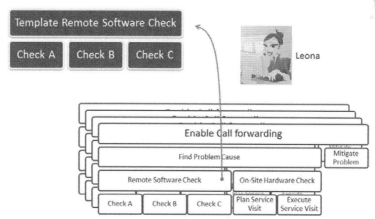

Figure 25: Creating a Template from existing Workitems

In our example, after having several similar cases, Leona recognizes that some checks for the software appear regularly, so it would be best to include them in a template. She thinks that if she can make the template available to John, a new colleague, she might ask him once in a while to perform the checks for her so that she saves some time. Therefore, she looks for the case that contains the checks she has in mind, copies the part that she wants into a new template, and edits the template with instructions so that John will be able to follow them (see Figure 25).

In the *AdaPro Workstream Platform* each Workstream has its own template library. Therefore Leona can create personal templates as well as templates for the telephone support. The template creation works with simple drag-and-drop. Leona drags a part of one workitem tree and drops it into the template library (see Figure 26); it then becomes a template. The template items do not have a status (see Figure 27). This then can be dragged and dropped into a new workitem. By this, all status values of the process snippet will be set to *Open* (see Figure 28). Now Leona can navigate to the workitem and edit the sub-workitems—independently from the template (see Figure 29).

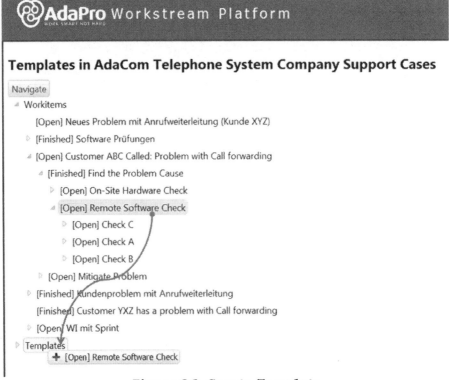

Figure 26: Create Template

So from now on, the work for Leona has become even easier. She has created a template in the template library for telephone service. John can now access the template. If John is on duty and he has a similar case, then he can copy the template into his case. And if Leona is on duty and has a similar case, she quickly copies her template into her case but assigns John to perform the checks. So in effect, Leona has saved some time for herself, while still giving guidance and instruction to John.

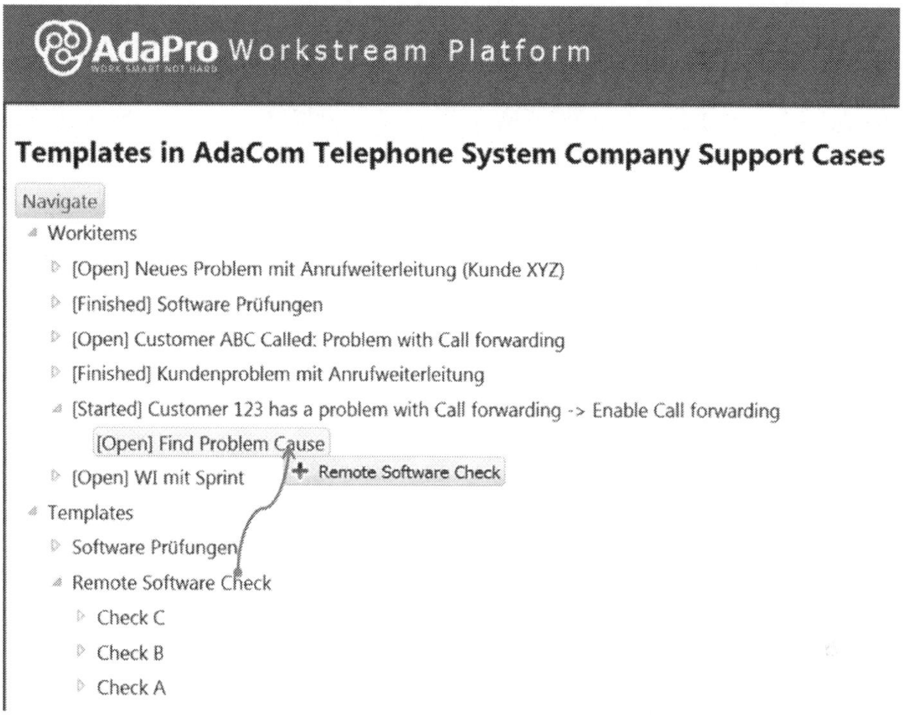

Templates in AdaCom Telephone System Company Support Cases

Navigate

⊿ Workitems

   ▷ [Open] Neues Problem mit Anrufweiterleitung (Kunde XYZ)

   ▷ [Finished] Software Prüfungen

   ▷ [Open] Customer ABC Called: Problem with Call forwarding

   ▷ [Finished] Kundenproblem mit Anrufweiterleitung

   ⊿ [Started] Customer 123 has a problem with Call forwarding -> Enable Call forwarding

      [Open] Find Problem Cause

   ▷ [Open] WI mit Sprint   **+ Remote Software Check**

⊿ Templates

   ▷ Software Prüfungen

   ⊿ Remote Software Check

      ▷ Check C

      ▷ Check B

      ▷ Check A

Figure 27: Use Template in new Workitem

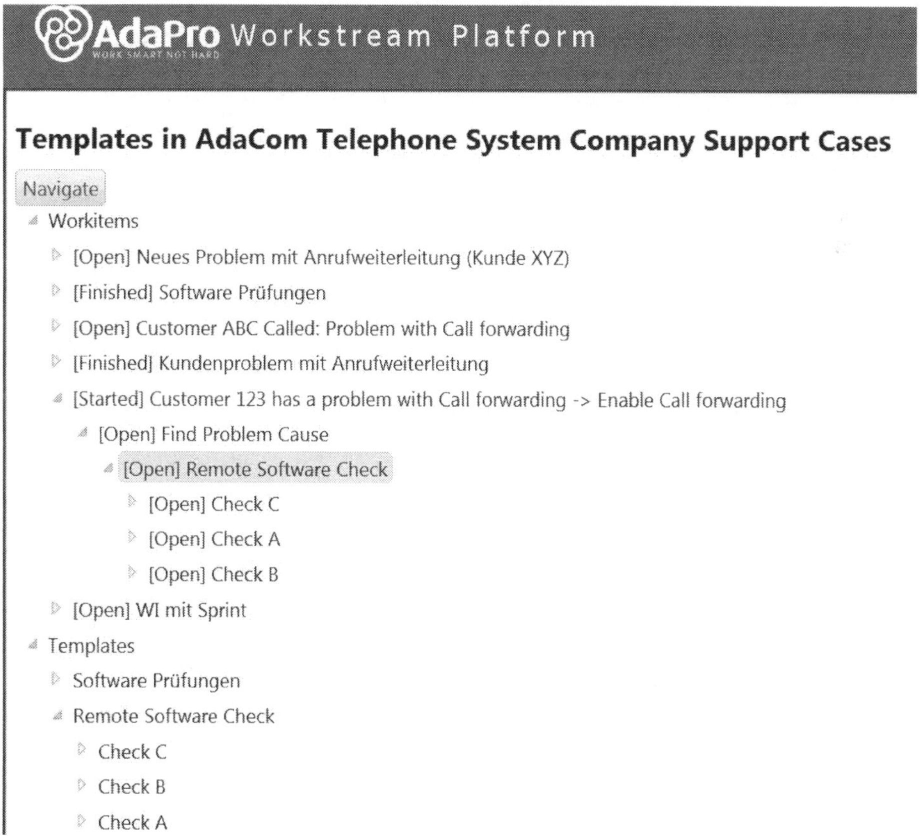

Templates in AdaCom Telephone System Company Support Cases

Navigate

⊿ Workitems

   ▷ [Open] Neues Problem mit Anrufweiterleitung (Kunde XYZ)

   ▷ [Finished] Software Prüfungen

   ▷ [Open] Customer ABC Called: Problem with Call forwarding

   ▷ [Finished] Kundenproblem mit Anrufweiterleitung

   ⊿ [Started] Customer 123 has a problem with Call forwarding -> Enable Call forwarding

      ⊿ [Open] Find Problem Cause

         ⊿ [Open] Remote Software Check

            ▷ [Open] Check C

            ▷ [Open] Check A

            ▷ [Open] Check B

   ▷ [Open] WI mit Sprint

⊿ Templates

   ▷ Software Prüfungen

   ⊿ Remote Software Check

      ▷ Check C

      ▷ Check B

      ▷ Check A

Figure 28: Resulting Workitems

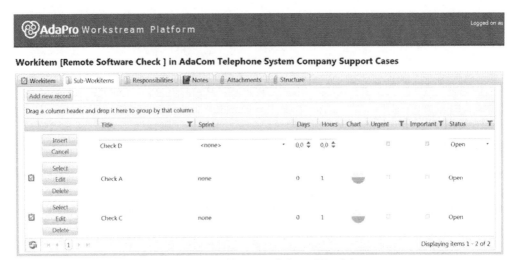

Figure 29: Edit resulting Workitem

By the way—the drag-and-drop functionality can also be used between one workitem tree and another one like it is needed in the example in Figure 30.

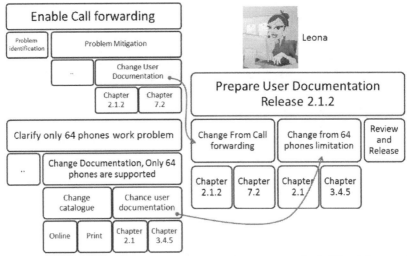

Figure 30: Using synergy by concentrating some Sub-Workitems into a new one

Leona had different customer cases that required documentation updates. Instead of doing each update separately and starting the review of the documentation change separately, Leona found it more practical to cluster the changes into a user documentation release and review it collectively. She could reassign these user documentation update work items into the case for the user documentation update. By clustering work, overhead for each change of the documentation is minimized, and again, time is saved that can be used for more important things.

You can easily imagine how the drag-and-drop will work in the *AdaPro Workstream Platform*. This is only one example for the so-called *patterns of knowledge work* that AdaPro has researched. These patterns describe how a knowledge worker typically manages his workstreams and processes. There are about 20-30 patterns of knowledge work known today, that cannot described here because of brevity. However the *AdaPro workstream platform* has been built to support these patterns in an optimized way—with special focus on user interaction. This makes the use of the *AdaPro workstream platform* feel natural—it is a natural flow of work.

SUMMARY AND FUTURE

First users especially appreciate that the workstream platform is a central storage for their knowledge work, accessible everywhere at every time. If they are at the site of their customers, for example, then they need not to install anything, they just can use any browser to access their knowledge work information needed for the project situation. It is easier for them to manage the workload including the regular interruptions of the work by phone calls and emails. It helps to create a workitem or some, give it a clear status and goal. Also it is helpful that there is always a clear status of all the knowledge work in question. This is especially helpful, if the manager calls and wants to know about a certain project situation. Also it is found helpful to see the progress of a workstream and to be able to guide less experienced workers in how to do certain things by creating workitems for them or using templates. This is the feedback by the first users. However also additional predecessor-successor relationships for workitems have been requested which is—as I said—part of a research project. Two other research projects are

- graphical display with simulation and
- process/workstream analytics.

There are great ideas, but they have not yet been finished. This is, because the solutions to these challenges must be different than in standard process modeling, if they are to be useful for knowledge work. Find out more at http://www.AdaPro.eu/

REFERENCES

(Kraft 2010) *F. M. Kraft, Mastering the Unpredictable (Editor: Keith D. Swenson).* Meghan-Kiffer Press, 2010, ch. 9: *Improving Knowledge Work*, p. 181 ff. See http://goo.gl/KxOPl

Author Appendix

EMILY BURNS
Principal, Product Marketing, Pegasystems Inc.

Emily heads Pega's cross-industry case management initiatives, driving product marketing and strategy. She spends a significant portion of her time working with clients, and analyzing market trends. Using these inputs she identifies key innovation areas to ensure Pega maintains its stance as the leader in dynamic case management in terms of product, methodology and delivery of case applications. Emily joined Pega in February of 2008. Prior to Pega, Emily worked at TIBCO driving BPM product marketing. Before moving to enterprise software, Emily worked as a strategy consultant to pharmaceutical and medical device companies. Emily holds a B.S. from Sweet Briar College with majors in biochemistry and music, and worked on a Ph.D. in neuroscience at The Rockefeller University.

DAVE DUGGAL
Founder and Managing Director, Consilience International LLC, the developer of the Ideate Framework™ (www.ideate.com).

Dave is a proven business leader who has made a career of building, growing and turning around companies over the last twenty years. The outspoken entrepreneur has been interviewed on Dateline NBC and presented at TED6. He is author of several academic papers on web-style software architecture, an inventor of a patent pending software framework, and has presented at many industry conferences. His passion for addressing fundamental business challenges was the genesis for his latest venture, Consilience International, which he founded with William Malyk in 2009. The company's Ideate Framework provides an EnterpriseWeb—a flexible interoperability layer for real-time integration and collaboration—so businesses can better manage variance and change. Dave's LinkedIn Profile http://www.linkedin.com/in/daveduggal1

LAYNA FISCHER
Publisher, Future Strategies Inc., USA

Ms Fischer is the Chief Editor and Publisher of Future Strategies Inc., the official publishers to WfMC.org. She was also Executive Director of WfMC and BPMI (now merged with OMG) and continues to work closely with these organizations to promote industry awareness of BPM and Workflow.

Future Strategies Inc. (www.FutStrat.com) publishes books and papers on business process management and workflow, specializing in dissemination of information about BPM and workflow technology and electronic commerce. As such, the company contracts and works closely with individual authors and corporations worldwide and also manages the renowned annual Global Awards for Excellence in BPM and Workflow and the new annual Adaptive Case Management Awards.

Future Strategies Inc., is the publisher of the business book series *New Tools for New Times*, the annual *Excellence in Practice* series of award-winning case studies and the annual *BPM and Workflow Handbook* series, published in collaboration with the WfMC. Ms. Fischer was a senior editor of a leading international computer publication for four years and has been involved in international computer journalism and publishing for over 20 years.

THOMAS M. KOULOPOULOS
Chairman, Delphi Group, USA

Chairman of Delphi Group, Past Managing Director of Perot Systems Thought Leadership practice, one of the industry's six most influential consultants, according to InformationWeek, author of eight books, professor at Bentley College Graduate School, lecturer at the Boston College Graduate school of management, and frequent contributor to national and international print and broadcast media, Mr. Koulopoulos is one of the industry's most prolific thought leaders. His insights provide a beyond-the-edge view of the turbulence created by the collision of technology and business. Tom Peters has called his writing, "a brilliant vision of where we must take our enterprises to survive and thrive." The late Management guru and 20th Century business icon Peter Drucker, said of Tom's writing "[it] makes you question not only the way you run your business but the way you run yourself."

FRANK MICHAEL KRAFT
Systems analyst and software architect, AdaPro GmbH, Germany

Frank Michael Kraft has 19 years of experience as a systems analyst and software architect for custom and standard software for business processes. In his last role at SAP AG, he defined the architecture for the model-driven development of the business processes of two hundred business objects as part of the business process platform that is the foundation for SAP Business ByDesign. These business objects cover the application areas of supplier relationship management, customer relationship management, logistics planning and execution, production, project management, human resources, and financials. Frank was responsible for the governance process for the business process management (BPM) models, and he conducted many thousands of model reviews, which included the design of many thousands of service operations as part of the service-oriented architecture. A special focus of Frank's work was the flexibility and adaptability of the modeled business processes, for which he developed innovative concepts. He is an inventor with various patents in the area of business process integration and design and flexibility. Recently, he was member of the BPMN 2.0 specification team and contributed in the area of choreography modeling, where he also published scientific articles. Frank's new role is founder of a company that will offer adaptive case management (ACM) software as a service (SaaS) including community library content, as well as knowledge products and coaching services in the area of business process design. Frank holds a Diplom. Inform. degree from the Technical University of Berlin. Visit www.adapro.eu for more information.

JOHN T. MATTHIAS, J.D.,
Principal Court Management Consultant, National Center for State Courts

John T. Matthias, J.D., is a Principal Court Management Consultant, National Center for State Courts. He has twenty years of experience as a management consultant and business analyst in courts of forty states and countries and ten years of law practice that includes five years of experience as a city prosecutor. As a consultant, John has directed or participated in over seventy requirements-gathering and process/technology evaluation projects. His domains of expertise include court performance metrics, information integration, and many aspects of courts, prosecution/defense, and adult/juvenile probation. He is certified to use the Justice Information Exchange Model (JIEM) tool and was active in development of Case Management Functional Standards for criminal and juvenile case types.

John holds a BA from the University of Iowa, an MA from Seton Hall University, and a law degree from New York Law School. John practiced law for ten years in Texas and Iowa, managing cases of all types and conducting investigations, bench trials, and jury trials. He is a Fellow of the Institute for Court Management's Court Executive Development Program (CEDP).

DERMOT MCCAULEY
Director of Corporate Developmen, Singularity, UK

Dermot McCauley is Director of Corporate Development at Singularity. Previous to joining Singularity in 2003, he held President and General Manager roles in publicly quoted, high-growth technology companies in the U.S. and Europe, including Cambridge Technology Partners (CTP) and Rare Medium Group. An executive in his own successful start-up that was purchased by CTP in 1995, Dermot has previously worked for JPMorgan Chase, Dun & Bradstreet, and Sema. Dermot holds a Mathematics degree from Imperial College, London. Singularity increases the performance and agility of business processes by the rapid implementation of its industry-leading business process management (BPM) and case management products. From offices in London, New York, Singapore, Ireland, and India, the company provides software products and professional services to increase the agility of organizations across the globe. Visit www.singularitylive.com for more information.

NATHANIEL PALMER
Chief BPM Strategist of SRA International and Executive Director, Workflow Management Coalition, USA., WfMC, USA

Nathaniel Palmer is a Principal with SRA International, serving as Chief Architect for some of the largest BPM initiatives. He also serves as the Executive Director of the Workflow Management Coalition (WfMC) as well as Editor of BPM.com, the industry's leading destination site on workflow and BPM. Previously he was Director, Business Consulting for Perot Systems Corp and spent over a decade with Delphi Group as Vice President and Chief Analyst. Nathaniel is the author of over several dozen research studies BPM and ACM, as well as co-author of the critically-acclaimed management text "The X-Economy" (Texere, 2001) plus several books on BPM and process improvement. He has been featured in numerous media ranging from Fortune to The New York Times, and also serves on the advisory boards of many relevant industry associations as well as was nominated to represent the Governor of Massachusetts on the Commonwealth's IT Advisory Board.

MAX PUCHER
Chief Architect, ISIS Papyrus Software, Switzerland

Max J. Pucher has a 37 year background in enterprise IT and has given the future of BPM substantial coverage in his writing and speaking. He has published two novels and is co-author of 'Mastering The Unpredictable,' the first book to discuss Adaptive Case Management. His passion is designing technology that empowers humans and uses his rich experience to simplify the use of powerful technology in the enterprise arena.

Max started his IT career with IBM where he worked for 15 years internationally—including three years in Saudi Arabia—in hardware engineering, consulting and sales. He is the founder and current Chief Architect of ISIS Papyrus Software, which provides process and communication solutions to Fortune 1000 clients worldwide. He holds software patents in the arena of Artificial Intelligence for real-time machine learning for process mining that discovers in real-time the complex user activity patterns representing 'actionable knowledge.'

Because of his belief in social networking concepts he joined forces in 2010 with the co-founder of ACT! Mike Muhney. Together they founded VIPorbit Software International, Inc. to offer Mobile Cloud solutions with VIPorbit®, the only full-featured Mobile Contact Manager designed for the iPhone.

BRUCE SILVER
Independent Industry Analyst and Consultant, Bruce Silver Associates,

Bruce Silver is principal of Bruce Silver Associates, provider of BPM consulting and training services, and founder and principal of BPMessentials.com, the leading provider of BPMN training. He served on the BPMN 2.0 technical committee in OMG, and is the author of *BPMN Method and Style*. He also writes the popular BPMS Watch blog (www.brsilver.com), offering reports and commentary on both BPMN and leading BPM Suites.

KEITH SWENSON
Vice President of R&D, Fujitsu America Inc., USA

Keith Swenson is Vice President of Research and Development at Fujitsu America, Inc. and the Chief Software Architect for its Interstage family of products. He is known for having been a pioneer in collaboration software and web services, and he has contributed to the development of workflow and business process management (BPM) standards. Keith is the Chairman of the Technical Committee of the Workflow Management Coalition (WfMC). In the past, he led development of collaboration software at MS2, Netscape, Ashton Tate, and Fujitsu. In 2004, he was awarded the Marvin L. Manheim Award for outstanding contributions in the field of workflow. Visit Keith's blog at http://social-biz.org

Case Studies
Adaptive Case Management

UVIT–Financial Services, Netherlands

Gold Award: Customer Facing

Nominated by EMC Documentum, United States

EXECUTIVE SUMMARY / ABSTRACT

The Univé-VGZ-IZA-Trias group (UVIT) is a Netherlands-based insurance company. During recent years, the people of UVIT have been facing increased challenges from Internet insurance competitors. Because of this, a main objective was to automate outdated processes that were primarily paper-based. To do this, UVIT chose EMC Documentum xCP for the creation of a case management application to process claims. The xCP platform is seamlessly integrated with the UVIT capture platform to digitize all incoming mail, especially the vast quantity of doctor and hospital bills customers forward for payment. The system is used by UVIT service, field, and insurance agents, while in the office, at home, and on the road.

With the new xCP system, UVIT staff now has instant access to customer documentation, which has helped improve customer response rates as well as overall processing efficiency. The amount of case documents they are now able to process is also huge– about three million in 2010, and they expect that figure to reach 50 million in the near future.

"EMC Documentum xCP has streamlined our claims processes substantially. Since using the new system, we have reduced costs by approximately 10 percent. We are very satisfied with the solution, and are expecting more added value when we begin using all of the features", said Pierre Kraakman, business analyst at UVIT. Documentum xCP orchestrates information through the process, end-to-end, while providing a 360-degree view of the case, in addition to supporting and documenting all human decision processes.

OVERVIEW

The Univé-VGZ-IZA-Trias group (UVIT), is an insurance company based in the Netherlands, with more than 150 satellite offices and about 4.2 million customers throughout the country. The company has its roots in the late 18th century and employs more than 5,000 people, 3,500 of whom work at the central organization and focus on product creation. The remaining employees are based in other locations, serving and consulting with customers. In 2010, UVIT revenue was approximately 11 billion Euros.

BUSINESS CONTEXT

UVIT's mission is to offer its customers top-quality products and services. As a partly profit-oriented entity, the insurance provider is always searching for ways to improve its business processes and provide better services to customers at lower cost. The company realized it needed to automate processes, many of which were paper-based and error-prone. It was definitely time for a change, as it often took hours, if not days, to locate all relevant documents needed to process a single claim. For compliance reasons and in order to strengthen competitiveness,

Unive Health Insurance, one of the group members, decided at the end of 2003 to introduce a document management system that would store multiple resources, such as fax, paper, web, and e-forms, as well as a variety of document types. "At the same time, we wanted a scalable solution that we could use enterprise-wide for different processes. The system also had to offer a Dutch-language front-end, authorization rules, and version control, as well as full-text indexing. And it had to automatically control retention periods," said Mr. Kraakman.

The Dutch archive law stipulates that all bills, letters, and contracts must be retained for seven years. Documents relating to corporate-level decisions from the board of directors, however, have to be kept for ten years. And certain medical files must not be deleted for a full 15 years after an employee has left the company. Therefore, it was crucial for Unive to select a system that would be reliable and stable enough to guarantee compliance with such legal regulations.

After a thorough evaluation of the most highly rated systems on the market, the organization selected EMC Documentum as its enterprise content management (ECM) platform and Documentum xCP for building BPM/case management applications.

THE KEY INNOVATIONS

4.1 Business

The new solution immediately began reducing the time required to locate claims and enrollment documents and it substantially improved customer service. Instead of lengthy document retrieval processes in response to a customer call, service agents now locate relevant documents in less than three seconds. The incidence of misplaced documents decreased as well. Providing the right person with the access to the right information in the right timeframe dramatically improves decision making processes. Tracking and documenting how information is processed and decisions are made is vital.

Decisions regarding a case is digitally recorded and stored, where management information can be easily extracted. Every case has a number of standard metadata that need to be filled; in addition, there are a large number of fields that contain information about why and how the decisions around this case have evolved. Any amount which is paid and details of how the case manager arrived at this amount are also saved.

4.2 Case Handling

The first deployment phase started at the beginning of 2004, with the implementation of EMC Documentum 5.3. With the help of EMC Consulting, the system went live in September 2004, and has been productive ever since. It is connected to Unive's old back-office Health system which has to be kept until 2015, when all data stored can be disposed of. It is also seamlessly integrated in the selected capture platform to digitize all incoming mail, especially the vast quantity of bills customers forward for payment to the respective doctors and/or hospitals. After scanning, the paper bills have to be kept for another three months before they can be destroyed, reducing physical storage costs.

Initially, Documentum served as a stable archiving solution. Unive then set up the first workflows, and initiated the process to digitize all application handling roughly one year after implementation. Finally, Unive included all contract management for doctors/hospitals. At the end of 2007, due to a merger with three other health insurance companies, Univé and the other members of UVIT decided to initiate phase two and to upgrade to EMC Documentum xCP.

"We wanted to set up the new system from scratch and connect it to the new back-office system. The goal was to include both incoming and outgoing document streams, which was clearly going to be a large project, so we split it into two parts: part one related to all health insurance cases, part two, to the claims management," said Pierre Kraakman. Implementation of part one started in January and took about ten months, while deployment of part two began in February and finished in December 2008.

In winter 2008, UVIT began using EMC Documentum 6.0 with Documentum xCP, which provides highly granular access control and includes various services. Content Services provides essential features for organizing, controlling, and delivering repository content. Process Integrator allows UVIT staff to gain integration with external applications through a service-oriented architecture (SOA) implementation; so far, it is connected with Oracle and Printnet. Microsoft Office and UVIT's HR solution were integrated in July 2009.

The repository is accessible through two clients: "Our claims adjusters, who use the Documentum xCP environment, have access through TaskSpace, which can be easily configured to our needs," said Pierre Kraakman. Additionally, it enables the service agents to rapidly build and deploy intuitive applications for functions such as case management. Agents, who work with Documentum 5.3, use the browser-based user interface Webtop, which handles insurance forms, faxes, e-mails, and paper-based correspondence. Field agents can also access Documentum from their home offices, via a Citrix environment.

To assess material damages, UVIT often receives short electronic videos and/or photos from car dealers. So, the insurance provider has to process many different image and office formats, including TIF and PDF, which are supported by the integrated IGC Brava Viewer for TaskSpace. Depending on the cost estimate, UVIT decides to either meet the costs or to send one of their claims adjusters to assess the damages on site. Another essential criterion to accelerate the business processes is the quick and flexible creation of intuitive, standards-based electronic forms. Forms Builder, part of Documentum xCP Designer, provides both high-accuracy and HTML-based e-forms. "By using TaskSpace or Webtop, our operators reduce costly paper handling. They can also add or remove fields or change the look and feel, according to their preferences," said Mr. Kraakman.

With Documentum Retention Policy Services, UVIT no longer has to ask itself how long it has to keep the various types of documents and when to clean up the files. The system automatically takes care of revision-secure content retention and disposition.

In order to increase transparency, agents must have an overview of the workflow or lifecycle states of documents at any time. Documentum Reporting Services provides control of the underlying workflows and the number of documents handled. The services mentioned were deployed at UVIT's selling and consulting department, the operational back office as well as the customer contact centers.

Each claim is considered a case and the claims process has several roles that are strictly divided. This is done because UVIT wants the "simple and laborious" tasks done by people who do not have or need extensive skill or specific knowledge.

Besides that, UVIT has legal and organizational rules about which step in the process is done by whom. The claims are processed by information workers who can then focus on the content of the claim and not about the process of collecting the correct documents or indexing metadata. After the claim is processed, the claim is checked and authorized for payment.

Documentum xCP greatly improves decision making because the claims worker only has to focus on the claim, not on administrative tasks. The claims can be processed by any number of specialists who can collaborate and work together because the claim information is digitally available instead of in a paper file. In this particular process, case managers can not influence the process steps, this is a design decision made by the organization. Case managers can invite specialists (damage specialists or legal specialists) to collaborate within the process. They are invited to look into the case with a specific question.

On the way to paperless case management and claim processing, UVIT's overall goal is to achieve virtually paperless transactions. Currently, approximately 12 scan operators are busy with scanning all incoming mail, such as applications, bills, or letters. The capturing system automatically delivers all documents scanned to the repository as index files in PDF or XML format. The documents have a view-only access. UVIT employs about 150 people to manage the processing of the relevant claims documents, plus 1,900 employees for the out-going letters for health insurance, which are automatically stored and can be dynamically recalled from the repository if necessary.

4.3 Organization & Social

The impact of Documentum xCP-based application on the employees and their jobs is significant. Instead of working with paper files, people have had to reorient to working with digital files. Every document is scanned at entrance and if there is no claim for this document a new claim is created. This has had a definite impact on the mailroom. There are now scan operators and workers who fill in the first metadata and verify if the claim is complete and can go to a case manager. The internal "mailman" has very little to do and several people with this role now have a different function. The people responsible for archiving have been reassigned.

HURDLES OVERCOME

Management

UVIT's management is very pleased but they did need to get used to the system. Digital case management works differently than paper case management. Before, a manager would have to walk the floor to see who was busy and who was not. If a case manager has a lot of paper on his desk he was busy, but now the manager can see if someone is very busy if he looks at the system reports.

Organization Adoption

After having had a half-day training session in order to familiarize themselves with the main features, about 1,500 employees now use Documentum xCP for their daily work. "We involved the users in the change management project at a very early stage, and showed them both the design and prototype, so they knew what to expect. What they appreciate most is the user-friendly interface, and the fact that they don't lose papers anymore," said Pierre Kraakman. UVIT plans to train more users in the course of the year.

BENEFITS

"EMC Documentum xCP has streamlined our claims processes substantially. Claims adjusters now have access to the documents they need within a few seconds only, and the incidence of misplaced documents has decreased. Since using the new system, we have reduced costs by approximately ten percent. We are very satisfied with the solution, and are still expecting more added value once using all of the features," said Pierre Kraakman.

6.1 Cost Savings / Time Reductions

Quantifiable benefits include:

- Claims process goes quicker, average one day
- Claim cases (or document belonging to a case) no longer get lost
- Quicker response to questions since everyone knows where the case files are and the right information and guidance is available to support the decision maker
- No personnel nor cupboards nor external contracts required for physical archiving
- Reduction of mailroom staff, reduction of administrative staff
- Reduced time-to-market and increased cycle time
- Higher availability and transparency—lower costs

6.2 Increased Revenues

Although difficult to measure at this time, improved customer service should improve competitiveness and expand the customer base.

6.3 Quality Improvements

Quality improvements include:

- Improve customer responsiveness– Case managers receive a message if a response from the customer is overdue
- The claim is paid quicker as well, so the customers are more satisfied
- Case managers can work from home, improves employee satisfaction and reduces facilities costs
- Management has better insight to process and they receive a message when a case is overdue
- Cases can be redirected more easily and quickly, allowing flexibility to reassign based on skills needed or availability.

The new solution dramatically reduced the time it took to locate claims and enrollment documents and substantially improved customer service. Instead of lengthy document retrievals in response to a customer call, service agents can now find relevant documents in less than three seconds. The incidence of misplaced documents decreased as well. Employees now have instant and simultaneous viewing access to customer documentation, which contributes to improving customer response rates as well as the overall processing efficiency.

The amount of data is huge: altogether, UVIT processed about two to three million documents last year but there is an upward trend. The insurance provider expects the figure to rise up to 50 million in the near future.

BEST PRACTICES, LEARNING POINTS AND PITFALLS

7.1 Best Practices and Learning Points

✓ *Digitization allows for more effective processes. Consider adapting the manual business processes along with the implementation of the system.*

At first, the business wanted a direct one-to-one transformation from paper to digital. Very quickly, we learned that this didn't work very well. We needed to adapt the business process along with the implementation of the system.

COMPETITIVE ADVANTAGES

Today's challenging economy requires all organization to be lean, quick, agile, and responsive to customer and market demands. "During recent years, we have been increasingly challenged by Internet-based insurance companies. That's why our main objective was to automate our processes, which were mainly paper-based. We selected EMC Documentum xCP because we felt that it would help us best achieve our objectives," says Kraakman.

TECHNOLOGY

UVIT choose EMC Documentum xCP as the foundation for building their case management application for claims processing. Built on the industry's leading ECM offering, EMC Documentum xCP provides a graphical toolset for building case-based composite applications. Providing enterprise-class information orchestration throughout the organization, xCP can accelerate process development to resolve many different business challenges.

UVIT is currently busy with adding the HR files to the system. In parallel, all medical files of its personnel will be included in the system as the insurance company also offers medical services to its staff. Another project has been set up to digitize all incoming mail in the new head office in Arnhem, which is designed to be an office mainly for knowledge workers. All employees will also have access to the system from home. The Web Content Management and SharePoint integration services are to be added soon. This will enable external users to log in to the UVIT web portal. Insured persons will be able to access personalized data and check the status of a process. They will be more and more involved in the whole case management process, and customer satisfaction will rise. All these changes will help avoid paper-based case management, in particular, and thereby generate cost savings.

THE TECHNOLOGY AND SERVICE PROVIDERS

EMC Documentum xCP automates knowledge-intensive processes and delivers information in context to reduce cycle time, improve business decisions, and ensure compliance. xCP is built on industry's leading ECM platform, which provides critical content management and control to all of your information assets. EMC Documentum features and offerings leveraged in this solution include:

- EMC Documentum Consulting
- EMC Documentum xCP
- EMC Documentum TaskSpace
- EMC Documentum Webtop
- EMC Documentum Retention Policy Services

Achievement Awards Group (Pty) Ltd, South Africa

Finalist: Customer Facing

Nominated by Pétanque Consultancy (Pty) Ltd, South Africa

1. EXECUTIVE SUMMARY / ABSTRACT

Adaptive Case Management (ACM) is imperative in enterprises where the exception to process becomes the process! ACM, a topic widely discussed and analyzed by academics, professionals and IT specialists, is what is needed whenever processes must react to changing and diverse customer or client needs and interactions to ensure efficient and effective outcomes. This means that defined, rigid processes become responsive to circumstances that require fluid processes in order to address specific requirements.

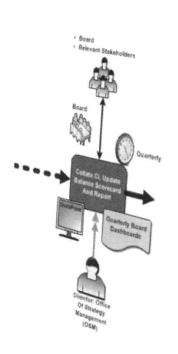

Achievement Awards Group (AAG), based in Cape Town, South Africa, recognized the benefits of adopting ACM as a critical success factor in attaining their strategic goals, and in response to their changing, diverse and unique customer requirements. The focus of AAG is to effectively and efficiently attain what they term "Customer Delight". The business of AAG includes predicting and responding to customer needs. No margin for error is allowed. Period.

This meant that absolute process agility had to be defined, designed, agreed upon and be continuously revisited. In the context of AAG, knowledge workers are the process executors, while stakeholders include customers and AAG shareholders.

A Customer Delight Framework, incorporating dynamic, unstructured process and process rules, was designed to deal with cases that require deviation from standard processes. These cases often require agility to ensure that desired process outcomes are achievable, regardless of the scenario.

Figure 1: A snapshot of VizPro® Process Step

The Customer Delight Framework was superimposed onto the business processes by using a collaborative, real-time and highly visual process mapping methodology called VizPro®. This easily understandable methodology clearly maps out who does what, why, where and how. It enabled role players to collaboratively design agile customer centric (outside-in) processes that are able to deal with a diverse set of cases or scenarios. In short, VizPro® facilitated an out-of-the-box mindset to design effective responses to customer needs.

What follows is a record of the roll-out of the Customer Delight Programme and the approach used to design dynamic processes which ensured quick management decision making, enterprise-wide adoption and execution of customer centricity.

2. CLIENT AND PROJECT QUICKVIEW

AAG (www.achievementawards.co.za) is a medium sized enterprise in the business of designing and delivering full-service incentive and performance improvement programmes for clients.

Profile
- It was established in 1980;
- the founder and current CEO is Geoffrey A. Amyot;
- the Head Office is in Westlake, Cape Town;
- the fulfillment centre/3260m² warehouse is also located in Westlake
- it has three certified Human Performance Technologists on staff;
- it is a single source provider;
- it has strong project management infrastructure;
- it has entered into a strategic partnership with Maritz Inc. (USA);
- it has produced more than 800 incentive programs to date;
- it has touched the lives of about 1.5 million South Africans to date; and
- its in-house services include a creative studio, a web/new media team, an IT development team, a banking/management information centre, a catalogue/supply chain team, an IATA certified travel agency and a VOIP enabled call centre.

Service portfolio

"Get a holistic perspective on your business; examine your cultural climate; support staff development through learning; motivate, recognise and reward performance; manage rewards and fulfillment requirements; and support back-end program requirements".

The project

The requirement was to partner in the development of an easily implementable Customer Delight Programme (CDP), based on the Disney Approach to Quality Management and Customer Care and effectively implement it by designing Customer Delight into process. The aim was to achieve customer excellence and continuous improvement.

The CDP comprised two aspects: First, the development of an operating model to address the requirements and challenges faced by the organisation. And second, an innovative design of customer-centric processes that would be easy to understand and implement, be aligned to business strategy, would be clearly defined, and would have the flexibility to deal with deviations that are part and parcel of the business of dealing with diverse customers groups. The CDP was to be infused into processes using VizPro®.

As one of the key outcomes, this programme created an AAG organizational-wide awareness amongst knowledge workers, support teams and management which resulted in buy-in that truly embedded customer excellence and a continuous improvement culture in all AAG activities.

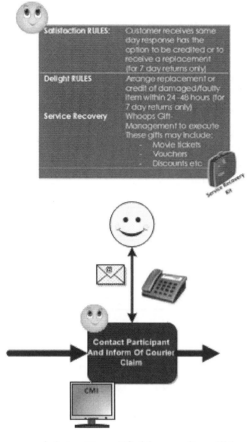

Figure 2: A snapshot of Customer Delight Rules, describing what will need to be done to attain a state of customer satisfaction, and what needs to be avoided.

Pétanque Consultancy (www.petanque-c.com) partnered with AAG, deploying one Specialist Consultant, two process architects and one project coordinator. The IT applied included two consultant laptops, MS Visio™, MS Office and data projectors. Key processes were printed on AO paper and the final output was framed and displayed in the AAG offices.

3. RESULTS

The feedback from the AAG Project Office four months after the initial roll-out stated: "Through our Customer Delight programme, we have been able to implement improvements in the After Sales Support, Courier and Stock Handling areas. As a result, we have cut down on back orders and delivery times. This has led to slight increases in our Customer Satisfaction Index (CSI) scores and compliments and also a reduction in complaints. Quantifiable results will be made available at the end of 2011."

Results in the following areas have been realized, and continue to do so:

- Cost saving through reduced time-to-customer and cycle time, as well as reductions in returns and queries;
- quality Improvements in how call centre and customer contact processes are executed; and
- clear performance indicators have been implemented.

4. KEY INNOVATION ELEMENTS

The principal success factors for this project were as follows:

1. to ensure Executive and Management Support,
2. to participate in developing and adopting a workable Customer Delivery Framework (see below), and
3. realise or actualise this Framework in the day-to-day operations by making use of a process mapping and management approach (VizPro®) that ensures clarity and alignment, and most importantly deliver results through buy-in and enterprise wide participation VizPro® is highly customizable and ensures clarity by using a detailed, storyboard format that produces real time mapping whilst simultaneously engaging knowledge owners and stakeholders in high energy, high impact work sessions (similar to JAD sessions). Innovation, adaptability and engagement converged to produce a project that was delivered speedily and which resulted in immediate, as well as medium and long term benefits.

5. SUCCESS FACTOR ONE: SENIOR AND EXECUTIVE MANAGEMENT BUY-IN

Strong, visible sponsorship was essential for the enterprise roll-out of the Customer Delight Programme. A project kick-off meeting was held whereby senior management and the executive team were introduced to the Customer Delight concept and particularly, how this needed to be integral to the what needs to done; (i.e. process), by whom-, why-, when- and how-steps. Throughout the project feedback on progress, issues and stumbling blocks were shared and addressed.

The innovation was in the **way that engagement and consensus were achieved**, using the VizPro® methodology, described below.

6. SUCCESS FACTOR TWO: CUSTOMER DELIGHT FRAMEWORK

A two-pronged approach to imprint Adaptive Case Management in AAG was followed, based on the questions "What will we do?" and "How will we do it?" The "What" needed to be defined in terms of Customer Centricity and Delight and the "How" needed to be expressed in activities, or processes—hence, the focus on the AAG Customer Delight Framework and Processes.

First, the Customer Delight Programme (CDP) was conceptualized, discussed, developed and agreed upon, using the Disney Approach to Quality Management and Customer Care as the departure point, followed by designing the CDP into processes This programme would drive the Customer Delight Framework for each relevant process where Adaptive Case Management was needed.

The Purpose of the Customer Delight Framework

The Framework was developed to describe the general directives of what and what not to do when specific circumstances present themselves. The purpose of the Framework was to identify, for each relevant process, the customer touchpoints and link them to the relevant categories (see below).

How the Framework was applied

Once the Framework was agreed to, the customer touchpoints were identified, added to the Change Controller (a VizPro® artifact that ensures process focus, as described below) and each touchpoint in the process defined.

The touchpoints were categorized as follows:

Customer Touchpoint category	Definition
Customer Satisfaction	Meeting customer requirements or delivering what has been promised.
Customer Delight	Touchpoints that will provide opportunities for delight or exceeding the customer expectations.
Service Recovery	Based on the understanding that in a service industry, things WILL go wrong, this answers the constant question "What steps must be taken in the event of service failure?"

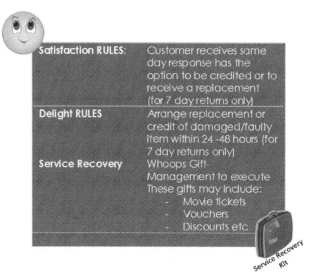

Figure 3: This is how a Delight Touch Point as referred to in figure 2 was elaborated upon.

Figure 3 shows how information was captured for one of the customer touch-points. The touchpoint was split into the Satisfaction, Delight and Service Recovery categories, and rules developed to satisfy each category's definition.

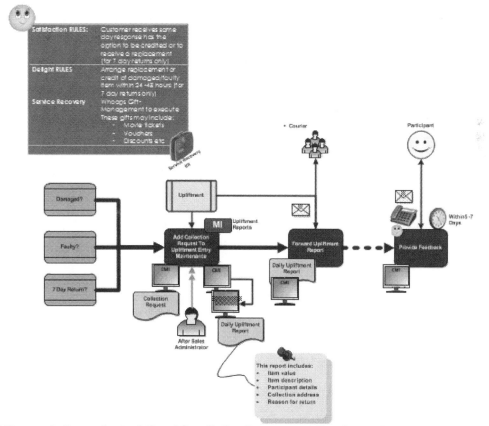

Figure 4: Snapshot of the After Sales Process, reflecting a Customer Delight Framework specific for this part of the process.

Figure 4 depicts how the Customer Delight Framework was applied. Each touch-point was analyzed and through facilitated work sessions, agreement was reached on a) what to do in cases of Service Failure (Service Recovery), b) what practices would meet Customer expectations (Customer Satisfaction) and c) what opportunities and actions would exceed customer expectations (Customer Delight). The key customer information collection touchpoints (listening posts) were also identified. This enabled AAG to generate customer intelligence that ensured better understanding of their customers which, in turn, fed into the AAG processes for continuous improvement.

Benefits of using the Customer Delight Framework

The benefits include:
- identification of critical touchpoint directives, or rules, to design customer centric processes;
- identifying ways of improving the customer experience and formulating these into framework directives for process role players;
- agreeing on ways to re-design areas with the greatest customer service inefficiencies in order to improve on responsiveness and, ultimately, profitability through customer retention and cost savings;
- a clearly defined action plan to drive behaviour change; and
- identification of and alignment on customer information collection points to generate intelligence that would facilitate customer centricity, continuous improvement and the development of metrics to monitor progress.

7. SUCCESS FACTOR THREE: PROCESS MAPPING AS THE VEHICLE TO PLAN, DEFINE AND DELIVER CUSTOMER DELIGHT

The Customer Delight Framework needed to be "dropped" into processes that were deemed too structured for an effective and efficient Customer Delight focus. In particular, the project participants identified the following as being the result of rigid structures:
- stifled creativity and innovation;
- slow responses to market changes as case-based solutions were not possible;
- non-adherence to the processes.

In addition, the following problems were identified:
- existing processes were not a true reflection of what was being practiced i.e. processes were not aligned with practice;
- there was a lack of efficient and effective communication, especially when there were service breakdowns i.e. when things went wrong;
- there was a lack of process accountability; and
- management and front-line staff were not aligned on how to deal with specific cases as they presented.

As a result of these insights, the following needs were identified:
- the need for a clear collective understanding of customers' needs and how to "wow" them; and
- the need for an agile processes that were easy to manipulate and quick to respond to market changes and customer requirements.
- the need for a Centre of Excellence to manage and maintain templates, business processes, version control, action lists, business improvement projects, etc.

It became evident that the project needed to incorporate the Customer Delight Framework into existing processes. In cases where there were gaps, new processes either had to be created or current activities had to be enhanced to ensure the inclusion of those elements needed to bring about Customer Delight.

7.1 The Motivation for deploying Process Mapping to fast track ACM into the enterprise

Process is the vehicle that states what activities are needed for specific outcomes. It also states who needs to do these activities. To be effective, process must clearly tell the "story" of the activity, i.e. identify the role players, pinpoint the risk areas, determine how to address exceptions and define the controls to be built into the flow; to list only a few of the many elements that are needed for a process "story". Each of the process elements must converge to synchronize people, activity, systems and artifacts to achieve agreed-to outcomes. These outcomes or results per process, in turn, must support the enterprise goals.

The process mapping methodology applied in this project was, and will for the foreseeable future be, VizPro®. It was chosen due to its ability to:

- build easy to understand, highly visual storyboard format processes;
- obtain immediate buy-in and support;
- build agile processes quickly and efficiently;
- gather corporate knowledge and expertise into process maps through interactive and collaborative work sessions; and
- build Customer centricity.

7.2 How Process was applied

Business process architecture includes understanding (i.e. analysis), developing, modeling, documenting and improving business processes, end-to-end. Unstructured or ad hoc processes are processes that cannot be clearly defined, and allows process stakeholders to develop the "what to do" as they execute the process, within defined guidelines or "the how-to" when many different scenarios present to the process role player. These are typically used in environments where there are many ways in which to execute and activity and execution is impacted by each circumstance

VizPro® lends itself to this by being a process documentation and analysis methodology that enables and facilitates Business Process design, architecture and buy-in. It applies the power of pictures and the effective use of narratives to show how processes support the enterprise goals—process-by–process and step-by-step. It engages process participants, role players and stakeholders in high energy mapping sessions where knowledge is captured and immediately converted into step-by-step maps. Workshops engage all session participants, thus leading to lively discussions that are informative and aimed at building improved practices. As a decision on the "who" does "what", "why" and "how" is taken, the information is captured and projected, thus creating a clear understanding of each step, along with immediate buy-in.

The following innovative process development, assessment, alignment and **mapping elements** resulted in multiple benefits and facilitated innovation in ACM in AAG.

8. ORGANIZATIONAL POSITIONING MAP

The Purpose and Creation of a Positioning Map:

Similar to enterprise architecture, but focused on creating links between processes and strategic goals, the aim of this map is to **link enterprise vision, mission and values** to a Performance Profile in which the strategic direction and goals are mapped. It furthermore identifies how each process will and must be designed and managed to achieve a common set of outcomes.

Each strategic directive and goal is linked to one or more critical success factor (CSF), which is in turn linked to a balanced scorecard focus area. Next, the processes that will impact on achieving those CSFs are identified and listed. The indicators per focus area are then recorded using process icons.

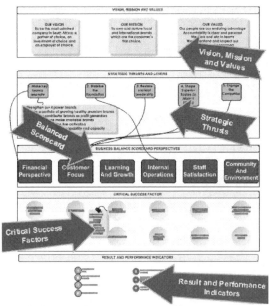

Figure 5: Snapshot of the Performance Profile

To complete the linkage between process, strategy and vision, a level one map is developed to show in five to six broad brush stroke steps what the enterprise "does". The processes to achieve these outcomes are then taken from the basket of processes defined in the Performance Profile (see figure 5). Having positioned the processes in the enterprise value chain, the group then agrees on which processes are critical to the outcomes and will bring the quickest improvement results if unpacked.

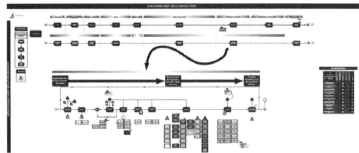

Figure 6: Positioning Map in which the processes that are needed to attain the value chain steps results, are identified and prioritised

How the Positioning Map was applied in AAG:

- The Positioning Map (figure 6) was developed with both the senior and executive management teams during a one-day work session. It depicts what value the organisation creates and required 8 hours to develop and complete.
- A key strategic objective for AAG is to actively manage the entire business to a customer focused value system. The management team agreed that the Solution Delivery Division should be "unpacked" as it would render the quickest and highest impact outcomes in respect of Customer Delight.
- The Solution Delivery Division contains many customer touchpoints, which means that this division needs to be highly adaptive and agile to each customer case that enters the process. Each of the Solution Delivery processes had to be designed to be fully aligned with the strategic objective(s) of being profitable, yet also being highly customer centric.
- The processes and activities thus needed to be designed to incorporate the characteristics of adaptability and agility whilst ensuring customer centricity, yet with enough flexible to deal with specific cases and enabling continuous improvement.

Benefits of using the Positioning Map:

The benefits included
- identifying and agreeing the key "must achieve" elements for each process that would collectively deliver results in support of enterprise goals;
- identifying the processes that make up AAG's value chain from start to end;
- identifying the critical processes needed in order to steer the business to being a customer centric organisation;
- providing direction in organising and developing a cross functional approach, instead of the traditional departmental approach;
- providing a high level view of the organisation and how all the processes interface to ensure effective service delivery; and
- identifying the scope, the process owners and stakeholders for each of the Solution Delivery Division processes and establishing the schedule for the Customer Delight Programme roll-out.

9. CHANGE CONTROLLER

Purpose of the Change Controller:

The purpose of the Change Controller is **to list those** minimum requirements that each process must adhere to in order to attain enterprise goals. These are derived from three sources, namely the CSFs and Performance Profile developed in the Positioning Map and from the "What Good Looks Like" (WGLL) statements developed by work session participants.[1]. These requirements are created by prefacing the source statements with the question "does this process..."

The Change Controller lists the "must do" elements in a matrix format. When reviewing each process against its particular Change Controller items, there are five status options (see Figure 7 and below). The status profile derived from the

---

[1] When defining desired outcomes, the term "What Good Looks Like" or WGLL, (pronounced "wiggle") is applied to guide responses in order to define what the desired process results must or should be.

Change Controller gives a good indication of the level of support a particular process lends to the enterprise goals.

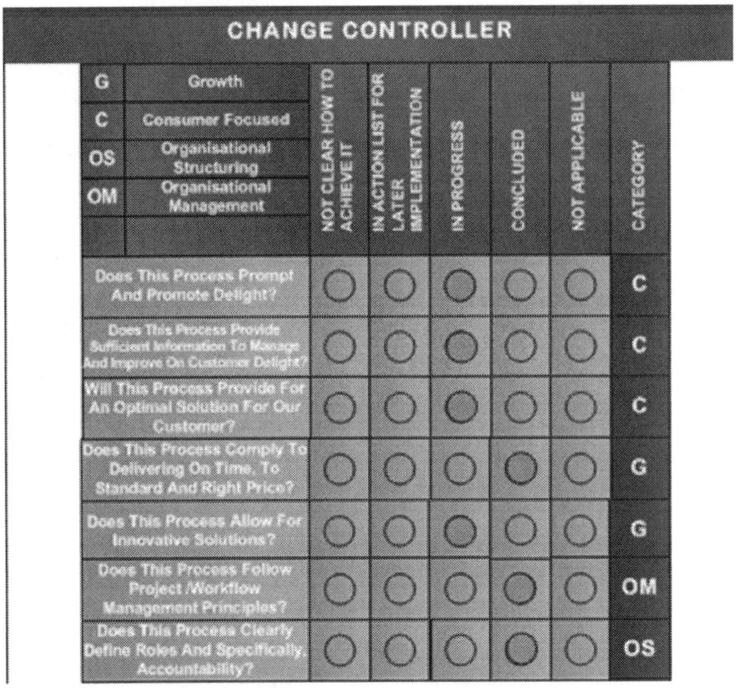

CHANGE CONTROLLER						
G Growth **C** Consumer Focused **OS** Organisational Structuring **OM** Organisational Management	NOT CLEAR HOW TO ACHIEVE IT	IN ACTION LIST FOR LATER IMPLEMENTATION	IN PROGRESS	CONCLUDED	NOT APPLICABLE	CATEGORY
Does This Process Prompt And Promote Delight?	○	○	○	○	○	C
Does This Process Provide Sufficient Information To Manage And Improve On Customer Delight?	○	○	○	○	○	C
Will This Process Provide For An Optimal Solution For Our Customer?	○	○	○	○	○	C
Does This Process Comply To Delivering On Time, To Standard And Right Price?	○	○	○	○	○	G
Does This Process Allow For Innovative Solutions?	○	○	○	○	○	G
Does This Process Follow Project /Workflow Management Principles?	○	○	○	○	○	OM
Does This Process Clearly Define Roles And Specifically Accountability?	○	○	○	○	○	OS

Figure 7: AAG Change Controller.

How the Change Controller was applied:

AAG's key strategic objective, as defined during the work session, included "to be excellent at servicing customers". To achieve this, the group agreed that it was necessary to address processes and align people and systems to:

- ensure that the organisation became more customer-focused;
- improve service delivery;
- develop customer centric business processes;
- develop agile processes that ensured quick management decision making;
- develop fluid processes that provided for innovative, creative and out-of-the box case-based solutions;
- create a customer excellence and continuous improvement culture;
- create a centre for excellence or Process Management Office (PrMO); and to
- create sustainable continuous improvement.

The Change Controller was developed to ensure that the Solution Delivery Division processes supported the company's strategic objectives. Each Case Manager had the opportunity to list their individual WGLL statements for the division. Once these statements were translated into goal definitions, the team agreed on what was critical for continuous improvement and to become a customer centric organisation. These prioritized goals were then added to the Change Controller. In the case of AAG, strategic goals were identified in the following categories:

- Growth;
- Consumer Focus;
- Organizational Structuring; and
- Organizational Management.

After each process mapping session, participants worked through the elements in the Change Controller to ascertain whether the process did indeed adhere to these requirements. These were categorised as such:

Status	Definition
"Not clear how to achieve it",	This means that there is a gap that needs to be addressed.
"In Action list for implementation"	This means that change actions have been defined, scheduled and assigned.
"In progress"	This means that it is incorporated in the "as is" or "to be" process, i.e. it forms part of what needs to be done and outcomes will reflect the process impact on the particular element.
"Concluded"	This means that the process outcomes are supporting the relevant element/requirement.
"Not applicable"	This means that the process is not intended to address the element.

Each Solution Delivery Division process map contained the same Change Controller against which the processes were tested to make sure that it contributed towards the strategic goals. A process would only be signed off once aligned to the Change Controller.

Benefits of using the Change Controller:

The benefits included:
- enabling Case Managers to list their process "WGLLS" and align these to enterprise goals;
- clarifying what each process should aim to deliver on;
- ensuring that there is a common direction when mapping processes in order to guarantee that the activities that occurred in each process would in fact bring about the desired results, as defined in the WGLLs and the CSFs; and
- ensuring final signoff of processes, since the Change Controller is the last step for final approval.

10. PROCESS MAPPING

The purpose of process mapping and processes

Each process clearly defines a number of related aspects, namely
1. what needs to be done,
2. who does it,
3. why is it done (i.e. "what outcome am I trying to achieve by doing this activity?"),
4. who is involved in each activity,
5. how does communication take place, and
6. how to achieve improvement where notes highlight specific "how" tips.

Each process step incorporates the value system of the enterprise by default and shows what needs to be done to achieve process outcomes. It also defines process management elements, such as what risks occur where, what controls are applied and where information is gathered with which to measure results (see figure 8).

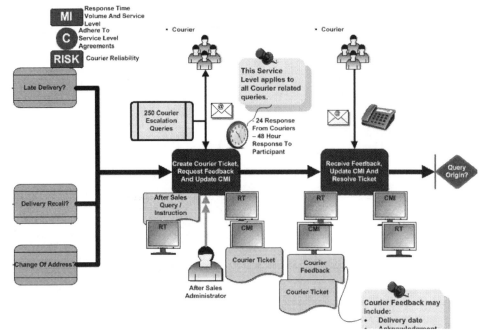

Figure 8: Snapshot of a VizPro® process map: section snapshot.

How the processes were mapped in AAG:

For each process the work session started with a blank screen. After agreeing the name of the map, the purpose and scope of the process was defined, discussed and recorded (refer to figure 9). From this starting point each process would be recorded, developed and improved upon—step by step.

The AAG Process Maps contained the following:

- customised icons;
- roles and responsibilities;
- customer touchpoints;
- opportunities for customer intelligence / feedback gathering; and
- areas where case-based solutions were needed and had to be executed according to response or activity Frameworks that incorporate Customer Delight Programme elements.

The Process Maps were developed in different versions:

Version 1:

Up to eight people were invited to unpack the "as is" (i.e. the status quo), adding notes on changes to be made, where needed. Discussion included subject matter experts, process stakeholders and management.

These sessions gave process stakeholders a forum to voice concerns and highlight challenges, problem areas and bottlenecks and to suggest solutions. It also aided in the collaboration of ideas and innovations whilst enabling the development of Frameworks on how to engage with customers in specific processes, and at specific points in the process. By doing this, the principles of Customer Delight could be built into each Framework ensuring the identification of the "do's" that would achieve the Customer Delights goals, as opposed to the "don'ts" that would compromise Customer Delight. Service recovery rules were developed to ensure sufficient guidelines for those occasions when service fails.

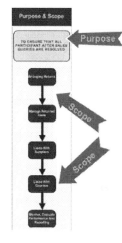

Figure 9: Snapshot of the Purpose and Scope of an AAG Process Map

The average time spent on each version one process map was between eight and 16 hours per process.

Version 2:

Up to 12 people joined this version to discuss, challenge and debate each of the Version 1 Process Maps, with the aim of adding improvements. This session included subject matter experts, external process stakeholders (organisational staff that had an impact on the processes) and cross functional management teams. This session provided opportunity for further design, collaboration and agreement that was particularly impactful in terms of information sharing and clarifying process risks and ACM.

Specific emphasis was placed on the following during discussions:

- Customer Delight and Service Recovery rules;
- risks and control points, specifically defining risks and the relevant mitigations that could be implemented;
- defining management information (MI) points where information is gathered;
- locating accounting points where cash or stock enter or leave the process and may impact on ACM;
- quality assurance points;
- key performance indicator (KPI) points, what indicator is applied to measure which element of performance and linking this back to the Performance Profile referenced above;
- burning points that resulted in bottlenecks or breakdowns in delivering services;
- points of escalations where the process executor required relevant Delegation of Authority to authorise certain transactions; and
- governance elements, including statutes, policies, standards and directives, ensuring that these were considered during ACM instances.

The average time spent per version 2 of the Process Maps was between 4-8 hours per process.

Benefits of using this approach to Process Mapping:

The benefits include:

- fostering an understanding by process stakeholders of the end-to-end processes in terms of who does what, with whom, when and how;
- identifying and improving process efficiencies, which positively impacted on cost, time and quality;
- clearly defining roles and responsibilities through the creation of visual Process Maps;
- highlighting the flow of documentation within the organisation, which ensures a clear audit trail;
- providing a cross functional view of the business instead of the traditional departmental view;
- ensuring that MI and KPIs are relevant and that they provide the right performance information at the right time to the right decision makers;

- defining process risks and agreeing on the controls to mitigate them;
- clearly defining and linking interrelationships between processes (within the organisation and within the Solution Delivery Division), people and systems;
- identifying process inefficiencies, bottlenecks, gaps and weaknesses;
- increasing performance and staff morale as people understood the "big picture" and the importance of their respective roles in it;
- knowledge transfer taking place and improving teamwork;
- enabling the development of training and induction material by using the process maps as a starting point;
- identifying competency level gaps and developing training programmes to address them; and
- ensuring a high buy-in into business changes since the process stakeholders were involved in the design of the process and understood the background of the change.

11. THE ACTION LIST

The purpose of the Action List

The Action List records the drivers for change. Whenever an item or an activity is identified during a workshop as an issue to be addressed, it is added to the Action List. The "who" and "when" is then agreed to by the participants.

Figure 10: Example of an Action List which records follow-on activities needed to ensure that change and improvement is executed.

How the Action Lists were used in AAG:

The Action Lists per process were populated and updated in real time during each mapping session. While working on processes, whenever a task needed to be recorded, the process architect would toggle to the Action List and record the action, stating:

- what the issue is;
- what needed to be done;
- what the desired outcome is;
- who needed to action the listed activity; and
- by when does it need to be done.

The benefits of the Action List:

The Action List:

- enhances ownership;

- it facilitates agreement of what activities or projects are needed to implement improvement, and
- it is a critical implementation management tool.

12. KEY BENEFITS

The key benefits of this process approach, which highlights the competitive advantages in addressing ACM as described in this case study, include:

- a saving of time—the work was concluded in 45.5 project days, over a period of six months utilizing one specialist consultant (six days), two process architects (31 and 7 days respectively) and a project coordinator (1.5 days);
- effective use of staff time, limiting the loss of work hours for the client—25 key people were involved in the project, impacting on approximately 150 co-workers, all of whom are part of the Customer Service delivery chain;
- it requires only low cost IT—MS Visio™ is used to produce the process maps and Microsoft Office Excel for the Action Lists. These documents are stored on the SharePoint Drive;
- recording a vast amount of knowledge in real time;
- enabling knowledge share and alignment through effective engagement;
- creating clarity on who does what, why and how and what the rules of each ACM instance are, as defined in the Customer Delight Frameworks;
- enabling a transfer of skills to update the process maps (1.5 days for training in AAG);
- aligning and linking each process to AAG's strategic direction and to specific business goals so that role players see the clear line between what they do and how it impacts on business goals;
- enabling group agreement
    - on actions to be implemented to ensure effective and efficient processes that are measurable;
    - on risks that need to be managed;
    - on how to attain Customer Delight; and
- agility as the tools and techniques are flexible and customisable to ensure that what is needed can be designed into processes and systems, provided that there is enterprise agreement and buy-in.

13. KEY CHALLENGES EXPERIENCED DURING THE PROJECT AND HOW THEY WERE ADDRESSED

Challenges	How they were addressed
Gaining senior management and executive buy-In	Senior management and the executive team were key in the development of the Organizational Positioning Map. In this work session the focus was on the benefits of having customer-centric processes and how it would impact on the bottom line. By focusing on these elements, immediate buy-in occurred through discussion and collaborative verification of the benefits, along with the commitment to ensure continuous benefit realization.
Overcoming functional thinking	Prior to the rollout of the project, AAG focused on traditional functional structures such as marketing, sales, operations, HR etc.
	The process sessions effectively communicated how approaching business processes from an end-to-end perspective would add value in service delivery. Once senior management and the executive team saw the outcomes of the

work session, which clearly identified the value stream from its origin to the end customer, there was immediate buy-in.

Business Change Management

Process stakeholders initially showed resistance to the work sessions, but after having been exposed to the VizPro® methodology, there was effective buy-in. This resulted in excellent, enthusiastic and high quality participation as it provided a platform for stakeholders from different levels of the organisation to contribute to the design of the customer-centric processes in a manner that addressed their specific process-related issues.

Process stakeholder availability

Many of the stakeholders felt that they had "more important" work to attend to. Once they experienced the VizPro® approach however, they saw the value it brought to their work lives. They also saw the project as being an opportunity to collaborate and develop innovative solutions to challenges faced on a day-to-day basis.

14. PITFALLS TO AVOID WHEN USING THIS METHODOLOGY

✘ Do not waste time. Deliver and show benefits and value as immediate value ensures continued participation and commitment from management all the way through to employees

✘ Do not underestimate the power of putting the right resources into the project. The relationships fostered in this way ensures the delivery of effective work sessions, and effective work sessions means delivering quick value to the client

✘ Do not waiver. Be secure and precise in the tools and techniques, be clear on the approach and explain in a way that every single person understands what is happening, why and what the end goal is

✘ Do not complicate matters. Keep it simple

✘ Do not underestimate the effort required. Prepare participants to what lies ahead and to the fact that it is hard work, with long, intense hours.

15. WHY THE INNOVATION IN THE PROJECT IS NOTEWORTHY

A number of reasons can be listed on why the innovation in this project is of significance:

- The approach was uniquely suited to introducing customer-centricity into the enterprise at every level as the easy-to-understand visible format conveyed the message in a simplified format which was easy to follow and implement.
- The approach fostered complete management support through its collaborative and interactive storyboard design work sessions;
- The project offered the holistic approach that was required by management and the relevant stakeholders to analyze the Solution Delivery Division processes in order to achieve realistic and practical customer improvements;
- The VizPro® methodology provided insight and a clear road map on how to achieve strategic objectives and organization-wide customer-centricity;

- The project required only simple, low IT to deliver a high impact methodology that enabled case-based solutions and highlighted essential customer touchpoints;
- The project, through its use of VizPro®, created participation and buy-in through interactive, high-energy workshops, resulted in user-friendly and information rich process maps. This moreover, led to the "wow" factor as abstract processes effectively come to life as visual storyboards through the use of icons that tell the story of each process in comprehensive detail. This is the unique characteristic of VizPro®.
- The project provided a voice to every knowledge worker participant that added to innovation and improved practices through effective collaboration.
- By facilitating discussions amongst process stakeholders from all organisational levels it enabled real-time collaboration of ideas and innovations that aided in designing, tailor-made customer-centric processes.
- The project ensured the best possible outcome by including stakeholders that lived the processes and its frustrations day-to-day, knew what to watch out for and have learned how to get past the hurdles. They have seen things go wrong and now had the opportunity to be part of the solution.
- The project provided clear programme elements. The Customer Delight Programme comprises the Customer Delight Framework, Customer Touchpoint Model, Positioning Map, Change Controllers, Process Maps and Action Lists which are all effective and easy access tools for the management of Corporate Knowledge.
- The project made smart use of technology by using MS SharePoint as the central repository system. The SharePoint was used to manage version control, process templates and to capture knowledge gained from lessons learnt in a timeous manner.
- A Centre of Excellence (COE) was established to design and document the core and supporting business processes.
- Skills were transferred to the COE team (Quality Champions) through on-the-job shadowing and formal training. The focus was on the VizPro® methodology and MS Visio™, and particularly, on how to effectively use technology.

The end result of the project was the creation of agile customer-centric processes allowing the AAG to embrace change rather than reject, control or suffer from change and the high demand on agility. The results included enhanced capability for knowledge workers and management to make quick decisions to ensure that processes generated the desired results.

Clear Programme elements:
- The Customer Delight Programme comprises the Customer Delight Framework; Customer Touchpoint Model Positioning Map; Change Controllers, Process Maps and Action Lists; effective and easy access to, and management of Corporate Knowledge;
- MS SharePoint was selected as the central repository system and is used to manage version control, process templates and the capturing of knowledge gained from lessons learnt;

- A Centre of Excellence (COE) was established to design and document the core and supporting business processes.
- Skills were transferred to the COE team (Quality Champions), through on-the-job shadow and formal training. The focus was on the VizPro® methodology and MS Visio™ on how to effectively use the technology;

Results: Agile customer centric processes were developed, allowing the AAG to embrace change rather than reject, control or suffer from change and the high demand on agility. The results included capability for knowledge workers and management to make quick decisions to ensure that processes generated the desired results.

16. CONCLUSION:

Achieving results through Adaptive Case Management is possible only when people, processes and system align and support one another. By creating a clear, easy to understand, management and staff supported Customer Delight Programme that includes a Customer Delight Framework and clearly defines in each relevant process "who" needs to do "what" to ensure that process outcomes *and* customer services are effectively and efficiently delivered, continued benefit is realized and results are monitored.

Global Banking Firm

Finalist: Customer Facing
Nominated by Virtusa Corporation, USA

1. EXECUTIVE SUMMARY / ABSTRACT

Our client, a global banking firm, required a global Payment Exception processing system for their client support managers operating across the globe.

The client has thousands of named users across the globe, who manage dispute-related enquiries 24x7 at its Call Centers through varied channels—email, phone, SWIFT message, etc. Each site used their own home-grown case tracking solutions and a few sites had little or no system support beyond spreadsheets. The Bank was unable to provide global service to their customers and had very little ability to see and report upon client activity globally. This was a major product capability and service gap compared with the banks' competitors.

Virtusa partnered with the bank to completely automate their end-to-end business processes and workflow using Pegasystems BPM/Pega technology. Our solution supports all relevant call center services, ticket tracking and integrated investigation and dispute management capabilities for Treasury products including cash, disbursements and wire transfer on an integrated global basis. Leveraging Pegasystems BPM technology provides our client with a scalable platform for that supports the full life cycle of the case management—Receive, Route, Report, Research, Respond. It accommodates real-time reporting with global, regional, and local views with enriched data security through Single-sign on based authentication and branch level entitlements. Virtusa leveraged its proven agile methodologies and techniques, which helped shorten the development cycle time by more than 30 percent, and mature global delivery model for flexible staffing structure and cost benefits to the client.

2. OVERVIEW

By implementing the new system, the client was able to mitigate operational risks and improved efficiencies by automating the transaction investigation and exception management system. The client was also able to improve the overall turnaround time for transaction investigations and exception processing, reduce overall operating costs through automation of the process, enhance internal user satisfaction through user friendly screens and made it easy to adopt.

With a vision for a single workspace solution, the abilities to do various searches from one system to create a case were a huge value-addition compared to the existing process where user had to check multiple systems for details of one case. The solution improved the collaboration and communication between the client and other financial institutions by implementing the common frameworks.

3. BUSINESS CONTEXT

The client had various legacy systems across different geographical locations that largely supported customers and currencies local to that region. A customer would contact the service center in their region who in turn would email information to the settling service center for research. While the Transaction Investigation process was pre-defined, but there was no guarantee that the process would be followed by different service center locations and there was no uniform system with controls in place. Service center support managers were able to deviate from the predefined processes. That resulted in inconsistent service for customers and lack of control for management. The client needed a way to close these loopholes and improve customer service and satisfaction by providing a consistent experience and service level across multiple countries and products to their corporate treasury clients.

Client wanted to build a system that would:

- ensure, timely, cost-effective resolution to investigations across a range of payments and cash management activities;
- allow them to more effectively respond to shortened settlement times, risk reduction initiatives, rising transaction volumes, and increased competition
- increase the productivity of their customer service team while improving the ability to manage business globally
- satisfy the demands of a diverse client base that includes corporate, correspondent, and institutional clients
- provide greater flexibility and time to market acceleration in responding to changes in business strategies and or customer requirements,

4. THE KEY INNOVATIONS

The transformational work resulted in the creation of a Single System for tracking all Treasury investigations

- The teams who have been using their own custom applications across the regions and branches were brought under one system. Management control and visibility increased significantly.
- New reporting capabilities were made available to customers.
- Various means of communications (Fax, Email, SWIFT, FED) were plugged in to the new system, started creating investigations automatically where possible.

Consistent High Quality Service

- Users across the globe who accessed the new system were using the same normalized version of case types. When one region raises an investigation request, it was very easily understood by the other regional offices whereas in the past when they had different systems, they needed to translate one team's case details to the other team's equivalent case details.
- Customer representatives cannot override the system process. They need to follow the correct process enforced by the system and serve all the clients in the same way.
- With the new system, the Bank was able to create tiered levels of service (e.g. platinum, gold, silver) and associated fee plans for each level.

Cost Savings

- Maintenance costs of individual applications were eliminated.
- Regional offices could save some operational costs which were centralized and needed less headcount due to the automated workflow capabilities.
- Onboarding of new service representatives was significantly reduced.
- CoEs (Center of Excellence) were able to cater to multiple regions around the clock from a single location where operational cost is low. This enabled the client to close down the operations where operational cost was higher.

Efficiency
- Establishing Center of Excellence led to higher productivity, higher efficiency and made available "around the clock" service for the customers.

Ease in Reporting
- The implementation of a single system globally allowed the Bank to employ standardized reporting for internal MIS and for external Customer reports.

Extensibility
- The project provided straight through automation of various means of initiation channels with the new system including: email, fax, IVR (Interactive Voice Response) and a self service portal to initiate their requests. They no longer needed to talk to a representative to create an investigation.

4.1 Business

This section describes the impact of the project on the way the firm engages its customers, partners and suppliers etc. (or other key stakeholders):

- All the client's customers are serviced using the same process globally. Customers are rated at different service levels and the SLAs were set appropriately, to the processes, to make sure the higher rated customers get immediate attention over the lower rated clients.
- Customers are able to engage with the system over multiple channels. The ordinary methods like Phone, Email, Walk-In, and modern methods like self service portal and IVR
- Management teams, senior management and stake holders were able to run ad hoc reports at any time to get the global view of the operations. Customers are able to get 24x7 service due to the global execution ability of the new system. The Straight-Through Processing model, which automated creating a case automatically from structured or unstructured electronic messages helped customers to be able to connect to the system 24x7 without even spending time talking to someone on the phone.

4.2 Case Handling Overview

How cases were handled before and after the project:

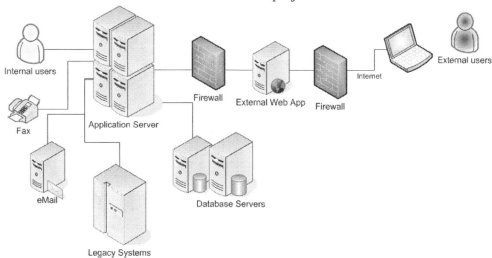

Application server sits in the data centre located in the US.

- The sites belonging to the client organization are connected to the application server using the Virtual Private Network.
- Email Server, Database Servers, Fax Servers and other in-house legacy systems also connect to the application server using the local network.
- External databases are in the US, but geographical location may differ.
- External application built for customers is deployed in the same application server. But the web application that holds the user interface is in a separate Web server outside of the network. The communication from Web server to Application server is protected by a firewall. The external user application is accessible via World Wide Web and it's protected by another firewall.

The key roles and how are they assigned/managed:

- The key roles in a transaction investigation would be the Transaction, Inquirer, Beneficiary, Credit Party, Debit Party, Owner of the case, Department of the person who own the case and the Investigator.
- Transaction is available in the client's transaction data base. Transactions can either be in Cash or Securities.
- The person who is requesting for an investigation is the Inquirer. The inquirer will provide the inquirer details. Based on the details given by Inquirer, and based on the details coming up in the investigation, the Beneficiary, Credit party and Debit party will be determined.
- Inquirer will reach the Investigator using the common communication channels such as Phone, Email, SWIFT message or they will use the self service application.
- Owner of the case is the responsible person for the case to be analyzed and resolved. It is derived by evaluating various other system factors. There are specific rules set to determine who should Own working on the case. For example, sometimes the inbound email address will be used to determine to which department the case should go to. Sometimes it will be based on other facts like, the inbound message type, the keywords defined in the message or sometimes it will be the person who takes the call or the person who gets the work after the initial phone call is over.
- One department/person can route the work to another department based on the investigation results, the owner will change to the new department/person
- The Department of the person which owns the case is the primary group who will be looking at the case. If the person who is working on the case is not available, it will be processed by someone else in the same department.
- The Investigator is the person who conducts the investigation on behalf of the Inquirer. The Investigators are the end users of the system. These users are authenticated against the company's Active Directory and they are authorized to carry out various functions of the system based on different levels of security points.
- Users are grouped in to different workgroups and they have been assigned different levels of access groups. Access groups will limit the main featured of the system at User Interface level. Different access groups will have access to different options when they log in.
- Once they are in the system, their work is restricted based on the entitled branches. User will see the work belongs to the branches he/she assigned

to. Even though the user is entitled to many branches, the work sometimes gets restricted at the department level. Some users may only pick cases belongs to his department and will not able to see anything outside his department.

- Some of the common functions that cannot be restricted by Branch, Department or Workgroup level, we have restricted the access to these functions based on a skill and a score. A particular user can have a skill bound to his user ID that enables him/her to do something others who does not have the skill can do. The Score comes in to play when there are many users having the same skill, but some are authorized to do full functionality and some should only be able to do just part of it. For example, if bunch of users have a skill to approve a payment, we can restrict the users with the same skill but a score of 5 to approve payments above 100,000.00 and who has the score of 1 to just approve payments less than 5,000.00

The main business entities and how they are maintained during the lifecycle:

- In this case, the case template is the case entry screen of the system.
- The data on the case entry screen is acceptable by all the parties and derived based on the various discussions at the design level. The template was improved during the pilot runs by accommodating real user's inputs
- Any change to the case template is announced for global user acceptance and only after getting global approval, change will be implemented.

4.3 Organization and Social

We describe the impact on the employees and what their jobs now entail compared to previously.

- The system resulted in improved productivity—users now have a central point to access all the data. Compared to the earlier practice of different regions accessing multiple systems to gain details related to the case, the new system gave them 360 degree view of the case to a single user.
- It is now possible to obtain an accurate global count of cases done in a day. Cases that are initiated and followed till resolution as well as cases that are prematurely ended because of the call line being dropped at the middle or misrouted calls, are also logged in the new system to show how many calls they received, how many were real requests and how many others, as "others" also require some effort from their time and should be counted as their work done.
- The new system increased the number of cases a user can complete in a day. That increased their productivity and compensation.
- Management teams were able to recognize the employees who were contributing well to the organization and also help the employees who were struggling or needed improvement.
- MIS greatly improved as client was now able to generate most reports automatically as well as see much activity summaries online real time.
- By developing a self service portal, the Bank extended its capabilities directly to clients and freed up time from customer service staff.

5. HURDLES OVERCOME

Organization Adoption

Management / Business

- Had to obtain buy-in from regional managers and regional stakeholders on the future operational vision
- Being able to show forecasted savings

Organizational Adoption

- This was done by region and by product.
- Clear and lengthy training sessions were conducted to make sure the users understood all the features of the system

Took an approach where we moved part of the users to work on the new system and kept the other half on the old system. Once the first half of the team was comfortable with the system, the 2nd half was moved in to the new system.

6. BENEFITS

6.1 Cost Savings / Time Reductions

- Most of the settings and decision making power of the system is configurable rule-based. Hence it makes easy to change the values as you do not need time from developers to do configuration changes.
- Most of the modules were implemented as frameworks, adding something to the framework takes less development time, results in lower testing time and lower development cost ($ value)
- Ability to solve the investigations in short time reduces the risk of the bank from paying high amounts as penalties. For example, a million dollar transaction that got deducted from party A's account didn't move to Party B's account on time will cause the Bank to pay Interest to party A and B both and also penalty fee, the loss could be thousands of dollars.
- Cost of marinating multiple applications reduced
- Reduced operational costs of some service centres by closing them down and move work to low cost CoEs

6.3 Quality Improvements

- Improved the time spent on one call / interaction. Earlier the response time to issue a case ID to the customer took longer time due to cross-checking multiple systems. Now in less than 10 seconds service rep can issue a case number.
- Quality of the service got improved with the unified process and fixed SLAs
- Quality of the reports got significantly enhanced with the ability to see global data
- Automated acknowledgements to customers and automated status notifications to clients made the client aware of the status of their investigation and kept them in the loop. Additional calls to service centres asking for the status have been cut down as customers now have much better access to information
- The self service interface made it easy to clients to update the case without contacting the service rep over the phone. That made the clients who are located in different location able to initiate or inquire on a case 24/7 without restriction to geography. The efficiency of opening and closing cases gained by the new solution improved productivity greatly. The Bank

was able to handle a 3x rise in volume without a corresponding rise in headcount.

7.1 Best Practices and Learning Points

✓ Identified common capabilities in the system, developed reusable components that standardize and improve the structure of information, user experience and productivity. These capabilities are a set of application features, system functions, rules tables, visual elements, usability and system guidelines, etc

✓ Implemented agile development methodology: Conducted hot-house with all the relevant stakeholders, gained consensus on the requirements from all the business groups. Build Self service application in 3 month cycle by deploying Virtusa's proven iterative methodology and best practices to the client satisfaction.

✓ Developed a scalable analytics platform for a historical trending analysis on the case tracking and performance across the globe.

✓ Decouple the reporting databases from transaction databases. A user running a expensive report at mid day will not cause the server to run slow and impact the other users.

7.2 Pitfalls

× Employ visualization techniques for demonstrating both look and feel but also new workflow to users.

× Use rapid development (agile) techniques so users can rapidly see results and provide feedback

× Ensure that the future state operating model is well defined before development commences.

× Do not write expensive SQLs. Make use of a DBA (Data Base Admin) to evaluate your DB calls. The SQLs you write can sometimes cause the server to crash on you

7. TECHNOLOGY

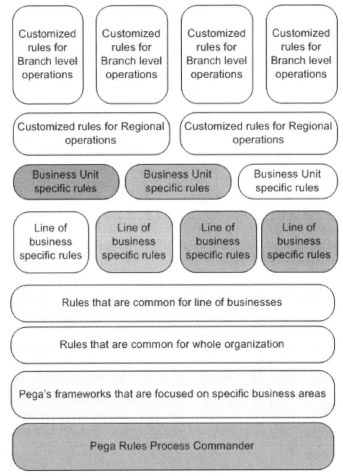

The rule stack

Above diagram shows how we placed our rules to make sure the reusability and concepts of productization are used to the maximum.

- All the re-usable components were kept in the base layers and each Line of Business or business unit specific rules have been stacked vertically.
- By using the frameworks given by Pega, we were able to provide services to the client such as quick solutions building for constant change requests and rapid defects remediation.
- Another step we took was to leverage standard PRPC functionality as much as possible and utilize the PRPC capabilities leveraging in integration.
- The out-of-the-box features like SOAP Connectors, Direct Database access and E-mail Listeners, SOAP Services, HTTP Connect integration and Active Directory integration for user authentication
- Apart from the benefits of using the above rule stack, we have done couple of tweaks to make the system perform the best.
- For almost all the communications with the legacy systems were done using the Message Queues and SOAP Connectors. Where ever we could not use SOAP (either because of the legacy system does not have ability to communicate to MQ, or the system is not having support resources to

build SOAP interfaces) we have used direct SQL calls to write the necessary data to Data tables.

- We schedule agents to process those data in batch processes.
- We have decoupled the transaction data table and the reporting data table to make sure the reporting requests that require massive data loads from the data table are not impacting the system's processing.
- We have implemented a nightly data archival process to back up the cases we created for the inquiries, services and investigations. The same process is populating the necessary data for reporting tables.

8. THE TECHNOLOGY AND SERVICE PROVIDERS

Pegasystems Inc., Cambridge, MA

Pegasystems is the recognized industry leader in business process management (BPM) and a leading provider of customer relationship management (CRM) solutions. Pegasystems help some of the world's largest companies achieve new levels of agility, enhance customer loyalty, generate new business and improve productivity. The company's patented technology enables organizations to realize rapid and significant business returns by directly capturing business objectives into fully automated processes and eliminating manual programming. Pegasystems enables clients to quickly adapt to changing business conditions in order to outperform the competition.

Virtusa Corporation, Westborough, MA

Virtusa provides end-to-end information technology (IT) services to Global 2000 companies. These services, which include IT consulting, application maintenance, development, systems integration and managed services, leverage a unique Platforming methodology that transforms clients' businesses through IT rationalization. Virtusa helps customers accelerate business outcomes by consolidating, rationalizing and modernizing their core customer facing processes into one or more core systems.

Virtusa delivers cost-effective solutions through a global delivery model, applying advanced methods such as Agile and Accelerated Solution Design to ensure that its solutions meet the clients' requirements. As a result, its clients simultaneously reduce their IT operations cost while increasing their ability to meet changing business needs.

Founded in 1996 and headquartered in Massachusetts, Virtusa has operations in North America, Europe and Asia.

BAA Heathrow, United Kingdom

Gold Award: Innovation

Nominated by Pegasystems Inc., USA

1. EXECUTIVE SUMMARY / ABSTRACT

At London's Heathrow airport, a new case is created by a system feed, every time an incoming plane is registered by air-traffic control, and closes when the plane is en route to its next destination. This event enabled case-management approach to aircraft turn-around has dramatically improved the overall efficiency of operations at Heathrow, including:

- An increase in on-time departures from 68 percent to 83 percent,
- A savings of 90 litres of fuel per flight, due to decreased time spent on the runway, yielding cost savings for airlines, and a positive environmental impact,
- A projected increase in retail revenues, by allowing passengers on faster-boarding flights to spend more time in the terminal rather than seated in airplanes awaiting take off.

The caseworkers in this case are the people responsible for the timely and efficient turn-around of airplanes—from airline teams, to stand planners, to air traffic controllers, to cleaning crews, to baggage handlers. With this new system, they are empowered with all of the information they need to make the right decisions—including a real-time visualization of planes on the runways—and to initiate the right processes, and allocate the right resources, based on the context of the situation from type of plane, to the plane's next destination. The imperative for adaptive case management is clear here, where the context is constantly changing due to external events such as weather or security alerts.

2. OVERVIEW

This example demonstrates just how broadly a case-based approach to work can be applied. In the most common applications of case management, people are the subjects of the work, whether they are customers, citizens, patients. Here the subject of the case is neither a person, nor even a business; the subject is an activity, a span of time—specifically, turning around an aircraft. Yet the approach is unquestionably case management. Personal experience tells us all how dynamic this type of case is; we know how many factors contribute to our flights taking off on time—or not. It is a true testament to the power of new adaptive case management approaches that case management can be applied to such a dynamic type of case.

Each case that is handled by BAA is like a performance of a well-coordinated jazz ensemble. In jazz, there are many sets of rules—tonality, rhythm, harmony—that govern what the players play. At the same time, the players improvise within this set of rules, constantly reacting to the actions of the other members in a perfect balance between structure and improvisation. At BAA, the different actors on the case whether people, departments or systems, are akin to the different instruments within an ensemble. Just as each instrument has a set range and sound that gives it a unique ability to contribute to the performance, so too each of these actors has a unique range of skills enabling them to contribute to the resolution of the case. Both the actors, and the skills they can apply, change with the context—one doesn't want a trumpet player belting out a fortissimo when the desired mood is pianissimo.

In the following pages, you'll read how BAA has harnessed this kind of controlled improvisation to substantially improve airport operations. Underpinning this was an undertaking by BAA to capture the rules of their operation, institutionalizing them such that every actor is able to perform to the best of his or her abilities in every situation. Because of the system-based nature, this is possible without years of training on what those policies and procedures are. In this way, BAA is able to fully empower the entire network of people collaborating to quickly turn around—literally—a jumbo-jet, without fear that regulations are being breached, or customer service is being overlooked.

3. BUSINESS CONTEXT

In 2008, over 145 million passengers passed through BAA's UK airports, including almost 70 million through the world's busiest International airport, London Heathrow. At Heathrow over 70,000 staff were engaged in helping those passengers to move through the airport as efficiently as possible.

Prompted by upcoming domestic and industry regulations such as the EU's Single European Sky ATM Research program (SESAR), in 2008 BAA initiated a program to simplify the complex set of operational systems that were used to manage the airport. One of the first goals of the program was to put in place a system that would allow the airport to optimize flight turnarounds, both in terms of time, and in terms of resources.

Prior to the program the resources that were employed to turn around a flight, including the stands, gates, check-in counters, refueling crews, cleaning crews, flight crew managers, and information from the systems—for example the air traffic control system—were managed by separate teams. Each of these teams was part of a separate line of business—or even part of a separate company. This organizational architecture yielded "optimization" at the department level, not at the airport level. At the airport level it was sub-optimal—on-time flight departures hovered around 60 percent. As one of the busiest and most inter-connected airports in the world, the ramifications of delayed flights extended globally.

Taking cues from other industries which have improved their customer service, BAA decided to take a case management approach, with the aircraft turn around being the case.

4. THE KEY INNOVATIONS

Describe the impact that resulted from the project (recommended).

4.1 Business

Since going live with this system, Airport Collaborative Decision Management or A-CDM, BAA has increased on-time departures to 85 percent from 68 percent which in turn decreases the amount they pay in penalties. The ability of managers to improve resource planning and allocation significantly improves the efficiency of terminal operations.

Because BAA now has visibility into which flights take the longest to board, whether based on how full they are, what the destination is, etc., they can optimize boarding to keep passengers in the terminal longer, rather than prematurely boarding them.

There are three benefits that arise from this practice:

- Passengers are happier, because they are free to move about rather than corralled in an airplane sitting on the tarmac.
- Passengers spend more time in the terminal shopping at retails outlets, or eating at dining establishments, improving the bottom line for these interests. Metrics for this are still being collected.
- The last benefit from this case-based approach to aircraft turnaround is that each airplane now spends less time on the runway, saving approximately 90 litres of fuel per flight. Not only does this decrease the carbon footprint, but—aggregated over time, it is a significant savings to the airlines flying in and out of Heathrow.

4.2 Case Handling

Case handling before implementation:

Prior to this program the resources that were employed to turn around a flight, including the stands, gates, check-in counters, refueling crews, cleaning crews, flight crew managers, and information from the systems—for example the air traffic control system—were managed by separate teams. Each of these teams was part of a separate line of business—or even part of a separate company. This organizational architecture yielded "optimization" at the department level, not at the airport level.

Case handling after implementation:

Now, when a flight bound for Heathrow enters British airspace, a system feed from air traffic control automatically creates the case. A template for how to handle it is applied based on a variety of criteria, including where the plane is coming from and going to, the size of the aircraft, etc. BAA thinks of these as resource plans. The template or plan that is used will also differ based on the current stress-level of the airport. The A-CDM system is then able to monitor the real-time aggregated volume of traffic in the airport and manage it based on pre-defined stress levels. These levels correspond to the amount of stress on airport resources and are constantly monitored to ensure that the current level reflects reality. The inputs to the level are various, but some are: weather, security status, daily and/or seasonal passenger volume. Each level has its own set of templates and policies that are applied for resource allocation, in order to ensure the optimal allocation given that particular stress level.

The key roles are:
- Airline Staff
- Air traffic control
- Stand planners
- Stand managers
- Flight crew managers
- Cleaning crews
- Repair crews
- Refuelling crews
- Baggage handlers
- Airport security

The assignment of a given crew or person to the turnaround of a specific aircraft at a specific stand is performed automatically by the system, based on the rules specified by the prevailing stress level. Up until the point that an aircraft is actually at the gate, these assignments (particularly the gate) are constantly in flux, ensuring the optimal resource allocation. Once the aircraft is at the gate, while the gate itself will not change, the allocation of other resources needed to turn the plane around will depend on the broader functioning of the airport, as well as any knock-on effects from air traffic at other airports. For example, an aircraft might be ready to turn around, Heathrow might have the capacity to send it on its way, but the destination airport may have an air traffic control delay in place. Given that situation, it may not make sense to deploy the resources to turn the plane around right at that moment, but rather to wait and address other turnarounds, whose aircraft may be in jeopardy of late departure.

The rules that are in force based on the stress level—which form the basis for the template, and the actions that are available—affect assignment and "routing" of aircraft and personnel. However, the actual work is still being performed by people, and their actions and updates impact how the system handles/allocates other resources, and what actions are available to others. The various managers of these resources act within the sets of policies that apply at that stress level. This means that they still have all the freedom they want to perform any action, as long as it isn't explicitly prohibited by the stress level. In this way, the case is extremely dynamic, as people and systems are constantly interacting to ensure the highest percentage of on-time flights, given the circumstances (or context) at the time. For example, an air traffic controller who decides to hold a plane on the ground automatically impacts the allocation and handling of all other aircraft at the airport.

"Caseworkers" also have a real-time view of the position of the various aircraft on the runway. This allows them to better understand how the work they are doing for a given turnaround case fits into the broader whole—the airport "case load" as it were.

Of course all of the rules need to be flexible and adaptable to manage situational flux. Firstly, different airlines want to manage their turnaround rules in a unique fashion, and therefore some of the rules within the case template are adaptable to define, for example, what the minimum turnaround time for each flight is. This automatically sets the goals and target times within the system for that flight. Also, as turnaround proceeds, some flights are delayed and others are ready ahead of the expected time. Therefore the airline has the ability to update its state of readiness and alert air traffic control that they will be ready to leave either earlier or later and the necessary processes (passenger boarding, pre-departure sequencing etc) can be amended accordingly. These are two examples of many functions in the system designed to allow the airport and the people working on its behalf to react promptly and consistently to constant change.

4.3 Organization & Social

Before the A-CDM system was deployed, the operating model was akin to moving from one "fire" to the next, as they were unable to anticipate, nor allocate work to address the flux in the amount of work. Now, while there are still certainly very busy times, in all except for emergency situations, they are able to plan for those, and staff accordingly. Even in emergent situations, the return to normal occurs in a faster and more orderly fashion. The appropriate policies for that stress level are applied, and these help to ensure that workers across the airport are able to handle the situation in the most effective way possible.

At the very outset of the process, BAA rigorously defined its business architecture, including a business capability and service map. This foundational work was necessary to being able to put together the resource plan templates, and also in meeting one of BAA's other goals—reusability. Further it has proven very valuable for helping BAA to manage the on-going changes being introduced by this new, ever-evolving, and expanding system.

5. HURDLES OVERCOME

Management
- Executive support throughout the project was essential, not only for requirements clarification but also to maintain the buy-in of the many external stakeholders. Executives were always aware of the importance of this project in the achievement of a range of BAA's corporate targets

Business (Operations)
- As above, this was achieved through clear and constant communication across the user community.

Organization Adoption
- The problems before CDM was delivered were that no one believed the information in their systems— everyone was looking at different 'versions of the truth'. This led to people putting poor data into the system or trying to use loopholes to their advantage. This system is coaching all users towards a more honest use of the system, including publicizing the accuracy of the data that each airline provides to the broader user community

6. BENEFITS

6.1 Cost Savings / Time Reductions
- Increases in on-time departures has reduced penalties paid to the airlines
- Save 90 litres of fuel/departure, as average time spent on the tarmac has been reduced
- Considerable reduction in system development, management and maintenance costs compared with off the shelf monitoring tools.

6.2 Increased Revenues
- Expected increase in retail revenues due to keeping passengers in the terminal as long as possible—without jeopardizing on-time departure.

6.3 Quality Improvements
- Increased on-time departures from 60 percent to 85 percent
- Airport running at 98.7 percent capacity

7. BEST PRACTICES, LEARNING POINTS AND PITFALLS

7.1 Best Practices and Learning Points
- ✓ *Make sure you have clear definitions of your business services and business capabilities, and how these are used throughout your organization.*
- ✓ *Identify and communicate the responsibilities for all stake holders*
- ✓ *When selecting a vendor, have a clear set of requirements. Ask each vendor to implement the requirements (some) in 1 day, then on the 2nd day, change the requirements. This will give you insight into how easy it will be for YOU to make changes when you need to.*

7.2 Pitfalls
- ✗ *User adoption*
- ✗ *Change management*

8. COMPETITIVE ADVANTAGES

Improving on-time departures ensures that Heathrow will continue to be a major hub for European and trans-continental travel. Without a demonstrated, on-going commitment to on-time departures and overall efficiency, BAA would run the risk of losing traffic to other major airports.

The A-CDM project is just the first step in a long-term plan to increase the efficiency of Heathrow.

9. TECHNOLOGY

The underlying technology infrastructure.

- The A-CDM system uses Pegasystems as its key technology. For the user interface, Pegasystems is combined with Microsoft SharePoint.
- In order to ensure that upgrades are easy, BAA has implemented a strict rule that only generally available functionality be used within the solution—no custom coding.

10. THE TECHNOLOGY AND SERVICE PROVIDERS

Pegassystems; implementation was handled by a joint team of Pega professional services and BAA Information Technology staff.

...ran & Sridharan, ...a

...l Courts

...are Technologies,

...vice Indian legal firm providing ...s in the domains of Tax, Intellec-...porate laws. The requirements of ...ated document management and ...rk allocations, knowledge manage-...their cases with excellence'. Further ...ing bills and tracking receivables. The u... improve efficiency in service delivery by enab... to work from anywhere outside the office and anytime o... ...uld provide flexibility in working for the professionals as well as guarantee availability of services to clients from any office. The system should also guarantee confidentiality and security of client information.

An optimum solution would support processes like data entry and case docket creation for various LOBs, contract management, capacity planning and fee estimation, effort estimation & work allocation, drafting by means of pre-configured templates and stored data in the database, court diary record keeping, timesheet maintenance, tracking of case progress and finances, customer billing, payments, collection and knowledge management. Additionally the solution needed to facilitate realization of the broader goals of L&S namely:

- Optimizing productivity
- Improving turn-around-time
- Sustained growth

The Newgen solution for L&S automated the core legal case management process and also integrated with the firm's accounting software (Navision). The Newgen solution has been able to supplement the achievement of the firm's goals by

- helping in improving excellence in service delivery
- assisting in improving cash flow by timely billing and effective receivables management
- aiding in optimal distribution of work and improved effective working of professionals
- facilitating distribution/allocation of work to the best suited professional for a particular case irrespective of location of the professional
- providing for dashboards and MIS reports to ensure real time monitoring and improved visibility

The solution has empowered L&S professionals across India that includes attorneys, chartered accountants, technologists and scientists. It has integrated the work of professionals with accounting. To ease the work of professionals, data capturing activities and other routine work has been grouped under a Docketing Cell to perform routine paralegal activities. This has been made possible because of Legal Case Management Solution (LCMS). The solution has the 3-in-1 features of a Case Management, Business Process Management and Document Management System. It is unique for combining all the three features besides having capacity to deliver consistently and accurately.

2. OVERVIEW

Lakshmi Kumaran & Sridharan (L&S) is a full service law firm in India specializing in the areas of Taxation, Intellectual Property Rights, International Trade and Corporate laws. L&S employs 208 professionals besides 100 support staff. L&S, through its six offices across India in New Delhi, Mumbai, Bangalore, Chennai, Hyderabad and Ahmedabad, provides litigation, dispute resolution and advisory services as also compliance reviews across each of its division. The Tax Division of L&S advises companies in all areas of tax including direct, indirect and international tax. The firm handles tax disputes and represents clients from the stage of the administrative authority to the Supreme Court of India.

The Intellectual Property Division at L&S has expertise in all the intellectual property laws including patents, designs, trademarks, copyrights and Plant Variety Protection (PVP). The team of IPR attorneys and professionals holding advanced degrees in Science and Technology at L&S, work closely with clients in litigation, preparation & prosecution, licensing and IP management.

The International Trade Division of L&S caters to WTO and International Trade disputes arising out of or involving India besides handling matters pertaining to Free Trade Agreements and safeguards. It has handled more than 150 anti-dumping actions besides investigation initiated by EU, USA, Korea, Indonesia, South Africa and Turkey against Indian exporters.

The Corporate Division at L&S provides corporate and commercial advisory, litigation and transactional services besides arbitration and alternative dispute resolution services. It provides services across a wide spectrum of sectors like mergers and amalgamations, infrastructure, real estate and private equity.

The Newgen Solution

Newgen proposed a comprehensive Legal Case Management for end to end tracking of cases by L&S. Key highlights of solution are:

- Built using Newgen's ECM & BPM Platform
- Automation of core legal case management process along with its supporting processes like Meeting, Visit, Expense and Bill to track all the activities performed in achieving case completion and delivery.
- In-built features like Contract Management, Fee Calculator, Effort Tracker, Capacity Tracker and Time Sheet are provided for better manageability, tracking, reporting and traceability.
- Integration with accounting software (Navision) for exchange of billing and collection related information.
- Dashboard and MIS reports

L&S has been reporting the following benefits:

- Improved customer service with reduction in turnaround time
- Timely raising of bills (invoices) leading to improved cash flow
- Seamless integration with accounting software
- Real time access to case documents

- Equitable distribution of cases among professionals
- Dashboard and MIS reports for real time monitoring and better visibility
- Knowledge Management and accessibility across the organization

3. BUSINESS CONTEXT

Before implementation of Newgen solution, cases were allocated in L&S based on manual process based on individual decisions without having a clear picture of work load of each professional within the organization and across the locations. The firm was experiencing difficulty in effectively utilizing an expert for a particular subject if he happened to be in a location other than the location of the client. Since the system was based on physical file movement, only one person could work at a time on the case.

Also, the body of institutional knowledge created over the years was fragmented and not available centrally for access to the professionals. Coupled with the above the client was not having sufficient information about the status of their case unless they came in touch with particular professional.

Lastly, although the case was delivered to the client, billing was not done simultaneously, leaving scope for revenue leakages.

4. THE KEY INNOVATIONS

4.1 Business

Legal Case Management Solution (LCMS) is a full-fledged case management system that has been tailored to meet the law firms' specific needs and requirements and allows them to organize all their contacts, case documents, deadlines and data within a proven, flexible workflow processes. Clients approach firms based on their reputation of delivering timely, excellent and effective advisory, litigation and compliance review services. LCMS helps to achieve this objective. LCMS serves two primary functions. First; assistance in improved use, management, consolidation, sharing and protecting case-related information. Secondly; LCMS tracks and shapes the business processes. As it integrates data with multiple systems, departments, professionals, and business entities, it increases a firm's business advantage.

4.2 Case Handling

How cases were handled before and after the project in L&S:
- At L&S all documents and correspondences were stacked in physical folders, creating a case docket (file). All the documents pertaining to a case were arranged in a chronological order of time of receipt / generation in the case docket.
- Any work assignment was done manually either on a piece of paper or by email by the HODs and TLs, referred as Owner 2 and Owner 1 of the case respectively.
- The resources (attorneys) had to work on several stand alone applications for different purposes. There was a separate application for filling up the timesheet and case wise occupancy in a day. There was a separate system to update the Court Diary after each appearance.

Further, all the documents were physically moved from one hand to another. For review and approval of the legal documents generated by the attorneys the documents prepared by the attorneys in MS Word format were printed and handed over to the experts (superiors). They would do the correction on the printed copies and hand them back. The documents were then edited by the resources. All these legal documents were stored in a mapped drive on a server. There was no proper document management system and the document copies would reside on the shared/mapped drive as well as the user's profile, resulting in document replication. Sometimes, multiple versions would exist for a document.

Apart from the above, L&S had a standalone system to capture the details of clients and cases. For billing there was a separate system in place leaving scope for slippages in billing and tracking of the outstanding amounts.

In the Newgen solution all these functionalities are tightly integrated with each other, ensuring proper tracking of each case handled by L&S. There are features to even create rate contract with the clients and vendors of the firm by means of the contract generator for a specified duration.

The Owner 2 of the case generates the Fee Quote for the case and gets it approved by the client before actual work delivery to enhance transparency to customers. The Owner 1s of the case do work allocation using Effort Calculator and Capacity Tracker. Each and every case expense is tracked and linked to a case by means of the supporting processes (visit, meeting, expense etc), which were not available earlier.

The same expense data is available in the billing process and the payments are captured in the workflow. The workflow based case management system is integrated with the accounting and billing software. Also the professionals fill the timesheet through the same system using the inbuilt Timesheet module.

The digitized and centralized Knowledge Repository of all the documents has been established across 6 branches of the firm spread across India.

System Architecture: The Legal Case Management System (LCMS) provides an efficient and cost effective enterprise wide system to track and execute the legal cases and the support activities.

Key highlights of the solution are:

- Built using Newgen's robust ECM & BPM Platform
- Automation of core legal case management process along with its supporting processes like Meeting, Visit, Expense and Bill to track all the activities performed in achieving the case completion and delivery.
- Inbuilt tools & features for Contract Management, Fee Calculator, Effort Tracker, Capacity Tracker and Time Sheet are provided for better manageability, tracking, reporting and traceability.
- Integrated with standard accounting software like Navision for ex- change of billing and collection related information.
- Provision to split the drafting work for collaborative working by multiple resources on a single case.
- Auto populated templates for creating responses to legal notices.
- Facility for sending emails from within the system. Further, all such emails are archived for future references.
- Powerful index-based searches with support for full text search for fast and efficient retrieval
- Knowledge Management: To help identify the required subject matter created over the last 25 years and available in any of the offices.
- Dashboard and MIS reports for better visibility to the top level management.

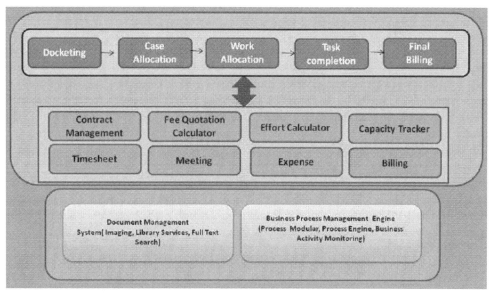

Legal Case management Solution Architecture

Legal case Management template: Newgen's Legal Case Management (LCM) solution provides features for end to end tracking and monitoring of legal cases.

Key activities involved in legal case management are as follows:

Docketing: Docketing center is the first contact point in the system and involves various important activities like work introduction, segregation, client/case creation and payment details creation. Most of these tasks are performed by L&S paralegals (supporting staff):

- *Work Introduction*—Any outside correspondence can happen either through hard copy or email. Hard copy correspondence from clients is scanned using Newgen OmniScan™ and introduced into the workflow. Similarly, mails coming to a dedicated email account are introduced into the workflow and a work item (WI) is created in the Newgen OmniFlow™ and all the documents are attached with it.

- *Segregation*—The correspondences thus received can be related to a New Case, Existing Case, Payment from Client or Junk (non case-related) etc. and based on the content they are segregated. The user has the option to search through the existing cases and view their details and if the correspondence is identified as an Existing Case, the people associated with the case are notified through email and all the documents are attached to the existing case file by the system. If identified as New Case, the work item is routed to a work step where the client and case details are captured. If identified as Payment related correspondence, the work item is routed to a work step where the payment details are captured and passed on to the accounting package. If it is a non-case related correspondence, it is discarded from the workflow.

- *Client & Case Creation*—For the new case, the client & case details are captured. If the client already exists in the system, the user just needs to select the client by searching through the existing list of clients or else the details related to offices and contacts of the client are captured in the system. Once complete case details are captured by Docketing Center, the-case is handed over to the head of the Group specializing in the case i.e. practice area.

- *Payment Details*—The Payment Details are captured at this stage against a client and the case. The data once validated is passed on to the accounting systems like Navision (Billing and Accounting Modules).

Case Allocation: At this stage, the owner of the case prepares a Fee Quote for the client using the inbuilt Fee Calculator and takes approval from the client on the quote. Rates used in the quotation are either from existing client contract or else the standard rate (if no valid contract exists with the client) is applied. The rates can be quoted based on the deliverable of the case as well as hourly basis based on the resource level. Owner of the case decides the target date for completion of case activities along with his subordinates.

Work Allocation: At this stage the work is allocated to the resources by the owner of the case. The Capacity Tracker helps the owner to check the resource availability and the Effort Calculator aids the user to allocate the tasks to various resources and also to identify the internal cost to L&S.

Task completion by resources: In this stage allocated tasks are completed by the resources and the case related expenses are declared, as and when incurred by the resources using the Expense Process. The resources also book their time in the Time Sheet against various cases (they are working on) on a daily basis. If any meeting and/or travel is required to complete the task, the resources use the Meeting and/ or Visit processes for the same.

Billing and Case Closure: The Owner of the case has an option to raise the bills from time to time. Once the case deliverables have been completed, if some amount is left to be billed, the Owner of the case raises the final bill to the client. Once all the tasks have been completed and collections received from the client, the Owner closes the case.

The key roles and how they are assigned/managed:
- Docketing Team
  - Docketing Team Leads—for QC of the docketing
  - Owner 2—Heads and expert of various domains, e.g. Excise expert,
  - CST Expert, WTO expert
  - Owner 1—Person junior to the Owner 2 and handling a team of resources (attorneys)
- Managing Partners—The heads of the company (L&S)
  - Accounts
  - Travel Desk—Travel bookings
  - Front Office—Receiving and recording the Incoming communication

The main business entities and how they are maintained / life-cycle:
- Customers
- Attorneys—The Knowledge Workers
- Accounts

How the case template is adapted in actual use by the case manager, and how those changes can be shared with others.
- The commonly used documents are all converted into templates. The captured data is automatically populated in the documents generated in MS Word from the templates, using the product Generate Response feature. The attorneys check out the documents and edit/ enrich accordingly.

4.3 Organization & Social

The L&S attorneys have found it easier to track the progress of the case and track and utilize their resources well. It was a bit of challenge convincing the senior attorneys in the beginning but once the benefits of the solution became prominent, their confidence increased. The younger workforce accepted the solution readily. Also the solution made the life of the attorneys easy. A fully-fledged docketing team was set up for data entry purposes.

The best beneficiary was the Accounts Department as billing and collection were streamlined.

5. HURDLES OVERCOME

Management
- Dashboard and MIS reports for better visibility to the top level management.

Business
- Auto populated templates for creating responses to legal notices.
- Facility for sending emails from within the system. Further, all such emails are archived for future references.
- Powerful indexed based searches with support for full text search for fast and efficient retrieval.

Organization Adoption
- Built using Newgen's robust ECM & BPM Platform
- Automation of core legal case management process along with its supporting processes like Meeting, Visit, Expense and Bill to track all the activities performed in achieving the case completion and delivery.
- Inbuilt tools & features for Contract Management, Fee Calculator, Effort Tracker, Capacity Tracker and Time Sheet are provided for better manageability, tracking, reporting and traceability.
- Integrated with standard accounting software like Navision for ex- changing billing and collection related information.
- Provision to split the drafting work for collaborative working by multiple resources on a single case.

The strategies and experience driving organizational adoption:
- A COE (Center of Excellence) was formulated at L&S and it works towards the continuous improvement of the processes. The operational metrics are not real time, which lead to proactive managerial intervention. The COE will be responsible for the faster roll out of new processes whenever required.

6. BENEFITS

6.1 Cost Savings / Time Reductions
- Greater visibility of the work and transparency to the client.
- Speedier processing of the cases
- Greater visibility in the bill processing cycle
  - Bills raised, payment received—ageing
  - Fixing of accountability through assigned activities
  - Intimation to managers on specific type of activity like discrepancy in bills

6.2 Quality Improvements

- Tracking and monitoring of resources utilization leading to increased productivity levels.
- Empowering the experts to get real time access to case documents
- Dashboard and everyday MIS for End to End tracking of cases
- Increased responsiveness via email notification to customers
- Access to the experts or access to the expert skills/ knowledge available in any one of the offices in India to the clients located elsewhere.

7. BEST PRACTICES, LEARNING POINTS AND PITFALLS

7.1 Best Practices and Learning Points

- ✓ Automation as a facilitator and not as a dictator for the resources working on it
- ✓ Simplicity, flexibility and robustness should be the prime focus
- ✓ Simple, lesser and similar interfaces across modules
- ✓ Transparency to clients.

7.2 Pitfalls

- ✗ Too flashy and complex looking interfaces can be distracting

8. COMPETITIVE ADVANTAGES

Outline of immediate and long-term plans to sustain competitive advantage:

1. Initially, cases were allocated based on a manual process and individualistic style, without having a clear picture of work load of each professional within New Delhi office of L&S and across the locations. It was difficult to make use of the expert for the subject if he happened to be in a location other than the location of the client. Since the system was based on physical file movement, only one person could work at a time on the case.
2. Now, the client has the flexibility to access any professional in L&S of their choosing, located anywhere in India, even outside the client's geo- graphic location.
3. Seamless Integration of processes with accounting software
4. Knowledge created over the past 25 years is now accessible to all L&S professionals centrally.
5. Provides the client with visibility about the status of their case
6. Has enabled simultaneous and streamlined billing leaving no scope for revenue leakages.
7. Integration of data with multiple systems, departments, professionals, and business entities, thereby augmenting the firm's business advantage.

9. TECHNOLOGY

The solution was built on top of Newgen's BPM Suite OmniFlow™ and ECM suite-OmniDocs™.

- Newgen's Legal Case Management (LCM) solution has been built using its core ECM and BPM platform. It also consists of various other modules to facilitate the end to end LCM process.
- OmniDocs™. It is an Enterprise Content Management (ECM) platform for creating, capturing, and managing, delivering and archiving large volume of documents. OmniDocs™ provides highly scalable, unified repository for securely storing and managing enterprise content. It provides centralized

repository for enterprise documents and supports rights based archival. It supports both centralized and distributed scanning with policy based upload. The platform manages complete lifecycle of documents through record retention, storage and retrieval policies. It supports exhaustive document and folder searches on date, indexes and general parameters as well as full text search on image and electronic documents.

- OmniFlow™: OmniFlow™ is a platform-independent, scalable Business Process Management engine that enables automation of organizational business processes. Built using open technologies, it has seamless integration abilities allowing it to be introduced into any IT infrastructure.

Newgen's Business Process Management Suit offers the following tools:

- **Business Process Modeler**: Used by business users to define the business process. Process is defined as set of activities in sequence, parallel, or loop.
- **Process Manager**: Enables efficient process management and administration using various people and process oriented real time reports.
- **Process Client**: Enables manual intervention in business processes through web.
- **Business Activity Monitoring Component**: Consists of a set of reporting tools for process owners, senior management, and other business users. eg: Real Time & Historic Reporting Tool and GUI Reports Builder
- **Simulator**: It is a de-risking tool that helps the process owner understand the effectiveness of the designed process even before its actual deployment in the enterprise environment
- **Contract Generator-**It is used for creating contract documents for the clients. Once a contract is created with the client, all the cases during the validity period are billed on the contracted rates. The contract can be based on individual line items as well as hourly rates of resources.
- **Fee Quotation Calculator-** It is used to estimate the fee & reimbursable expenses for the case. The fee can be based on hourly rates (maintained separately for different levels in organization) or based on deliverable (where there is a fixed deliverable for the case). It also has provision to give discounts, generate fee quote in MSWord format and confirm the quote (post which it cannot be modified).
- **Effort Calculator-** It is used to assign work to resources based on their availability. There is provision to allocate TAT and efforts to the resources for the activity assigned. It also provides facility to estimate the cost to company for individual task and complete case execution.
- **Capacity Tracker-** It is used to determine the availability of a resource on a day to day basis and for subsequent weeks. Daily as well as weekly consolidated booked hours are displayed for each resource.
- **Time Sheet-** In this module an interface is provided to book the time for various billable and non billable activities by the resources against each case as well as for other organization tasks like Knowledge Transfer, Learning, and Administration etc. It also has provision for notification and escalation mails to the Reporting ID, if time sheet is not filled.
- **Meeting Process-** This module keeps track of the details of all the major meeting conducted with the client for a particular case. On completion of the meeting, the meeting requestor prepares and circulates the Minutes of the Meeting (MOM) to the concerned people.

- **Visit Process**—This module keeps track of the client visits made during the course of the case and expenses involved. The attorneys can also make ticket booking requests to the Travel desk using this process.
- **Bill Process**—It is used to raise and track the bills for a case. Only the items covered in the confirmed fee quote can be raised in the bill. To eliminate client surprises at the time of bill, once bill items are validated by the case owner, the data is passed to accounting software to generate invoice. The invoice generated is mailed from the system to the client's billing contact. A provision is made to follow-up with client for payment. As and when payment is received, the outstanding amount is updated. Once the outstanding for the bill becomes "0", the bill item is closed.
- **Outgoing Correspondence Management**—An integrated correspondence process is provided at all relevant stages. Users can send emails from within the system instead of opening the MS Outlook or web mail each time a case related email is required to be sent. Standard templates are also provided to the user, on selection of which the email body content is automatically generated. The user has the option to use the template language or customize the email body as per the requirement.

10. THE TECHNOLOGY AND SERVICE PROVIDERS

The solution has been implemented at L&S by Newgen Implementation team and no third party team was involved in it.

The system study, solution design and implementation were carried out by Newgen professionals.

Pinellas County Clerk of the Circuit Court, Florida, USA

Silver Award: Legal and Courts

Nominated by Global 360, Inc., USA

1. EXECUTIVE SUMMARY /ABSTRACT

Assuring justice for the nearly one million residents in the most densely populated county in the state of Florida requires both personal dedication and the right technology. For the Pinellas County Clerk of the Circuit Court that meant an adaptive case management solution that could serve the Clerk of the Court office, the courts, and the entire Pinellas County judicial system and its citizenry.

Ken Burke, the Clerk of the Court, was originally inspired to implement their Global 360 case management solution by his vision to "go paperless." The solution has achieved that and more for Pinellas. It positions them for compliance with state legislative mandates on e-filing and access to public records, ensures that all court files and supporting documents are securely available within the judicial system, and provides improved collaboration, court file workflow and audit trails.

With case management Pinellas have revolutionized how their work gets done. They have created a team-centric environment with collaborative access to court files, documents, tasks, deadlines, and threaded discussions from within a single virtual case folder, using an interface tailored to each individual's roles and privileges. The result is improved service levels and a reliable platform for future growth.

Today, Pinellas has successfully leveraged their case management implementation to get "paper off the floor," eliminating the filing and re-filing burden and reducing costly storage facilities and transport - both a "green" and a cost savings achievement for this local government!

2. OVERVIEW

The Pinellas County Clerk of the Circuit Court office is responsible for maintaining court records and pleadings, securing court evidence, collecting and disbursing court fines, and a variety of other functions within the County's judicial system.

By serving as the primary information collection department for the County's judicial system, the Clerk's office is instrumental in ensuring that the County courts efficiently serve its citizens. However, like many counties experiencing rapid growth, Pinellas County experienced process inefficiencies fuelled by millions of paper-based records that hampered its ability to effectively support and service the public, county judges and attorneys, the judiciary, and the state and county legal community as a whole. The system was plagued by inefficiencies due to the time required to sort, copy, distribute, file, secure, and store court file documents.

The Pinellas County Clerk of the Circuit Court needed a case management solution that would not only make court files and their supporting documents collaboratively available to all Pinellas County judges, lawyers, office staff, the public, and the entire County judicial system, but also one that would provide improved court file workflow and guidance, and create an improved audit trail within the system. Moreover, the Clerk's office wanted to position itself to be in compliance with the state's legislative mandate.

The solution would be used by the Clerk of the Court office staff, the Records Manager supervisor, the Intake and Audit department who "prepare" cases, and the judges, magistrates and lawyers, as well as the public. Transitioning from a paper-based workflow system to document imaging and a case management system presented the biggest challenge to a culture that was steeped in two hundred years of a paper-based legal system. Other significant challenges involved integrating work processes and business processes between different agencies and making sure that the business needs of each agency and their individual users were fully understood and met.

The chief goals were to improve efficiency and productivity in case files management by transitioning from paper files to electronic files through imaging, make all court files and their supporting documents electronically available to all Pinellas County judges, lawyers, office staff, the public, and the entire County judicial system, provide improved court file workflow and create an improved audit trail within the system, and position the Clerk's office to be in compliance with the state's legislative mandate requiring them to support e-filing and make records publicly available via the Internet.

Since moving to their Global 360 case management solution, the Pinellas County court system enjoys the following benefits:

- Going "green" and eliminating the need to handle, file, and route court files and paper documents has resulted in an **annual savings** potential in the $ millions.
- Improved information access has reduced lost or misplaced documents and files and **improved collaboration and decision making**, with simultaneous online access to electronic records by staff, multiple judges and judicial staff members. The robust search and retrieve functions enable case retrieval times to be shortened from days to seconds.
- Increased **customer satisfaction and ease of use** enables Judges to read, sign, approve and take actions electronically anywhere, anytime
- The solution has delivered **better business control** for visibility and productivity across the legal system, workload balancing for fine tuning intake document performance, and audit trails that meet operational and governance requirements.

3. BUSINESS CONTEXT

The Clerk's Probate office was burdened working in a clerical environment with inordinate amounts of paper coming into the office on a daily basis. Most of the office staff's time was spent dealing with the paper—either scanning it, processing individual pieces of paper or preparing the files, filing documents away, and then also pulling cases and sending them to other locations.

They spent an enormous amount of time looking for missing pieces of paper or files. And if they were behind in maintaining current case files, this increased the volume of paperwork they would have to go through to locate requested documents and files. This often resulted in the very slow turnaround of documents critical to lawyer's cases or judge's rulings.

Delays in accessing required files impacted the entire spectrum of Probate customers. The staff, judges and magistrates who did not receive files in what they considered a timely fashion, the public, which needed to be able to view files, and attorneys, who might be waiting for closing documents critical to their cases.

Compounding the problem was an inability to determine the priority of each request, resulting in less critical document requests sometimes being fulfilled ahead of more critical requests.

Since 1999, the Clerk's office had been scanning all new Probate cases as they entered the office, but a method for accessing and distributing those images to the court for review had never been developed and the internal staff had no way of leveraging those images for their own work as well. The staff grew as a result of this dual system by 25-30 percent and it became increasingly difficult to maintain it given budget considerations. In 2006, the Clerk's office began imaging everything that came in—not just new cases but all pleadings.

Since then, the Clerk's office had been looking for a way to create a collaborative bridge to this information that would enable them to get this information to the court for their review and interaction and back to the Clerk's office for review, access, and archiving.

In addition to the desire to enable *a better way to support court collaboration*, there were a number of internal and external motivating factors that drove adoption of the new case management and workflow system for the Clerk's office:

- Sustainability. The Clerk's office is dedicated to taking the necessary steps to reduce paper use to save trees and move towards more "Green" initiatives.
- Regulatory requirements. The Florida Supreme Court adopted electronic access standards for a statewide Internet portal allowing attorneys and the public to access court records, make payments and electronically file documents. Court clerks in all 67 counties were mandated to begin implementation by October 1, 2009.
- Information agility. Demands were increasing from Judges, lawyers and the public for online access to court files and records in near real-time from their offices, homes, and mobile devices.
- Cost efficiency. The need to eliminate the nightmare of dealing with and managing paper case files and the slow time issues around retrieval was a powerful motivator, as was the need to reduce the high cost of purchasing supplies in support of court case files. There were also extremely high storage costs, especially since many of the records such as felony and probate records have retention periods that are 50 or 75 years. And, there was a need to secure records in the most affordable yet secure way possible. The stored paper records are very vulnerable in Pinellas facilities, as they are a coastal state subject to hurricanes.

4. THE KEY INNOVATIONS

4.1 Business

Since the case management solution went live, the paper, storage and transport costs have been significantly reduced - a particularly important business impact in the current economic climate. The impact on service delivery has been impressive as well, freeing all of the stakeholders to focus on more value-added activities. Judges, attorneys, legal firms, staff, and the public can now immediately view entire case files and court records and all their supporting documents 24x7 from any computer, enabling better customer service to the Judiciary and the public.

Both transparency and service level to key stakeholders has increased exponentially.

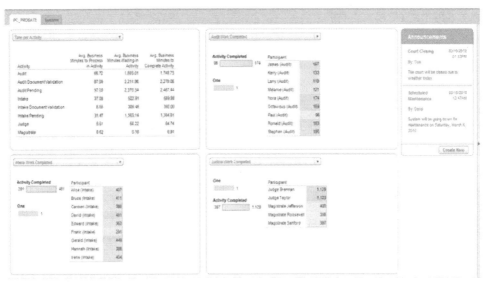

4.2 Case Handling

The Probate Department handles estates, guardianships and mental health cases. The Clerk's office receives the cases, the estates or guardianships, from the public and attorneys and the cases are processed.

In the past, attorneys would take paperwork directly to the court for review and approval. This could potentially be delayed if the court was unavailable or at another location and unable to view the file. Once the court reviewed the files, these signed records might be taken home with the attorney and never come back to the court. Other times, a judicial assistant might bring it down to the Clerk's office, which may take a day or two resulting in several days passing before the paperwork was properly processed with the Clerk's office.

Now, the submitted paperwork is reviewed, scanned and then forwarded to the court electronically to become a part of the virtual case folder and for action to be taken as necessary. Then the court electronically signs the papers, they come back from the judge, are prepared for distribution and copies are made as necessary. The case is also processed per any instructions handed done by the court.

Architecture.

The Global 360 case management implementation in the Probate Department at Pinellas County incorporates document management and workflow processes that integrate with the core systems and other applications already serving the county. Paper documents are captured at the front-end and as a part of the virtual case folder made available to four major groups of individuals: Intake, Audit, Magistrates, and Judges. The system allows Intake and Audit users to "prepare" cases for the Magistrates and Judges by identifying the key documents to be reviewed and acted upon, as well as the additional supporting documents that may be needed for proper handling of the case. Where appropriate, the Global 360 case management solution will pass information to and from the mainframe-based docketing system used by the County. This allows users to review the docket history on a case without having to exit the case solution. When document processing is complete, images are placed in the system for permanent storage. A subset is also made available via an Official Records subsystem that allows for public viewing of documents.

The design was guided by the following principles:

- A fundamental goal was to convert the processing from one in which documents were processed as paper (and then scanned at the back-end when complete) to one in which documents were scanned at the front-end and processed as electronic images.

- The workflow process assumes that the users as knowledge workers knew their jobs and were capable of making decisions with only minor guardrails for direction. Thus, the solution allows for several queues from which to draw work, and places to which work can be routed. Few automated or predefined paths are used since the intention is to allow the users to decide on the appropriate destination for any given item of work. The absence of pre-defined workflow paths in the core workflow process means that in one sense the process has run-time adaptability. Users have the knowledge and authority to select the appropriate destination based upon the type of document and the processing required, and are not forced to route work to the same "next step."

- A user-centric "Persona-based" design maximizes flexibility by making the system as dynamic as possible. Documents are loosely linked together based on a unique reference number that is applied to each document as an index. This approach allows new documents to be available in the case folder as soon as they are indexed with that reference number. All users can therefore access all the documents in the case immediately, regardless of where they are in the process. In addition, the user interface is dynamic with the data and available options available changing automatically depending on where one is in the process, and what one's role is. Thus, Intake workers, Record managers, Magistrates and Judges will have different Persona-based views of a case based on their work objectives and roles.

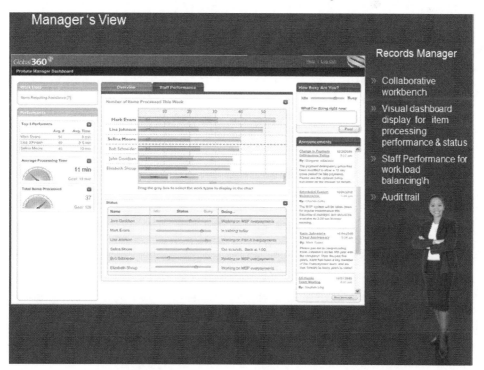

- The solution integrates with and leverages the services of external components. For example, the mainframe-based docketing system used by Pinellas is automatically updated by a step running in the case management process. As documents are completed, this step accesses web services that add docket entries that correspond to the documents being processed. The user interface in the case management solution also provides the ability for users to add docket entries, or to list existing ones, using similar web services.

4.3 Organization & Social

The new solution and workflow has changed the way work gets done within the Clerk's office, making all the employees more efficient and effective at delivering data and services. A natural hesitancy at first has given way to realization that improved processes have benefited all aspects of the organization's day-to-day activities.

The solution has increased collaboration and value-added interactions. Clerk office staff is receiving fewer phone calls from attorneys and the public requesting case file or record request statuses as they now have online access. This has freed the staff to focus on more value-added activities within the office, eliminating time spent on clerical activities. The staff takes a tremendous amount of pride in providing excellent customer service and customer satisfaction. They pride themselves in processing work quickly and accurately and getting responses back to the attorneys or other people waiting for the data.

The staff no longer spends time looking for lost cases and pleadings, which took a tremendous toll on the staff morale when these incidents occurred. It is now very rare for a case file or supporting document to be lost. The staff no longer has to spend time preparing files to be moved to other remote locations and tracking the movement and securing of those files. Office staff's desks are no longer cluttered with files as they have gone almost completely paperless.

"It has revolutionized the office," according to the Manager of Probate Court Records. The time saved on clerical duties has enabled the staff to cross-train on a lot of different functions. The staff employees have enjoyed the opportunity to learn new things and it has changed how everyone views the work conducted within the office. They now can engage in more constructive work within the case management system. The employees are happier and they feel more motivated to do their work. They can constantly see the amount of work pending in their queue and are more concentrated on their work. They are no longer diverted by having to pull files, look for pleadings, and file cases back. Even assisting customers on the phone is easier. Employees feel more confident with the information they are providing because they can see the documents, so if they say the case file or document is with the court, they can be confident the court has it.

Management and staff have visibility to and are able to monitor their work queue, which has increased productivity. In fact, it has almost become a competition within the Probate department to see who can get their work done the quickest and keep their work queue empty.

5. HURDLES OVERCOME

Management

The organization of the County posed some challenges in trying to integrate business processes across different agencies. The Pinellas County management, from the Probate Department, through the Court and Operational Services, and on up to the Clerk himself were deeply involved in the project. In addition there is a Clerk's Technology area and a Business Technical Services area that provide services to the various departments. On the Court side there are the Court Administration area, including the judges and magistrates, and a Court's IT area. The challenge was to coordinate *all* of these resources and to reach management consensus. The approach then was to ensure active participation from all of the key stakeholders, and to ensure the team stayed active and involved throughout the entire process improvement and implementation project.

Business

The County was comfortable with the design goals of the system. They had no problem giving up paper and static document imaging to move to a collaborative case management solution. One hurdle though was getting the judges and magistrates to approve the use of electronic signatures for signing imaged documents. They were concerned about the security of the signature itself, and wanted to make sure that no unauthorized person could access and apply the signature. They needed to be accessible only by the individual judge or magistrate. This hurdle was overcome by demonstrating the approach that would be deployed, and assuring them that the signature was tied to the users' logon ID. As long as the ID was secure, the signature would be too. They were also concerned about the general use of an electronic signature, rather than one signed in ink. Before agreeing to a solution the Court sought the opinion of higher courts and administrative bodies in the State of Florida to ensure that electronic signatures were acceptable and that hurdle was met.

Organization Adoption

The Probate Department was so committed to the new system that it was deployed rather smoothly. Because users were involved up front in the design—one of the fundamental tenants of the Global 360 Persona-based approach—the way to adoption was smoothed. Train-the-trainer training was conducted, after which the end-users received training and had time to spend on the test system. Procedures were adopted by the department that eased the transition.

The Court Administration area did experience some adoption difficulties. While some judges became proficient quickly, others required more assistance. To address this, views were created to make it easier for the judicial and magistrate assistants to organize work going to and from the judges and magistrates. The increased attention received by these groups made them more comfortable with the system.

6. BENEFITS

6.1 Cost Savings / Time Reductions

Pinellas has an estimated savings potential of millions of dollars annually for file storage costs - in many cases for files that have retention periods of 50 and 75 years, lower transportation costs associated with not having to move documents between offices, and savings from not having to purchase supplies in support of paper court case files.

The typical case file work cycle has been cut in half, reduced from 4 to 2 days for the **Clerk's office staff.** Previously, paperwork was received, sent to a judge where it might sit for a day or so, and then be returned to the Clerk's office for Probate processing. This could take up to three to five days. Now, incoming paperwork can be received, imaged, sent to the judge and returned signed to the Clerk's office in as little as 60 seconds.

At the **Audit** level, locating and pulling requested files could take up to a day or more. Now, requested files can be located for printing or electronic distribution almost instantaneously.

The ability to file a document with the Clerk's office and have it immediately processed and sent to the Judge for signature has been very well received by the Bar (attorneys). **Attorneys** have filed documents, anticipating a week's delay in needing to request a service before the document "posts" to the docket, only to find out that the document was processed and docketed within a day. These attorneys have now changed their procedures, requesting services much sooner after filing.

At the **Judicial** level, Judges are able to receive documents for review within 24 hours of receipt in the Clerk's department. Judges can help other judges from the location of their choice, whether from home, office or some other remote location. Judges can work weekends or any time that suits them. One Judge who was in court all week, was able to catch up with a queue that had reached 200 items.

For **the public,** they can access public records, such as deed histories or mortgage information, from the comfort of their home, office or any internet access point 24 hours a day.

6.2 Increased Revenues

The case management implementation and the change in policy have expedited electronic subscriptions, creating additional revenue ($60 sign-up charge) for the county.

6.3 Quality Improvements

The case management solution has enabled a number of quality gains. Pinellas are now able to process higher volumes of court documents correctly and with fewer staff resources, reducing lost or misfiled case documents. Work can be properly managed even though it is being handled at more than one location. Management has full visibility into all Clerk's office work queues so the staff always knows exactly what work is pending and can escalate a case is the situation calls for it, making the office more responsive to emergent cases. The workflow improvements have standardized all of the basic procedures for processing court files and documents, so training is easier and faster, and everyone can cross-train on different roles and responsibilities.

The solution has also improved the county's ability to plan for and recover from a disaster or other disruption in operations, enabling business continuity and service to constituents.

7. BEST PRACTICES, LEARNING POINTS AND PITFALLS

7.1 Best Practices and Learning Points

- ✓ *Start with a manageable project as your first case.*
- ✓ *Work closely with your vendor to ensure best practices are explained and in force right from the beginning of the project.*
- ✓ *Take the time to ensure that all partners and stakeholders are aligned and have a very clear understanding of the project's overall goal and the project milestones along the way.*
- ✓ *Ensure that you have cooperation from "process owners"—clerk of the court and judges - and the IT departments they have supporting them.*
- ✓ *Use a solution and approach that considers the end user from the beginning to make user adoption and acceptance considerably easier.*
- ✓ *Communicate, communicate, communicate!*

7.2 Pitfalls

× *Do not fall into the trap of forcing end users to learn a system not adapted to their role within the process*
× *Do not forget to keep continuous process improvement in mind.*

8. COMPETITIVE ADVANTAGES

Achieving "competitive advantage" in the public sector equates to improving service delivery for constituents and stakeholders.

Going paperless with the new case management system has meant cost savings and efficiency improvements that allow multiple people to be working on the files at the same time. Improved service is delivered as Clerk staff, judges, attorneys and the public are able to review and work on files simultaneously and from any location.

Another advantage to the Clerk's office is the improved and more agile workflow between the Clerk's office and the judge. The staff is able to ensure that the oldest work is processed first, ensuring better customer service to all requested services. And, the Clerk's office is able to have the judge apply his digital signature to the cases and send those files and orders back to the Clerk's office electronically. This flow and efficiency in being able to turn work around quickly makes the Clerk's office more responsive and efficient. It also enables judges to work when they want to and where they want to, giving them greater flexibility in getting their work done. During hearings, judges are able to pull up records and transcripts online faster than attorneys can produce hardcopies.

Judges conduct what they call "ex parte" where they meet with attorneys to discuss specific paperwork and provide help. Attorneys can now enter the office, have their paper work scanned into the system, visit with the judge, have the judge sign the paperwork electronically, and by the time the meeting is over, copies can be provided to the attorneys if they need them. This process can take less than half an hour. Previously it might have taken several days to complete.

The public, as well as attorneys' offices can now view a Judge's docket and be able to see that, for example, a proposed "audit" has been submitted and forwarded to the court. They can then see when the docket code changes status, indicating it has been signed. This is very important to the public and to attorneys.

9. TECHNOLOGY

For Pinellas, the Global 360 case management solution includes imaging and document management capabilities that provide a more secure environment, make documents available to multiple users simultaneously, and facilitate retrieval. All documents and work are organized in the virtual case folder and accessed by user roles. Returned documents are archived for permanent storage, a subset of documents is recorded as public records. Attorneys and others can access documents on a public website.

The Global 360 case management technology is a rich application that combines the capabilities of document and business process management tools into a single adaptive case management solution. Case360 handles the complexities of both collaborative and ad-hoc business processes, providing a team-centric environment through access to documents, tasks, deadlines, and threaded discussions from within a "virtual folder," called a case folder. Within this case folder, all the information needed to process a case is readily accessible and available to all, yet tailored to an individual's roles and privileges.

The result is a unified and integrated view of case data, giving organizations complete visibility and auditable control.

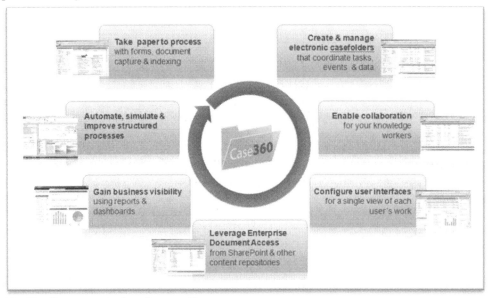

10. THE TECHNOLOGY AND SERVICE PROVIDERS

Global 360 was the sole case management solution vendor, integrator, and consultant for this project. (www.global360.com)

About Global 360

Global 360 helps organizations to better manage processes today and make improvements for tomorrow. Our market leading process and case management solutions improve business performance by maximizing the productivity of all participants in a process. To accomplish that, we address the unique requirements of all key roles that are critical to improving a process. Providing the industry's first Persona-based business process and case management software, Global 360's viewPoint delivers an intuitive, configurable, and personable user experience, accelerating time-to-deployment while reducing the development costs typically associated with complex BPM user applications. And with real-time performance data, managers can find and fix problems before they impact customers and extend these efficiencies to customers and partners. Building on our strength in financial services, government, insurance, consumer packaged goods, manufacturing, and the retail sector, Global 360 has helped more than 2,000 customers in 70 countries reduce paper, automate processes, and empower individuals to truly change how work gets done. Global 360, Inc. is headquartered in Texas with operations in North America, Europe, and the Pacific Rim. For more information about Global 360's process and case management solutions, visit the company web site at www.global360.com.

Velindre Hospital Integrated Care Pathway[1]

Gold Award: Medical and Healthcare
Nominated by Cardiff School of Computer Science and Informatics, Cardiff University, UK

EXECUTIVE SUMMARY / ABSTRACT

Teamwork, collaboration and coordination are key aspects of the patient-centric approach taken by modern healthcare. Although many projects have been and are currently being undertaken to improve support for health care professionals, adequate support for teamwork, communication and coordination has yet to be achieved. The delivery of the healthcare service is very challenging as it involves heterogeneous distributed systems, multi-professionals and dependent tasks among each. In addition, the treatment journey of each patient is unique, as decisions are usually made according to several constraints related to the patient, medical condition, patient's choice, available resources and\or feedback from doctors' consultation.

We believe that, in order to provide the required support, it is necessary to explicitly acknowledge the patient's medical state within their treatment journey. This project proposes the use of a Business Process Management (BPM) system that uses associations between patients, health care professionals, and the Integrated Care Pathway (ICP) to provide improved support for healthcare professionals as individuals and as members of integrated care teams. Moreover, mapping the ICP onto the BPM system will help support the implementation of the best practice according to the national guidelines. By leveraging the information contained in these associations, and understanding the patient progress along the dynamic care pathway this proposal indicates and supports tailored context-based actions. This includes automated notifications, alerts, scheduling and timers as well as support for change management as the patient progresses throughout their treatment journey. Clinicians and developers feedback on this proposal has been very positive.

OVERVIEW

Modern healthcare has seen an ongoing move towards a patient-centric approach. This approach emphasizes teamwork and collaboration as key aspects of the healthcare process. Patients within such a collaborative model follow an Integrated Care Pathway (ICP). This treatment journey usually involves multi-professional care team members providing different healthcare services at distributed sites. This process requires an effective mechanism to support the interaction and collaboration among the care team members as well as management of potential interactions between complex care pathways being followed by a single patient. Current Hospital Information Systems (HIS) used at different healthcare organisations were originally designed to support the traditional disease-centred delivery model. The challenges imposed by political influence and dealing with legacy systems, add to the challenge of the complex nature of the domain with its

---

[1] Authors: Hessah Al-Salamah (H.alsalamah@cs.cf.ac.uk), Prof. Alex Gray & Dr. Dave Morry.

many conflicting requirements and confounding factors. It has been a priority to support the implementation of modern healthcare, however it is not yet adequately supported by HISs [1]. Many proposals have been made and followed to address different aspects of this problem, but there are still many challenges which have not yet been addressed, such as: teamwork collaboration with respect to member's roles, actual care progress and case specific needs.

This project considers the dynamic requirements of health and care practitioners which are beyond the traditional decision support and knowledge management systems provisions. We believe that, in order to address this problem fully, it is necessary to take account of the activities of practitioners as members of a dynamic team handling the treatment of a patient. Moreover, it is important to have this linked to the flow of a patient's treatment(s) and the dynamic processes involved, and to do this in a patient-centric way. This includes associating the patient record with the involved care providers and connecting both back to the patient's ICP. The work described includes tracking care teams and individual team members dynamically as the patient progresses along the dynamic care pathway. It proposes the integration of a Business Process Management (BPM)[2] system into the HISs as it will better support both the individual work of health and care practitioners as well as improve support for team communication, and care coordination throughout the patient's care. A proof of concept prototype was developed to test our assumptions and investigate the capabilities of the BPM system and how much support it could give in the treatment process. Moreover, the prototype will be used to demonstrate the features of the proposed system when multi-professional care team members and HIS developers are evaluating it. The development challenges involve: first, maximising the flexibility of the system to support the patient's dynamic state as they usually don't follow the anticipated care pathway but follow multiple pathways at the same time. Second, maintaining the logical sequence (dependencies) of the treatment stages depending on the patient's medical state while ensuring that the system is fully controlled by the users. Finally, the individual information requirements of practitioners with different specialties or the dynamic communication requirements beyond pure provision of information are taken into account.

The proof of concept prototype showed that the application of Workflow Technology in the healthcare domain is a very promising development. It can be used to evolve the functionalities of existing HIS, so that they can be used to support implementation of ICP services and associated treatment flow for a patient. It is believed that these functionalities are important as they result in safer more effective and efficient care and treatment. Functionalities of the proposed system include: providing a pro-active system, routing and information filtering.

BUSINESS CONTEXT

This research was conducted at Cardiff School of Computer Science & Informatics in her PhD research by Hessah Alsalamah, supervised by Professor Alex Gray. It is based on a joint project between Cardiff School of Computer Science & Informatics at Cardiff University and Velindre NHS Trust cancer centre in Wales, UK. Velindre NHS Trust is one of the largest tertiary specialist cancer centers in the UK. At Velindre, the Information System for Clinical Organisations (ISCO) HIS

---

[2] BPM and WFMS are used interchangeably throughout this document. This is based on the studies stating that WFMS is part of BPM. Conversely, BPM is a superset of WFMS with more control over processes, integration and optimisation. Source: http://www.opensystems-bs.com/Portals/0/BPM+vs+Workflow.pdf

was evolved and developed, which is currently used across Wales as Cancer Network Information System Cymru (CaNISC) [2].

There is a long-term cooperation between Cardiff School of Computer Science & Informatics and the Clinical Information Unit (CIU) at Velindre. Dave Morry the Head of the CIU and his team usually bring to our attention problems they have with their HIS and we research these issues and recommend solutions. These solutions are evaluated by the developers and healthcare providers at the centre. If the CIU team is convinced by our ideas, they adopt them for implementation by their team in a future evolution. This project concentrates on one of these suggestions to show how the interaction works.

THE KEY INNOVATIONS

The implemented proof of concept prototype showed that adapting the Workflow Technology into the HIS will evolve the CaNISC system positively. Specifically by mapping the ICP into a BPM system and incorporate IT into the existing HIS will help extend the offered functionalities by these systems. This will have a positive impact at business, case handling, and system levels in the treatment.

4.1 Business

This is not a proposal for a completely new system but a proposal to evolve an existing HISs and improve its support functionalities. This can be done by mapping the clinical guidelines into a BPM system engine and having this operate as an invisible intermediate layer between users and an existing HIS (see Diagram 1). This aims to make the support for care teams more proactive by taking appropriate actions with regard to the support needed at the treatment stage, while utilising the information and facilities of the existing HISs. The extensions will follow the best clinical practice available to healthcare professionals through the National Institute for Health and Clinical Excellence (NICE) [3] and other projects, such as the Map of Medicine (MoM) [4]. These clinical guidelines aim to enforce quality standards to achieve: clinical effectiveness, patient safety and improved patient experience through the support given by the enhanced system [5].

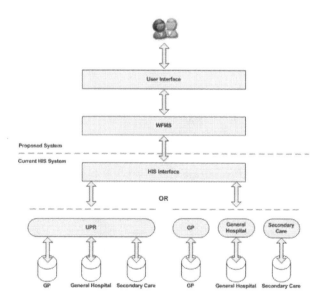

Diagram 1- System's Architecture

The strength in the BPM system is in its ability to invoke existing systems at any stage during the process flow in a way which overcomes the system heterogeneity challenge. This makes their data available through the system as an aid to the medical team's decision making.

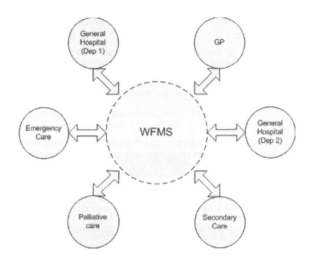

Diagram 2- WFMS Operating as a Hub

BPMs can be adjusted to enforce a specific sequence and\or enable an extremely flexible order of processes. In the breast cancer scenario, some stages of the treatment journey are pre-structured examples, for instance single tasks performed in subprocesses such as tests. While other stages are dynamic as the process flow cannot be predicted in advance. This commonly occurs among patients who have multiple diseases. In order to achieve maximum flexibility, the system should be driven by the patient's condition yet fully controlled by the multi-professional care team members. The proposed system provides suggestions and support for the process according to best practice guidelines; however the final decision is taken by medical team users. This is to ensure and stress the fact that this proposal represents a tool to support the treatment process and is not meant to takeover the treatment flow decisions from the care team members.

At a business level, the system will facilitate multi-professional care team communication and therefore care coordination across the multiple healthcare organisations involved in the treatment of patients. The direct advantage will be support for implementation of an ICP used in the modern NHS.

4.2 Case Handling

The diagnostic breast cancer clinical guidelines were selected as the trial scenario to be used in the proof of concept prototype development, since there is extensive information about cancer and its clinical guidelines online which made searching and understanding the treatment process easier; the process is complex enough to show the challenges involved in the treatment delivery, as it involves interaction among different systems, organisations and care team professionals; and our co-operation with the Velindre cancer unit has occurred over the last 20 years.

The guidelines for diagnosing breast cancer and the treatment choices used in the implementation of the prototype are taken from the MoM diagnostic for breast cancer [6] and treatment options [7]. These guidelines show the different stages of the treatment process and have an attached document explaining the details about the organisations involved, information required, roles involved, flow logic and any constraints. By using this information, a good sense and understanding of the treatment process was achieved.

The scenario represented in Diagram 3, is a version created by combining [6] and [7]. It starts with a General Practitioner (GP) suspecting a patient has cancer and therefore referring the patient to a Surgeon Oncologist. The Surgeon Oncologist checks the patient's history and requests assessments such as an examination, imaging, fine needle aspiration, and core biopsy.

The results of these tests will then be reviewed at a Multi-Disciplinary Team (MDT) meeting to decide whether there are any abnormalities, if more tests are needed, or if there are positive findings. In the case of no abnormalities, the patient will be reassured and discharged to primary care. In the case of more tests being needed, the MDT will decide whether a surgical or core biopsy is needed before the patient is reviewed again in an MDT meeting. In the case of a positive finding, the reviewers will decide whether it is benign or if cancer is confirmed. If a benign disease is confirmed, the patient will be educated on the principles of management and the patient will be discharged to primary care. If breast cancer is confirmed, the GP will be informed.

This will be followed by a number of care stages until the care reaches a point where a decision is made on the treatment options for this patient, which could be a surgical or non-surgical option, such as radiotherapy or chemotherapy.

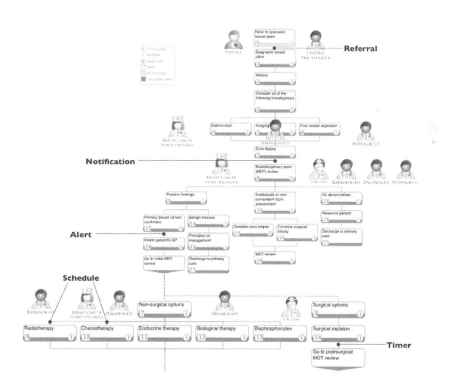

Diagram -3- ICP of Breast Cancer Treatment

By looking at the flow in MoM guidelines and its associated documents, and the literature, we can identify the treatment stages where there is a need for communication and care coordination among the different MDT care professionals involved in this flow. Diagram 3 highlights the different critical stages of the treatment flow, which are:

- Referral from the GP to the surgeon oncologist. This is initiated by the GP, performed by the primary care nurse and sent by the administration at the GP surgery. The referral is picked-up by the administration at the secondary unit, scheduled on the secondary care system and picked up by the breast cancer nurse to be processed by the surgeon oncologist.

- Notification of MDT reviewers about the triple assessment results and clinical examination notes; these have to be gathered and made available to the team before the MDT meeting. The notes will be forwarded by the breast cancer nurse to the haematologist, radiologist, and pathologist from the stored information in the secondary care records, (haematology laboratory system, radiology system and pathology system). The results are gathered by the MDT coordinator so that they can be discussed at the MDT team meeting involving a surgeon oncologist, radiologist, pathologist, clinical and medical oncologist, and a nurse.

- Alert of a patient diagnosed with breast cancer, this informs the patient's GP. It is initiated by the surgeon oncologist, performed by the breast cancer nurse and sent by the administrator at the secondary care unit. The message is picked-up by the administrator at the GP surgery, scheduled by the primary care nurse to inform the GP and update the patient's record in the GP surgery system.

- Alert of a patient undertaking chemotherapy or radiotherapy. This is used to avoid any conflict. It is usually managed and controlled by the clinical oncologist using available information about the patient's medical and treatment history and the medical information revealed by the patient.

- Scheduling required if the patient is under both chemotherapy and radiotherapy; a minimum break of two weeks must occur between these two treatments. This is managed and controlled by the clinical oncologist using available information about the patient's medical and treatment history and the medical information provided by the patient.

- Time lapse before referring patients to their oncologist to allow recovery after a surgical operation. This is usually a specified waiting time. The patient's condition is reviewed at a post-surgical MDT meeting to agree on the treatment plan after surgery. This will be requested by the surgeon oncologist, performed by the nurse and picked up by the MDT.

Diagram 3 shows a simple flow with no complications which is not the usual case. Patients do not usually follow the anticipated care pathway and each patient's flow is unique as many elements interact to affect its progress.

At the case handling level, the information system will support the critical stages of treatment flow which require support at critical stages. Support includes taking the following actions alert, notify, refer, schedule, and set timers. These are all customised to the patient's condition and controlled by the users interacting with the system who are the actual decision makers of the care process.

4.3 System

The proof of concept prototype showed that the application of Workflow Technology in the healthcare domain is very promising. It can be used to evolve the functionalities of existing HIS, so that they can be used to support the implementation in the ICP and associated treatment flow for a patient. It is believed that these functionalities are important as they result in safer more effective and efficient care and treatment of a patient. Functionalities of the proposed system include: providing a pro-active system, routing, task automation and information filtering. These functionalities are:

- Pro-active System: this is the primary advantage of using Workflow Technology in the healthcare domain. It is the difference between having a reactive or a proactive system. In the case of a reactive system, which most traditional HISs are, reactions are a response to requests made by users while proactive systems are capable of identifying the need to take an action and the activities it activates. The workflow engine within the workflow management system can be coded to fetch triggers, understand which of the users or roles are affected by this trigger, how they are affected and finally, take appropriate actions to inform them. These pro-active functionalities can be used to execute many different actions, such as: alert, notify, refer, schedule and set timers.

- Alert: is fired when urgent or immediate action is required, or when specific information about a patient's condition needs to be noticed (e.g. a patient under chemotherapy).

- Notify: this is gathering the information required at a certain stage of the process flow so that members are fully informed when taking decisions (e.g. gathering all requested test results before a clinic patient's visits).

- Refer: this is done automatically and targeted not at the organisation but to the exact administrator or even to the specific role. This is done by delivering a referral letter to a targeted user and making it available in their in-tray\inbox (e.g. GP referring a patient to an Oncologist when new symptoms appear).

- Schedule: is needed to formalise a process. This involves maintaining pre-requisites or a sequence of steps which are essential and required in the care process (e.g. a patient stops taking aspirin two weeks before scheduled surgery, or maintaining two weeks waiting time between chemotherapy and radiotherapy sessions for a patient).

- Set timers: these are required when a certain action needs to be processed at a specific time. This is important in ensuring continuity of care and that patients do not get overlooked in the process. This functionality is carried out by making sure that information is delivered to a targeted user before the time it is needed. This can involve: sending letters to a user's in-tray, executing alerts, sending notification, and/or doing referrals (e.g. at end of two weeks recovery period following surgery, a patient needs to be scheduled for a clinical visit, and reminders sent after a certain waiting time).

- Routing: this helps the system determine the sequence of the processes and the consequences of any decision made. This is either by suggesting the next stage or automating a set of processes. While routing is a tool that WFMSs provide, routing is only made with a user's approval or suggestion. This is done by providing a message to the user showing the alternative routes according to the ICPs' logic, and the user can approve any route or simply skip it (e.g. MDT referral after a set of examinations for a patient is performed, and the system suggests an imaging test according to age (mammogram for older than X or an ultrasound otherwise)).

- Task automation: is performed when a number of tasks need to be processed as a set. In this context, it includes tasks that do not require user interaction.
- Information extraction and filtering: to ensure summary of important information is visible to healthcare professionals when viewing a patient's records. This aims to facilitate tracking a patient and improving the decision-making process by making healthcare professionals aware of the development of the care process and therefore making better use of their time. This includes improved visibility of: treatment history, milestones, order and time, and acting healthcare professionals.

At the system level, the HIS will become more pro-active and capable of performing the following actions: alert, notify, refer, schedule, and set timers. It also provides a flexible system that handles dynamic changes happening during a patient's treatment. This includes routing the flow and performing automatic tasks. Moreover, the workflow system provides a tool to track patients and ensure continuity of the flow by filtering and extracting important information. The treatment information extracted includes: history, milestones, order and time and involved care team professionals.

HURDLES OVERCOME

This is a research project. It aims to investigate a specific problem and propose solutions to address it. This involves implementation of a proof of concept prototype and its evaluation which leads to recommendations. Different factors are considered in the study. These include adoption barriers as well as users' resistance, and cost. This is meant to identify ways of evolving a system Nevertheless, users and developers of current HIS system are involved at different stages of the research for validation. The main approach considered in this study was to follow the evolutionary framework. Here we work on enhancing existing systems rather than proposing a totally new system. This is aiming to: First, reduce cost and failure risk. Second, overcome the technical and political barriers of adoption. Finally, reduce the changes made to the environment as unnecessary changes can lead to increased users' resistance. Moreover, users were involved from the early stages of this research to ensure that their needs are considered and met as the top priority.

Although the current proposal has been demonstrated to show its potential, there are still several areas requiring further investigation. These include assessing the impact of alerts on working practise and interface usability. Future work will also identify the data needs of the different roles to be extracted from the patient record, the information requirements of each and how they would like to receive it. The focus of this research was on a Breast Cancer scenario and its requirements. Future plans include specifying a generic pattern flexible enough to accommodate more medical scenarios. This will ensure that the system is capable of accommodating any national or local ICP and that it has maximum flexibility. Currently, automation within the system is done according to treatment history and current treatment stage. Future work will include considering the anticipated care pathway in the automation process. This will improve care efficiency and reduce costs by avoiding redundancy and future complications. It will allow the system to inform practitioners whether a complication is likely to affect upcoming patient appointments, and to schedule tests to fulfil not only current requirements but also those likely to occur in the near future and thereby improve planning and scheduling of patient treatment.

BENEFITS

The technical aspects and usefulness of the prototype were examined at the evaluation stage. The technical evaluation was conducted by implementing a proof of concept prototype and interviewing members of the CIU at the Velindre Trust to evaluate the possibility of adopting the proposed ideas. The usefulness evaluation is conducted through a literature survey and sessions with medical users (brainstorming sessions and one-to-one interviews with actual users of the current Trust HIS CaNISC).

An evaluation session with a group of six developers at the CIU at Velindre will evaluate the possibility of getting this proposal implemented in practice. This will include the technicalities involved in mapping, integrating, and interacting with the system. However, we have had several sessions with technical experts in BPM and HIS, who agree on the possibility of these ideas being implemented in reality. BPM experts are the developers and founders of Alia systems Ltd. (see section 9), and they assured us that it is technically possible to implement this proposal using current systems.

The coordination problem was originally brought to our attention by the team at the CIU at Velindre Trust. They pointed out their need for a more intelligent proactive system. They highlighted that there is a need for a system that facilitates following patients up and providing interaction. In discussion sessions about our proposal, they confirmed that the functionalities that workflow technology can provide are already in their agenda for the current system's improvements and more. Members of the CIU agreed the general ideas and assured us of their need for a more proactive system to help support the current system in use.

Finally, five one-to-one semi-structured interviews with care team professionals with different specialities in cancer treatment were conducted. These one hour interviews aimed to evaluate the multi-professional care team member's opinions on this proposal in terms of its usefulness, advantages, disadvantages and to identify any concerns. All five care team members interviewed agreed on the potential benefits that could be gained from having such a system. They agreed that there is need for a more proactive system that facilitates care coordination among care team members. The majority provided examples where they had been unable to make a decision due to inappropriate or unavailable information at a clinical visit. They also highlighted some of the difficulties they face in using the existing system to search for certain information and that it would be very useful to have highlights of the case visible in one place. They all agreed that it would not reduce their current work load, as this is mainly spent with patients, however it would save them time searching for medical information in a patient's records. A physiotherapist interviewed highlighted that she can see the benefits of having this proposal implemented for care team members other than physiotherapists, as she believes that the physiotherapist's role in cancer care rarely requires urgent reaction unless they are in-patients and that she finds manual communication tools to be effective and so there is no need for a change. An oncologist interviewed discussed his concerns that it would lead to information overload and being over-alerted about his cases. He suggested giving the users an option to turn the private alert messages off and having a patient's information visible only when viewing the patient's case. However, he stated that having important information highlighted in a patient's records would be beneficial. He also identified that we need to measure the benefits gained by implementing this system against the effort and cost required for implementation. The oncologist later explained that the information gathering process for his cases is conducted by a general oncologist before cases are transferred to him, which explains why he did not experience similar challenges to his colleagues.

COMPETITIVE ADVANTAGES

In recent years, there has been wide exploitation of Information Communication Technologies (ICT) in the healthcare domain. Recent informatics projects emphasise the implementation of standards and providing access to knowledge resources and patient data. Examples of these ICT projects include: Electronic Patient Records (EPR) (e.g. [8]), knowledge management systems (e.g. [9]), triage systems (e.g. [10]), assessment systems, prescribing systems (e.g. [11]), test ordering and result delivery systems [12]. Within the National Health Service (NHS) in the UK, notable projects in this domain include: developing and making available guidelines and standards through NICE and MoM, the Scottish emergency care record [13], and proposals for a shared, unified patient record accessible at any location, when required [14, 15].

We believe that, while these projects are an important first step in improving healthcare support systems, there is still more work to be done. For example, shared patient records support the treatment process in terms of provision of patient information and medications prescribed. However, they do not actively indicate to practitioners that relevant information is available, nor do they consider the individual information requirements of practitioners with different specialties or the dynamic communication requirements beyond pure provision of information. Similarly, decision support and knowledge management systems support coordination between different tasks or processes by managing their sequence. This is suitable for patients following the anticipated treatment pathway; however a patient's state is dynamic, and often patients needs evolve and they follow a non-predicted care pathway. As each patient is unique, changes to the treatment plan can happen at any time and in many ways. This requires support for dynamic team allocation and the management of changes along the care pathway as it is an extremely dynamic process.

TECHNOLOGY

The following sections will detail the criteria of the system selected and the mapping technique.

8.1 System Characteristics

Different WFMSs were investigated in order to determine the most appropriate engine to address the collaboration problem in the healthcare domain. These different WFMSs were tested and compared taking account of aspects such as: availability, portability, functionality, operation, behaviour, information and organisation [16], and also the characteristics of the WFMSs engine that had been identified as making the approach. These were:

- **Business Workflow:** This is required to model the huge number of processes interacting in a healthcare system. Business workflows support human interaction with the system. This is necessary in healthcare systems, where different care team professionals interact with the system which supports their decision making process and therefore the routing of the flow. Moreover, the ability to set security and privacy controls is extremely important in such a domain, as is assigning activities to different roles or associating a role with a team member. Human interaction is a major element that must be considered in a healthcare system to support security and privacy. Another benefit from using business workflows is the ability to set timers that

are capable of starting activities and alerts, as this can add enormous benefits to a HIS's support.

- **Activity-based Workflow:** This is where the centre of the process is the activities. Activities represent all the treatment and diagnosis options a patient
  can follow. These options should be modelled in the WFMS and form the
  main block of the system.
- **Support Control Flow:** This can be coupled with an activity-based workflow
  system. It is normally the controller of the routing process along the flow. In
  the healthcare scenario and for our proposal, the system should be state-
  driven. This means that a patient's medical condition is the main driver
  along the treatment journey. Other drivers could interfere in the routing
  process, such as the available resources and the decisions of multi-
  professional care team members.
- **Support Data Flow:** This option is also extremely important in the healthcare scenario as information referencing the patient should also be sent
  along the flow to relate the running process\activities to a patient.
- **Support Workflow Patterns:** The variety of the patterns supported by the
  WFMS must ensure that multiple cases can be mapped. This is extremely
  important for patients with multiple conditions as the treatment journey becomes very complex. If the system does not support different patterns, it
  should provide tools to implement them.

8.2 Process Mapping

After selecting the scenario it is mapped into our chosen BPM. The Stateframe
process designer tool is used. This mapper uses Microsoft Visio with a custom-
ised-user template. The map designed by the mapper is linked dynamically to the
system's engine. The data about the flow logic and the cases processed is stored
in the process server database and organised as an entry in the User Data Properties (UDP), which is used at runtime to manage the process. The process map
consists of the following elements:

- A Process: this is the actual workflow map of the clinical guidelines. Each
  process could be a representation of a specific task within the guidelines or
  the whole disease treatment. Sub-processes representing specific tasks
  within a treatment could be internally (within the map) linked to the task.
  Tasks repeated along the treatment pathway could be mapped in separate
  processes which will be called when required. For this project, the whole
  treatment journey represented in Diagram 3 was mapped into a single process. The scale of the project is small and therefore it did not require splitting
  the treatment guidelines into multiple processes. However, to improve the
  visibility of the processes and for a more organised manageable mapping, the
  map is divided into separate sheets, each representing a different role, or location the patient is referred to. Diagram 4 is a sample of a process map
  showing an MDT's sheet. It shows a small portion of the whole process map
  representing Diagram 3, however the different steps are linked with anchors
  to sustain the flow of the treatment according to clinical guidelines.
- An Activity: the steps of the clinical guidelines. Activities represent tasks
  which provide productivity gains throughout the process flow. An activity can
  be: a prompt for manual decisions, an automated referral, an automated
  step where no user interaction is required, or a decision support tool (ASP
  activity) where relevant information is displayed to the user and their decision is expected. Activities along the map will be associated with the acting

roles (if any) which will be then linked to the patient as he/she progresses along the treatment journey. In this project, each stage within the treatment flow of the breast cancer diagnosis and treatment was represented by at least one activity. The choice of type depends on the nature of the task. These activities can be coded to add constraints to the logic and access related data when additional information is required.

- A Process object: this provides control or audit to the case according to its state. As a state-driven engine, the actual driver of the flow is the case process object state representing the patient's status or condition at certain points of the treatment. Process objects can change the state of another object, initiate an activity or just state a condition. Activities, on the other hand, change the state of the process object that initiated them. Process object states identify the state of the case. This is usually defined before and after each activity by showing the initial state and the resulting state after processing the task. For this project, process object states are a representation of either the treatment flow progress or the patient condition. In most of the cases, treatment flow progress is used. Examples include: examination start or examination completed (see diagram 3). When the object state initiates an activity, it should identify its state before and after it is processed. The patient condition state is used at some stages in the process map, such as MDT review decision of malignant, benign or no abnormality (see Diagram 4).

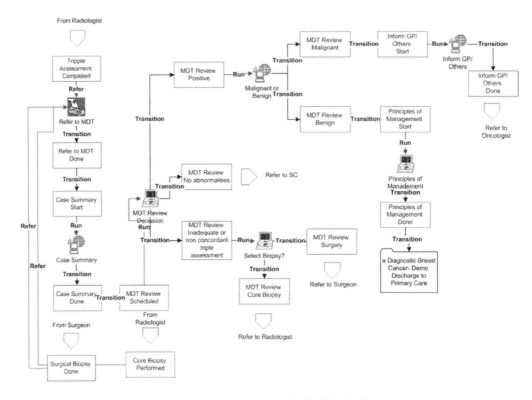

Diagram 4- Process Map of MDT's Actions

- A case: this is the scenario in progress. Each case represents a patient's treatment flow. For each patient, the treatment pathway is unique and is processed by considering a patient's health condition and the available resources. The case hierarchy at run time usually shows treatment history, the progress, the state in each and the roles or users involved in different stages.

At runtime, as the patient's case progresses along the care pathway, the reference to the patient's record will be passed through. The driver of the case progress will be the process object state. When an activity gets activated, if a role is associated with the activity, the role will be associated with the case. Moreover, if a rule is associated with the activity, the rule will be processed by considering the different roles involved with the patient.

THE TECHNOLOGY AND SERVICE PROVIDERS

Stateframe BPM system at Alia Systems Ltd. is the system used for implementation. The developers of the system agreed to support a number of our research projects including this research. They support the installation and development of our prototypes and we investigate and present their system's capabilities in different areas.

Alia Systems Limited Website: http://www.stateframe.com/

REFERENCES

[1] Campbell, H., et al., Integrated care pathways. BMJ, 1998. 316(7125): p. 133-137.

[2] Informing Healthcare. CaNISC. [cited 2008 24 September]; Available from: http://www.wales.nhs.uk/sites3/page.cfm?orgid=770pid=33639.

[3] NICE. National Institute for Health and Clinical Excellence - Home Page. [cited 2011 16 Jan]; Available from: www.nice.org.uk.

[4] Map of Medicine. Map of Medicine - Home Page. [cited 2008 16 June]; Available from: http://www.mapofmedicine.com/.

[5] NICE. National Institute for Health and Clinical Excellence- Quality Standards. [cited 2011 16 March]; Available from:
http://www.nice.org.uk/guidance/qualitystandards/qualitystandards.jsp

[6] Map of Medicine. Map of Medicine - Diagnostic Breast clinic. [cited 2011 20 March]; Available from: http://www.mapofmedicine.com/.

[7] Map of Medicine. Map of Medicine - Breast Cancer - Advanced. [cited 2011 20 March]; Available from: http://www.mapofmedicine.com/.

[8] NHS Wales. Informing Healthcare - Home Page. [cited 2009 1 May]; Available from: http://www.wales.nhs.uk/IHC/.

[9] Map of Medicine. Map of Medicine - Home Page. [cited 2011 16 Jan]; Available from: http://www.mapofmedicine.com/.

[10] NHS Direct. NHS Direct - Home Page. [cited 2009 30 June]; Available from: http://www.nhsdirect.nhs.uk/.

[11] NHS Connection for Health. NHS Connecting for Health - Home page. [cited 2009 1 May]; Available from:
http://www.connectingforhealth.nhs.uk/.

[12] Natasha, M., et al., A national survey of computerized decision support systems available to nurses in England. Journal of Nursing Management, 2009.

[13] Scottish Executive Health Department. Your Emergency Care Summary: What Does it Mean to You? 2006 [cited 2009 30 June]; Available from: http://www.scotland.gov.uk/Publications/2006/08/16152132/1.

[14] Informing Healthcare. Welsh Clinical Portal. 2007 [cited 23/01/2008]; Available from: http://www.wales.nhs.uk/ihc/page.cfm?pid=23396.

[15] Connecting for Health. Connecting for Health- Home Page. 2007 [cited 2007 07 August]; Available from: http://www.connectingforhealth.nhs.uk/.

[16] Al-Salamah, H., et al., Change Management Along the Integrated Care Pathway (ICP), in International Symposium on Health Information Management Research (ISHIMR). 2009: Kalamar, Sweden.

The authors of this chapter are: Hessah Al-Salamah, Alex Gray & Dave Morry. Hessah Alsalamah is a PhD student at the Cardiff School of Computer Science & Informatics and lecturer in the Department of Information Technology at King Saud University in Saudi Arabia (e-mail: h.alsalamah@cs.cf.ac.uk). Alex Gray is a Professor of Advanced Information at Cardiff School of Computer Science & Informatics. Dave Morry is the Head of the Clinical Information Unit at Velindre Hospital in the UK.

Los Angeles County Information Systems Advisory Body, USA

Gold Award: Public Sector

Nominated by Global 360, USA

1. EXECUTIVE SUMMARY / ABSTRACT

Los Angeles County DNA Offender Tracking System (DOTS)

Los Angeles County is one of the nation's largest counties with 4,084 square miles, an area some 800 square miles larger than the combined area of the states of Delaware and Rhode Island. It has the largest population (10,347,437 as of July 2008) of any county in the nation, and is exceeded by only eight states. Approximately 27 percent of California's residents live in Los Angeles County. There are 88 cities within the County, each with its own city council. All the cities, in varying degrees, contract with the County to provide municipal services; 37 contracts for nearly all of their municipal services.

The Information Systems Advisory Body (ISAB) is a multi-agency, multi-jurisdictional policy sub-committee of the Los Angeles County Countywide Criminal Justice Coordination Committee (CCJCC) established in 1982 to oversee the coordination, planning and development of major justice information systems.

In response to the passing of Proposition 69, the "DNA Fingerprint Unsolved Crime and Innocence Protection Act," Los Angeles County ISAB developed a plan to implement a centralized, web-based DNA Offender Tracking System (DOTS) using Global 360's case management solution, Case360, as the application platform.

The Case360-based DOTS system is used for tracking the collection of DNA samples for the estimated 1,200 daily criminal arrests, as well as for the more than 21,000 incarcerated inmates. The DOTS system:
- Tracks the collection of criminal offender DNA samples
- Identifies subjects in custody who are eligible for DNA sample collection
- Integrates with various criminal justice systems
- Implements legislative rules governing DNA collection
- Makes the DOTS DNA check and eligibility determination functionality available to other systems using web services
- Meets the following goals set forth by the State of California:
- Utilize DNA evidence to support conviction and exoneration of persons accused of crimes
- Solve current and COLD cases by increasing the population of DNA profiles in CODIS

More than 500 law enforcement personnel across 40 law enforcement agencies in Los Angeles County use DOTS, including the sheriff's department, municipal police departments, and probation officers,.

Results:

Los Angeles County now enjoys visibility and control over the third largest DNA database in the world while meeting legal requirements for obtaining, submitting and utilizing DNA evidence to support conviction and exoneration of persons accused of crimes, as well as solving cold cases by increasing the population of DNA profiles in the FBI's CODIS database.

- The DOTS system streamlined DNA sample collection rate while ensuring compliance with legal requirements.
- Most manual errors were eliminated by DOTS, and it reduced cost and complexity of maintaining multiple systems.
- DOTS enables information sharing with other state, local, and federal law enforcement agencies and databases.
- DOTS saves LAC staff around 20 minutes for every DNA collection case they process. With LAC processing more than 1,200 criminal arrests every day, the result is an additional 400 hours of time a day that LAC personnel can spend on other value-added activities.

DOTS tracks collections that enable payment from a state-provided reimbursement fund for every collection made. With each collection costing around $30 and an average 7,465 DNA samples collected every month, this automated payment method ensures that local law enforcement agencies quickly recover almost $225,000 in expenses every month with little to no manual effort.

2. OVERVIEW

In November 2004, State of California voters passed Proposition 69, the "DNA Fingerprint Unsolved Crime and Innocence Protection Act," to expand and modify state law regarding the collection and use of criminal offender DNA samples and palm print impressions to help solve crimes and increase public safety. Proponents of this proposition argued that too many crimes went unsolved because California did not have a comprehensive DNA database with samples from all convicted felons. Citing statistical evidence that suggested stronger DNA collection laws enabled more crimes to be solved, they also argued that requiring convicted felons and arrests for rape/murder to submit DNA helps solve crimes, prevents false imprisonment, stops serial rapists, and brings California law enforcement in line with 34 other states. Prior to proposition 69 being enacted, California solved only five percent of crimes utilizing DNA evidence, compared with 40 percent of crimes solved in states with larger DNA databases.

Proposition 69 requires all criminal offenders arrested for certain qualifying charges or convicted of certain crimes to provide deoxyribonucleic acid (DNA) for analysis and inclusion in the California DNA and Forensic Identification Database and Data Bank program.

The responsibility to collect DNA samples from eligible offenders is shared among 40 law enforcement agencies in Los Angeles County (LAC), including the Sheriff's Department and other municipal police departments. Faced with tracking and processing more than 1,200 criminal arrests in LAC every day, as well as the more than 21,000 incarcerated inmates, LAC needed an automated, collaborative, and rules-driven way to identify and determine a suspect or inmates DNA collection status while maintaining legal compliance with existing DNA collection eligibility legislation.

Additionally, LAC needed a way to exchange and share this information with other state, local and federal agencies, and ensure the county met the following Proposition 69 requirements and rules for obtaining, submitting, and utilizing DNA evidence to support conviction and exoneration of persons accused of crimes:

- Meet legal requirements for taking a DNA sample
- Avoid taking DNA from subjects with DNA already on file

- Submit DNA for processing to the appropriate DNA Crime Lab
- Submit DNA profiles to the FBI Combined DNA Index System (CODIS) database for multi-agency crime solving
- Reimburse DNA collection agencies for processing costs ($30/specimen)

Since going live in July of 2007, the DOTS system records, shares, and archives an average 7,465 DNA collections per month.

Eliminated manual errors—most manual errors were eliminated by DOTS, and it reduced cost and complexity of maintaining multiple systems. The DNA collection process has been streamlined, automating simple decisions and processes and eliminating the need for repetitive and wasteful human interaction.

Information sharing with outside stakeholders—DOTS enables information sharing with other state, local, and federal law enforcement agencies and databases. It empowers LAC with web services technologies, supporting new applications and consistent user access to information spread across multiple applications and organizations.

Improved productivity—DOTS saves LAC staff around 20 minutes for every DNA collection case they process. With LAC processing more than 1,200 criminal arrests every day, the result is an additional 400 hours of time a day that LAC personnel can spend on other value-added activities.

Quickly recover expenses—DOTS tracks collections that enable payment from a state-provided reimbursement fund for every collection made. With each collection costing around $30 and an average 7,465 DNA samples collected every month, this automated payment method ensures that local law enforcement agencies quickly recover almost $225,000 in expenses every month with little to no manual effort.

3. BUSINESS CONTEXT

Prior to DOTS, the process for checking an offender's eligibility for a DNA sample was completely manual and mostly paper-based. See the case handling section below for more details.

4. THE KEY INNOVATIONS

4.1 Business

The Case360-based DOTS system is mission-critical for the criminal justice agencies in LAC. It has streamlined the business process to check and collect DNA samples from qualified offenders, enabling LAC to better serve the public interest by solving more crimes, preventing false imprisonments, and removing serial rapists from the streets. The system automates the cross-checking of jail inmates with the DNA database, eliminating slow and manual checks as to whether or not the inmate has already had their DNA collected.

Moreover, these DNA samples, which are processed by the State of California and added to the State and FBI DNA databases, serve as a critical component for helping to solve both local, state and national crimes using case management technology. The FBI CODIS database currently has more than 6,625,752 offender profiles for which crime-scene DNA is compared against to identify the culpable and exonerate the innocent. Case360 has made the sharing of DNA collection data between multiple law enforcement agencies possible by integrating with and combining data with the Consolidated Criminal History and Reporting System (CCHRS) and DOTS. Updates between the two systems are carried out in real time, creating a bi-directional interface with CCHRS that allows DOTS updates to occur automatically. By automating the retrieval of the CCHRS RAP sheet into an electronic case folder, end users no longer need to access separate applications to gather this data, and all data entries are validated by the system, saving time and removing the chance of data entry errors.

Additionally, the DOTS system tracks collections that enable payment from a state-provided reimbursement fund for every collection made. With each collection costing around $30 and more than 30,000 DNA samples collected in the first eight months of the DOTS program alone, the expense adds up quickly. This automated payment method ensures that local law enforcement agencies recover their significant expenses quickly with little to no manual effort.

4.2 Case Handling

The old process to check an offender's eligibility for a DNA sample was completely manual. The arresting officer or the jail personnel had to check multiple systems at different terminals for the offender's Record of Arrest and Prosecution (RAP sheet), print the RAP sheet and review the data to determine if DNA was needed. This manual process increased the risk of error in DNA eligibility determination. Moreover, when criminal intake processing became extremely busy, the DNA eligibility check might get skipped, or the collection would be made, but the state billing would not get processed.

If a DNA sample was collected, a paper-based card would then be filled out, providing yet another opportunity for data to be captured inconsistently, incorrectly, or illegibly, resulting in a high percentage of DNA samples being rejected. It was estimated by the county that this process typically took anywhere from 20 to 30 minutes for jail personnel to complete.

Moreover, the lack of a centralized tracking system made it extremely difficult and costly to ensure process compliance and management oversight. There was no way to easily share this information with other law enforcement agencies or submit results and statuses to the FBI CODIS database.

The ISAB determined that a phased approach would best meet the needs and requirements of the project and ensure functional success and future scaling opportunities. Therefore, the deployment was broken down into the following three phases:

- Phase I – County-wide deployment
- Phase II – Automatic daily screening of jail population to determine DNA sample collection
- Phase III – Integration with Live Scan screening system

Phase I – County-Wide Deployment

The DOTS County-Wide Deployment phase was designed to meet the following requirements:

- Retrieve the Consolidated Criminal History Reporting System (CCHRS – pronounced "cheers") RAP sheet automatically
- Pre-populate the DOTS Arrest Booking Interface with data from CCHRS
- Validate the user-entered data on the DOTS Arresting Booking Interface
- Update CCHRS with DNA collected status in real time

Phase 1 of the DOTS deployment enabled all law enforcement agencies in LAC to track the collection of criminal offender DNA samples using the Case360 DOTS Arresting Booking Interface. The system enables the user to check the status of an offender's DNA sample online by searching the DOTS database by State ID (SID) using a web service query. If no record is found, another web service query is made into the CCHRS system. The system then retrieves the offender's RAP sheet from CCHRS and saves it as justification and documentation for DNA sample collection. The system also updates the DNA offender's DNA status in CCHRS in real time. For all new records, the DOTS application creates Case360 case folders and stores a copy of the RAP sheet and related information.

Phase II – Automatic Daily Screening of Jail Population to Determine DNA Sample Collection

Phase II of the DOTS application extended the Phase I functionality by adding process management capabilities. Phase II of DOTS enables all County Jail Sheriff Personnel to identify subjects who are in custody and are eligible for DNA sample collection. With the daily population of the County jail at a proximately 21,000, the County relies on a system to monitor the status of subjects in custody. For example, when inmates are transferred within the County jail, or transferred from the jail to a courtroom and back. The system generates a data stream of XML messages, which are broadcast through a countywide messaging system.

DOTS then utilizes Case360's Capture Broker to process and evaluate these XML messages, retrieves RAP sheet data from CCHRS, and uses its DNA Eligibility rules engine to decide if a DNA sample is required. The system categorizes these records into work queues: To Be Collected, Collected, No Need To Collect, Currently Collecting, etc... Jail staff is then able to process these queries and collect DNA samples from eligible offenders in custody. The system has resulted in significant improvements in the efficiency, effectiveness, and productivity of the jail staff.

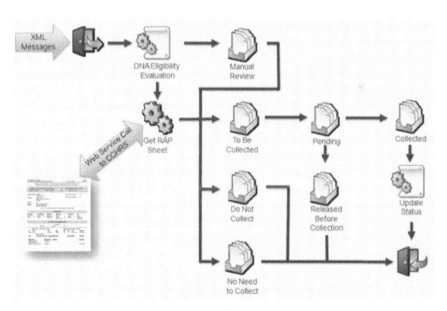

DNA Eligibility Process Flow

Phase III – Integration with the LiveScan Fingerprint System

Phase III of the DOTS application deployment focused on integrating DOTS functionality with the county's fingerprint-based booking system, LiveScan. To accomplish this integration, a web service interface was developed for DOTS that leveraged the Phase II workflow screening logic and integrated it with the Fingerprint Identification systems used for all LAC bookings and probation monitoring.

This new integration provides a consolidated business process for booking subjects and streamlines the systems interaction to just one system, LiveScan. The lookup and verification of DNA collection status happens automatically at the time of fingerprinting, eliminating the manual lookup that was required as part of Phase I.

5. ORGANIZATION & SOCIAL

DOTS has empowered law enforcement officers and jail staff in Los Angeles County to better enforce public safety laws by providing a centralized database of DNA sample information and an automated and integrated system for verification and eligibility determination. The ability to take DNA samples from eligible suspects and offenders during the booking and transfer processes

Los Angeles County LiveScan Fingerprint Kiosk

enables police to conduct more accurate and efficient investigations, further helping them ensure public safety.

For jail personnel monitoring the status of subjects in custody, DOTS has resulted in significant improvements in their efficiency, effectiveness, and productivity. An informal study by the LA Police Department indicates that on average, the DOTS system saves LAC staff around 20 minutes for every DNA collection case they process. With LAC processing more than 1,200 criminal arrests every day, the result is an additional 400 hours of time a day that LAC personnel can spend on other value-added activities.

When inmates are transferred within the county jail or transferred from the jail to the courtroom and back, the DOTS system automatically retrieves RAP sheet data from CCHRS and uses its DNA eligibility rules to decide if a DNA sample is required. Once the system makes this determination, that information is provided to the jail staff as work queues, such as: To Be Collected, Collected, No Need To Collect, Currently Collecting, etc. Jail staff is then able to process these queries and collect DNA samples from the eligible offenders in custody with no additional research or processing necessary.

6. HURDLES OVERCOME

Management

The organization of the County posed some challenges in trying to integrate business processes across different agencies, to coordinate all of these resources and to reach management consensus. However, because ISAB is a multi-agency, multi-jurisdictional policy sub-committee that oversees the coordination, planning and development of major justice information systems, it was easier to overcome those challenges by gaining active participation from all of the key stakeholders and ensuring the team stayed active and involved throughout the entire process improvement and implementation project.

Business

The County was comfortable with the goals and design of the system and was ready to significantly reduce the amount of paper being used in processes. However, before agreeing to a solution LAC ISAB sought the opinion of other county law enforcement agencies and administrative bodies to ensure that the case management system would meet their needs and integrate with systems being used by stakeholders outside of LAC.

Organization Adoption

LAC was so committed to the new system that it was deployed rather smoothly. Because users were involved up front in the design the way to adoption was smoothed. "Train-the-trainer" training was conducted, after which the end-users received training and had time to spend on the test system. Procedures were adopted by the department that eased the transition.

Benefits

Since deploying the case-based DOTS system, LAC has experienced a number of benefits. The County now enjoys unprecedented visibility and control over the third largest DNA database in the world while meeting legal requirements for obtaining, submitting and utilizing DNA evidence to support conviction an exoneration of persons accused of crimes. They have greatly enhanced the business process for collecting DNA samples from eligible offenders, eliminating most of the manual errors that plagued the older process and made it difficult to ensure compliance with state legislative mandates.

By utilizing Case360 as the collaborative content and process management foundation for DOTS, LAC now has a single, trusted repository of DNA collection data that has reduced the cost and complexity of maintaining multiple manual and paper-based archives. The DNA collection process has been automated and streamlined, automating simple decisions and processes and eliminating the need for repetitive and wasteful human interaction.

Moreover DOTS empowers LAC with web services technologies, supporting new applications and information sharing with other state, local, and federal law enforcement agencies and databases for consistent user access to information spread across multiple applications and organizations. By integrating with back-end systems and repositories and enabling the consistent reuse of data and documents, LAC personnel get more than just a portal view to conduct their DNA collection process, but a seamless and simple way to ensure that DNA collection processes are consistent with legislative mandates so that the DNA collected may be utilized as evidence to support conviction and exoneration of persons accused of crimes, as well as solving current and COLD cases by increasing the population of DNA profiles in the FBI's CODIS database.

Since going live in July of 2008, LAC averaged 2,638 DNA collections a month in the first six months alone, and has increased collection to an average of 7,465 collections a month.

LAC anticipates that tracking a larger pool of potential and probable repeat offenders through DNA collection will lead to higher rates of crimes solved and decrease overall crime rates for improved public safety.

6.1 Cost Savings / Time Reductions

The DOTS system saves LAC staff around 20 minutes for every DNA collection case they process. With LAC processing more than 1,200 criminal arrests every day, the result is an additional 400 hours of time a day that LAC personnel can spend on other value-added activities.

6.2 Increased Revenues

The DOTS system tracks collections that enable payment from a state-provided reimbursement fund for every collection made. With each collection costing around $30 and an average 7,465 DNA samples collected every month, this automated payment method ensures that local law enforcement agencies quickly recover almost $325,000 in expenses every month with little to no manual effort.

6.3 Quality Improvements

- Eliminated most manual errors, reduced cost and complexity of maintaining multiple systems
- The DNA collection process has been streamlined, automating simple decisions and processes and eliminating the need for repetitive and wasteful human interaction.
- Information sharing with other state, local, and federal law enforcement agencies and databases
- The DOTS system empowers LAC with web services technologies, supporting new applications and consistent user access to information spread across multiple applications and organizations.

7. BEST PRACTICES, LEARNING POINTS AND PITFALLS

7.1 Best Practices and Learning Points

- ✓ Take the time to ensure that all partners and stakeholders are aligned and have a very clear understanding of the project's overall goal and the project milestones along the way.
- ✓ Using a phased approach to implementation ensures functional success and future scaling opportunities.
- ✓ Ensure that you have cooperation from "process owners" – in this case law enforcement personnel—and the IT departments they have supporting them.
- ✓ Use a solution and approach that considers the end user from the beginning to make user adoption and acceptance considerably easier.

7.2 Pitfalls

- ✗ Do not fall into the trap of forcing end users to learn a system not adapted to their role within the process
- ✗ Training of managers and end users is critical. Failing to provide training and continued support will result in personnel finding 'workarounds' for parts of the process they don't understand how to do.

8. COMPETITIVE ADVANTAGES

Achieving "competitive advantage" in the public sector equates to improving service delivery for constituents and stakeholders. DOTS has empowered law enforcement officers and jail staff in Los Angeles County to better enforce public safety and significantly improve their efficiency, effectiveness, and productivity.

DOTS supports information sharing with other state, local, and federal law enforcement agencies and databases for consistent user access to information spread across multiple applications and organizations outside of LAC.

Ensuring that the collection of DNA complies with all legal requirements, and records confirmation of compliance within each case folder, aids the LAC District Attorney in prosecuting criminal offenders.

9. TECHNOLOGY

The Global 360 case management technology is a rich application that combines the capabilities of document and business process management tools into a single adaptive case management solution. Case360 handles the complexities of both collaborative and ad-hoc business processes, providing a team-centric environment through access to documents, tasks, deadlines, and threaded discussions from within a "virtual folder," called a case folder. Within this case folder, all the information needed to process a case is readily accessible and available to all, yet tailored to an individual's roles and privileges.

The result is a unified and integrated view of case data, giving organizations complete visibility and auditable control.

10. THE TECHNOLOGY AND SERVICE PROVIDERS

Global 360 was the sole case management solution vendor, integrator, and consultant for this project. (www.global360.com)

About Global 360

Global 360 helps organizations to better manage processes today and make improvements for tomorrow. Our market leading process and case management solutions improve business performance by maximizing the productivity of all participants in a process. To accomplish that, we address the unique requirements of all key roles that are critical to improving a process. Providing the industry's first Persona-based business process and case management software, Global 360's viewPoint delivers an intuitive, configurable, and personable user experience, accelerating time-to-deployment while reducing the development costs typically associated with complex BPM user applications. And with real-time performance data, managers can find and fix problems before they impact customers and extend these efficiencies to customers and partners. Building on our strength in financial services, government, insurance, consumer packaged goods, manufacturing, and the retail sector, Global 360 has helped more than 2,000 customers in 70 countries reduce paper, automate processes, and empower individuals to truly change how work gets done. Global 360, Inc. is headquartered in Texas with operations in North America, Europe, and the Pacific Rim. For more information about Global 360's process and case management solutions, visit the company web site at www.global360.com.

Los Angeles County Department of Public Social Services (DPSS)

Finalist: Public Sector
Nominated by KANA, USA

1. CHALLENGE

With over 10 million people, Los Angeles County is the largest county in the United States. The Los Angeles County Department of Public Social Services (DPSS) currently serves over two million participants each day and a caseload of over 1.6 million across its various public assistance programs—more than any other jurisdiction except the states of California and New York. Even though the County has developed standardized processes and workflow, the unpredictability of people and the sheer volume of cases in Los Angeles create an often overwhelmed situation. It is the goal of the Call Center personnel, who are classified as Eligibility Workers, to determine individual benefits eligibility.

Through DPSS, the County provides a range of programs including CalWORKs (California's Temporary Assistance to Needy Families (TANF) program), CalFresh, Medi-Cal (California's Medicaid program), and General Relief. Eligibility determination for all of these programs is provided through a case management system called LEADER (Los Angeles Eligibility Automated Determination Evaluation and Reporting). With demand for these programs and the complexity of administering them ever growing, LA County's DPSS needed a solution that would increase case worker accessibility, improve operational efficiency and enhance the overall customer service experience.

2. SOLUTION

In August 2006, DPSS selected Lagan to collaborate on the implementation of a centralized customer service call center for approximately 86 eligibility workers designed to service the San Gabriel Valley District Office with an annual caseload of 30,000. This was the first wave of a planned enterprise roll-out that ultimately will touch approximately 6,000 case workers and potentially, 600 to 800 Customer Service Representatives (CSR).

The Call Center went live in January 2007, achieving a key project milestone early on— integration with the existing LEADER system—thanks to Lagan's open interface toolkit. Lagan and LEADER created an interface that allowed case information to populate on the Lagan application and case comments to automatically populate on the LEADER system without retyping the comments.

CSRs have direct access to over a million eligibility case records in the County's LEADER system while fielding live calls in a contact center environment. Later that year, the County added two more district offices, and as of June 13, 2011 has expanded to eight district offices serving a combined caseload of 400,000 clients. Average monthly call volume is 110,000, with monthly tracking tickets averaging 35,000.

In January 2008, the County implemented a self-service component through an Interactive Voice Response (IVR) system giving callers 24 hour access to case information, such as benefit amounts and case status, as well as emergency hotlines. Today, the IVR system helps screen the calls that are purely informational in nature before ever reaching a Call Center agent. The calls that are taken are documented by the Computer Telephony Integration (CTI) and Requests for Information (RFIs) are supported by the software solution that front-ends the County's eligibility system (LEADER).

Actions that need to be performed by Case Workers or other District Office workers are initiated as tickets from the software solution that then assigns tasks that need to be completed in order to resolve case issues for a County welfare participant. Every case is unique because every family is unique. The number of family members, ages, relationships, parents, step-children, foster children, adopted children, locations, educational levels, etc., vary greatly from case to case. There may be similarities to case and the process workflow helps to identify those similarities to aid in greater efficiency. The LA County DPSS Customer Service Center (CSC) project team analyzes reports and data extracts through Business Intelligence (BI) reporting and utilize that data to make changes in the Business Process management (BPM) module of the software solution.

In June 2010, the County implemented an Outbound Dialing System to further improve communication and customer service. The system places reminder calls to DPSS participants and assists in reaching the most vulnerable participants in case of emergency.

Through the call center, participants have access to service information Monday through Friday from 7:30 a.m.–5:30 p.m. via an 800-number. Support is provided in five languages—English, Spanish, Mandarin, Vietnamese and Cambodian. As a result of a well-developed knowledgebase and system ease of use, approximately half of the calls received can be handled directly by the customer service center without the need to generate additional work for the case workers. The remaining calls are automatically routed via a tracking ticket to the district office for case worker follow-up. Supervisors have instant access to case files and can track progress in real time. Reports and notifications are automatically generated to inform supervisors where bottlenecks and issues may be occurring, making it far easier to manage the day-to-day work of the agency.

3. RESULTS

LA County DPSS deployed the solution in a fraction of the time it would have taken for a traditional solution; the initial phase of the project took less than six months from contract signature to implementation and rollout.

Today, LA County DPSS customer service center receives about 190,000 calls per month, of which an average of 74,000 reach a Customer Service Representative. Approximately 74,000 tracking tickets are generated each month, fielded by the 222 representatives in the call center.

There were several key factors that have made the deployment of Lagan Human Services and the expanded customer service center capabilities a success: defining processes up front; encouraging involvement of case workers, supervisors, customer service representatives and the technology department throughout the process; garnering support and buy-in from top administrators; and fostering collaboration between Lagan and the County.

The successful collaboration between department and vendor was critical to reach the goal. Defining the business process along with input and feedback from users was integral to the success of the project and will ensure success though expansion.

Preliminary customer satisfaction surveys have yielded a 99 percent satisfaction rate. Through the centralized call center, participant access to case information has increased from two hours a day to ten hours a day. The self-service option ensures that more questions can be answered with a single phone call, with fewer visits to the district offices. The response, both internally and externally, has been excellent.

The net results:

- For staff, the opportunity to excel by providing more responsive and accurate guidance to participants
- For supervisors, higher levels of accountability since all data is being tracked in real time
- For the County, a highly cost-effective means of improving accessibility to services through the application of non-invasive technology
- For the participant, a completely new way of interacting with DPSS—one which saves trips to the district office and yields positive outcomes in shorter periods of time

Today, the customer service center handles calls for eight line district offices. The goal is to expand support to handle calls for all 36 LA County district offices. Plans are also in place to extend the IVR system and expand county-wide with multiple full-service contact center locations serving as one virtual center. The customer service center has implemented an Electronic Document Management System (EDMS) which will allow DPSS to begin its transition to a paperless environment by scanning all case documents. Longer term, the county seeks to streamline its operations more strategically, incorporating other programs, additional customer service and hotline numbers, and internet-based automated services.

4. LA COUNTY DPSS CALL CENTER SUCCESS AT A GLANCE

- Access hours expanded from two hours/day to ten hours/day, 7:30 a.m. –5:30 pm.
- Self-service interactive voice response system adds 24/7 access to case information and program and emergency hotlines
- Eight district offices now supported with a combined caseload of 195,000
- Monthly call volume: 190,000 of which 96,000 are handled by the Customer Service Representatives
- Monthly tracking tickets: over 74,000
- Trained call center customer service representatives directly handle approximately 77 percent of inquiries
- Customer satisfaction survey rates are 99 percent.

5. ABOUT LAGAN, A DIVISION OF KANA SOFTWARE

Lagan, a Division of KANA Software, Inc., is the global leader in G2C (government to citizen) solutions connecting government and citizens worldwide. Lagan enables governments and citizens to communicate online, on the phone and on the move. With 200 public sector customers worldwide, Lagan helps local governments serve the everyday interests of more than 60 million citizens.

Lagan's solutions for Service Experience Management have been designed to streamline the service delivery functions of government, enabling improved efficiency and more citizen-centric public services. Lagan manages the interactions between citizens and government and provides full support for a wide variety of government service delivery processes. Lagan's solutions have proven utility for state and local governments and offer a range of flexible delivery methods: on-premise, on-demand and hosted. Learn more at www.kana.com.

Appendix

Glossary of Terms
Adaptive Case Management

To have a meaningful discussion, we must start with clear definitions.

- **activity**—A description of a piece of work that forms one logical step within a process. It is the basic unit of work within a process. Presumably, work could be subdivided into units smaller than a given activity, but it is not meaningful for the organization to track the work to that level of detail. Synonyms include node, step, and task.

- **adaptive case management (ACM)**—A productive system that deploys not only the organization and process structure, but it becomes the system of record for the business data entities and content involved. All processes are completely transparent, as per access authorization, and fully auditable. It enables nontechnical business users in virtual organizations to seamlessly create/consolidate structured and unstructured processes from basic predefined business entities, content, social interactions, and business rules. It moves the process knowledge gathering from the template analysis/modeling/ simulation phase into the process execution phase in the lifecycle. It collects actionable knowledge—without an intermediate analysis phase—based on process patterns created by business users. ACM differs from business process management (BPM) and from human interaction management (HIM) in that the case information is the focus and the thing around which the other artifacts are organized. And it is the case information that persists for the long term.

- **ad hoc process**—See emergent process.

- **agile methodology**—To move quickly and lightly. In reference to solution development, it is a method where many short iterations are used, with many quick (internal) releases, so that the nontechnical customer of a solution can be more actively involved in guiding the course of development. The agile approach to development is known to produce solutions that better meet the needs of the customer, and it also allows for greater responsiveness to external changes in requirements.

- **analytics**- A mechanism for collecting and processing statistics. Process analytics will gather and process statistics about the running of processes in such a way that it is useful for evaluating how well the process is running.

- **best practice**—An approach to achieving a particular outcome that is believed to be more effective than any other approach in a particular condition or circumstance.

- **business operations platform (BOP)**— A next-generation technology platform oriented toward continuously designing, executing, monitoring, changing, and optimizing critical business processes proposed by Fingar (2009).

- **business process**— A set of one or more linked activities which collectively realize a business objective or policy goal, normally within the context of an organizational structure defining functional roles and relationships.

- **business process execution language (BPEL)**—A standard executable language, based on XML, for describing a process that uses web service calls to communicate with the outside world.
- **business process management (BPM)**—The practice of developing, running, performance measuring, and simulating business processes to effect the continued improvement of those processes. Business process management is concerned with the lifecycle of the process definition. BPM differs from adaptive case management (ACM) and from human interaction management (HIM) in that its focus is the process, and it uses the process as an organizing paradigm around which data, roles, and communication are organized. Process models are prepared in advance for particular situations, and the performance can be measured and monitored so that over time the process will be improved.
- **business process management suite/soft ware/system (BPMS)**—A soft ware system designed to support business process management. The acronym BPMS is used to distinguish the technology product from the management practice of BPM.
- **business process modeling notation (BPMN)**—A standard set of graphical shapes and conventions with associated meanings that can be used in modeling a business process.
- **business process orientation (BPO)**—A concept that suggests that organizations could enhance their overall performance by viewing all the activities as linked together into a process that ultimately produces a good or service.
- **business rules engine (BRE)**—A soft ware system for managing and evaluating a complex set of rules in a business processing environment. A business rule is a small piece of logic that is separated from the application logic so that it may be managed separately from the application code. Rules are oft en expressed in a language that is more accessible to non-programmers.
- **case**—The name given to the specific situation, set of circumstances, or initiative that requires a set of actions to achieve an acceptable outcome or objective. Each case has a subject that is the focus of the actions—such as a person, a lawsuit, or an insurance claim—and is driven by the evolving circumstances of the subject.
- **case file**—Contains all of the case information and processes, and it coordinates communications necessary to accomplish the goal for a particular case. A case file can contain information of any type including documents, images, video, etc.
- **case management**—A method or practice of coordinating work by organizing all of the relevant information into one place—called a case. The case becomes the focal point for assessing the situation, initiating activities and processes, as well as keeping a history record of what has transpired. Beyond this generic definition, case management has specific meanings in the medical care, legal, and social services fields. For this book, we see case management as a technique that could be used in any field of human endeavor.
- **case owner**—A person (or group of people) who is responsible for the outcome of a case. The case owner can change any aspect of a case and is actively involved in achieving the goals of the case.

- **clinical pathway**—a method that medical professionals use to standardize patient care based on accepted practice guidelines.
- **commercial-off -the-shelf (COTS)**—Describes software or hardware products that are ready-made and available for sale to the general public. This term is used to distinguish such product from custom software and hardware made specifically for a purpose that is presumed to be more expensive to produce and maintain.
- **crowdsourcing**—Identify evolving trends and best practices through continuous analysis of social interactions and conversations[2]
- **customer relationship management (CRM)**—Technology to manage a company's interactions with customers and sales prospects.
- **dynamic case management**—support real-time, incremental and progressive case-handling in response to changing events by leveraging collaborative and information-intensive BPM.[2]
- **emergent process**—A process that is not predictable. Emergent processes have a sensitive dependence upon external factors outside of the control of the process context, which is why they cannot be fixed according to their internal state. Workers involved in an emergent process will experience it as planning and working alternately or at the same time, such that the plan is evolved as the work evolves. Synonyms include *ad hoc* process and unstructured process.
- **enterprise content management (ECM)**—Strategies, methods, and tools used to capture, manage, store, preserve, and deliver content and documents related to organizational processes. ECM strategies and tools allow the management of an organization's unstructured information, wherever that information exists.
- **enterprise resource planning (ERP)**—Computer system used to manage resources including tangible assets, financial resources, materials, and human resources.
- **extended relationship management (XRM)**—a discipline of mapping and maintaining relationships between any type of asset in very flexible ways, for the purpose of leveraging those relationships in business rules or business processes.
- **goal-oriented organization design (GOOD)**—The change management methodology associated with human interaction management (HIM), which defines 3 standard Stages: Design (scope definition, business motiation modeling, benefits definition), Delivery (requirements management, stakeholder management, operational transition, risk management) and Optimization (marketing & communications, benefits realization). Each Stage has associated Roles, Activities and Deliverables.
- **human interaction management (HIM)**—The practice of describing, executing and managing collaborative human activity according to 5 standard principles (effective teams, structured communication, knowledge management, time management and dynamic planning) so as to achieve optimal results. HIM differs from business process management (BPM) and adaptive case management (ACM) in that its focus is definition of goals, assignment of associated responsibilities, and management of

---

[2] Forrester Research, USA

the resulting knowledge. Templates describing Stages, Roles, Activities and Deliverables are used to generate executable Plans that evolve during usage and may be re-used as new templates.

- **knowledge work**—A type of work where the course of events is decided on a case-by-case basis. It normally requires a person with detailed knowledge who can weigh many factors and anticipate potential outcomes to determine the course for a specific case. Knowledge work almost always involves an emergent ACM/BPM process or HIM Plan template.
- **knowledge workers**—People who have a high degree of expertise, education, or experience and the primary purpose of their job involves the creation, distribution, or application of knowledge. Knowledge workers do not necessarily work in knowledge intensive industries.
- **lifecycle**—This book uses lifecycle only in regard to the work of creating a solution. The development lifecycle of a solution might start with definition of requirements, development of a process definition, development of forms, testing, deployment of the solution into production, use of the solution by many people, and finally the shutting down of the solution. The lifecycle of a solution may involve monitoring the running process instances and improving those process definitions over time. Note: A solution has a lifecycle that takes it from start to finish; a case has a process or processes that take it from start to finish.
- **model**—A simplified summary of reality designed to aid further study. In the business process field, a process model is a simplified or complete process definition created to study the proposed process before execution time.
- **node**—See activity.
- **online transaction processing (OLTP)**—A class of systems where time-sensitive, transaction-related data are processed immediately and are always kept current.
- **organizational agility**—That quality of an organization associated with sensing opportunity or threat, prioritizing its potential responses, and acting efficiently and effectively.
- **predictable process**—process that is repeatable and is run the same way a number of times. Synonyms include definable process, repeatable process, and structured process.
- **process definition**—A representation of a business process in a form that supports automated manipulation, such as modeling or enactment by a process management system. The process definition consists of a network of activities and their relationships, criteria to indicate the start and termination of the process, and information about the individual activities, such as participants, associated IT applications, and data. Synonyms include process diagram and workflow.
- **process diagram**—A visual explanation of a process definition. Synonyms include process definition, process model, and process flowchart.
- **process flowchart**—See process diagram.
- **process instance**—A data structure that represents a particular instance of running of a process. It has associated context information that can be used and manipulated by the process. A process instance plays a role in a business process management suite (BPMS) that is very similar to but not exactly the same as a case in a case management system. A particular case may have more than one process instance associated with it.

- **process model**—A simplified or complete process definition created to study the proposed process before execution time. Synonyms include process diagram.
- **records management**—Management of the information created, received, and maintained as evidence and information by an organization in pursuance of legal obligations or in the transaction of business.
- **role**—An association of particular a user, or users, with a particular set of responsibilities in a particular context. In this case, responsibility means the expectation to perform particular activities for that context. routine work— Work that is predictable and usually repeatable. Its predictability allows routine work to be planned to a large extent before the work is started. As the name implies, routine work is considered normal, regular, and it is not exceptional.
- **scientific management**— An early twentieth century school of management that aimed to improve the physical efficiency of an individual worker by carefully recording precisely what must be done for a particular task, and then training workers to replicate that precisely. It is based on the work of Frederick Winslow Taylor (1856–1915).
- **scrum**—An agile software development methodology emphasizing iteration and incremental development. Originally referred to as the *rugby approach.*
- **service-oriented architecture (SOA)**—An approach to system design where the software functionality is deployed to a specific logical location (a service) and programs requiring that soft ware functionality make use of communications protocols to access the service remotely. SOA has oft en been discussed together with business process management (BPM), but this connection is coincidental. While BPM might benefit from SOA the way that any program/system would, there is no inherent connection between managing business processes and the system architecture that supports them.
- **social business**—An organization that has put in place the strategies, technologies and processes to systematically engage all the individuals of its ecosystem (employees, customers, partners, suppliers) to maximize the co-created value.
- **social BPM**—Leverage social networking tools and techniques to extend the reach and impact of process improvement efforts.
- **social network analysis**—Pinpoint historical activity patterns within social networks through the statistical mining of complex behavioural data sets.
- **social process guidance**—Apply crowdsourcing and social network analysis techniques to deliver real-time contextual advice and guidance for completing a process task or activity.
- **social software**—A class of software systems that allows users to communicate, collaborate, and interact in many flexible ways. Generally, such software allows users to form their own relationships with other users and then exchange messages, write notes, and share media in different ways.

- **solution**—A package of artefacts (configurations, forms, process definitions, templates, and information) that have been prepared in advance to help users address particular kinds of recurring situations. A solution may embody best practices for a particular kind of situation.
- **sphere**—a collection of people or other assets. Inclusion in a sphere can be based on business rules or can be a nested collection of other spheres. Spheres can represent nodes in a network of relationships or process flow in a workflow system
- **step**—See activity.
- **straight-through processing (STP)**—The practice of completely automating process and eliminating all manual human tasks. This term is typically used in the financial industry.
- **subject (of a case)**—An entity that is the focus of actions performed in the context of a case. For example, a person, a lawsuit, or an insurance claim.
- **task**—See activity.
- **template**—The general concept of something that is prepared in advance approximately for a particular purpose with the anticipation that it will be modified during use to more exactly fit the situation. A process template does not define a process in the way that a process definition does.
- **unstructured process**—See emergent process.
- **work**—Exertion or effort directed to produce or accomplish something. Organizations exist to achieve goals and work is the means to achieve those goals. The smallest recorded unit of work is an activity. Activities are combined into procedures and processes.
- **workflow**—The automation of a business process, in whole or part, during which documents, information, or tasks are passed from one participant to another for action according to a set of procedural rules. Synonyms include process definition.

These definitions are licensed under Creative Commons—you are free to copy and use them in any way that helps the pursuit of knowledge. It is not strictly necessary to reference this glossary, but we would appreciate a link back to this book. The bulk of this glossary is derived from the work done by Keith Swenson at http://social-biz.org/glossary and was originally assembled for inclusion in Mastering the Unpredictable[3]."

Accreditation guide: "Taming the Unpredictable" 2011 published by Future Strategies Inc. Lighthouse Point, FL. http://FutStrat.com

---

[3] Mastering the Unpredictable: How Adaptive Case Management Will Revolutionize the Way That Knowledge Workers Get Things Done, published by Meghan-Kiffer Press, April 2010

WfMC Structure and Membership Information

WHAT IS THE WORKFLOW MANAGEMENT COALITION?

The Workflow Management Coalition, founded in August 1993, is a non-profit, international organization of workflow vendors, users, analysts and university/research groups. The Coalition's mission is to promote and develop the use of workflow through the establishment of standards for software terminology, interoperability and connectivity among BPM and workflow products. Comprising more than 250 members worldwide, the Coalition is the primary standards body for this software market.

WORKFLOW STANDARDS FRAMEWORK

The Coalition has developed a framework for the establishment of workflow standards. This framework includes five categories of interoperability and communication standards that will allow multiple workflow products to coexist and interoperate within a user's environment. Technical details are included in the white paper entitled, "The Work of the Coalition," available at www.wfmc.org.

ACHIEVEMENTS

The initial work of the Coalition focused on publishing the Reference Model and Glossary, defining a common architecture and terminology for the industry. A major milestone was achieved with the publication of the first versions of the Workflow API (WAPI) specification, covering the Workflow Client Application Interface, and the Workflow Interoperability specification.

In addition to a series of successful tutorials industry wide, the WfMC spent many hours over 2009 helping to drive awareness, understanding and adoption of XPDL, now the standard means for business process definition in over 80 BPM products. As a result, it has been cited as the most deployed BPM standard by a number of industry analysts, and continues to receive a growing amount of media attention.

WORKFLOW MANAGEMENT COALITION STRUCTURE

The Coalition is divided into three major committees, the Technical Committee, the External Relations Committee, and the Steering Committee. Small working groups exist within each committee for the purpose of defining workflow terminology, interoperability and connectivity standards, conformance requirements, and for assisting in the communication of this information to the workflow user community.

The Coalition's major committees meet three times per calendar year for three days at a time, with meetings usually alternating between a North American and a European location. The working group meetings are held during these three days, and as necessary throughout the year.

Coalition membership is open to all interested parties involved in the creation, analysis or deployment of workflow software systems. Membership is governed by a Document of Understanding, which outlines meeting regulations, voting rights etc. Membership material is available at www.wfmc.org.

COALITION WORKING GROUPS

The Coalition has established a number of Working Groups, each working on a particular area of specification. The working groups are loosely structured around the "Workflow Reference Model" which provides the framework for the

Coalition's standards program. The Reference Model identifies the common characteristics of workflow systems and defines five discrete functional interfaces through which a workflow management system interacts with its environment—users, computer tools and applications, other software services, etc. Working groups meet individually, and also under the umbrella of the Technical Committee, which is responsible for overall technical direction and co-ordination.

WORKFLOW REFERENCE MODEL DIAGRAM

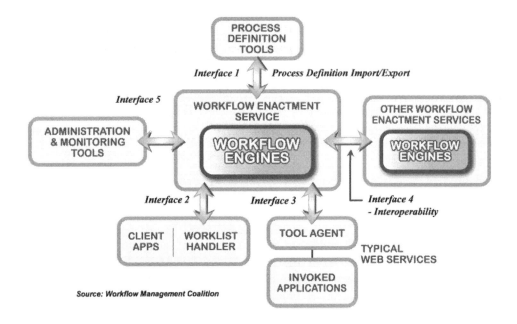

WHY YOU SHOULD JOIN

1. Gain Access to Members-Only Research and Q&A Forums
2. Participate in Members-Only "Brown Bag" Networking Sessions and Industry Speaker Series
3. Receive Free Admission to Business Process Focused Events and Programs (a Benefit Worth $1,000s Annually)
4. Access to the Industry's Largest Research Library on Business Process Modeling, Workflow, BPMS
5. Assistance in Product Certification and Conformance, as well as Requirements Analysis and Procurement Strategy

Being a member of the Workflow Management Coalition gives you the unique opportunity to participate in the creation of standards for the workflow industry as they are developing. Your contributions to our community ensure that progress continues in the adoption of royalty-free workflow and process standards.

MEMBERSHIP CATEGORIES

	Full Member	Associate Member	Individual Member
Annual fee	$3500	$1500	$500
Hold office	Software Vendors, IT & Professional Services Firms, Government, Non-Profit & Commercial	Government or Non-Profit (incl. academic); Any Commercial Firm Not Selling Software or IT Services	All open to all organizations; limited to observing roles, not eligible for officer or committee participation
Limitations	Eligible for All Offices & Committees	Eligible for All Offices & Committees	Observer Only
Events/Research	Full Admission to WfMC Events (up to 3 individuals) and Full Access to the WfMC Research Library (up to 3 log-ons)	Full Access to the WfMC Research Library (single log-on) and Free Admission to All WfMC Events	Full Access to the WfMC Research Library (single log-on) and Free Admission to Select WfMC Events
Promotional Benefits	Logo on All WfMC Pages; Free Use of WfMC Banner Serving; Detailed Company Profile in WfMC Publications	Listed on WfMC Members List and Within Member Directory	N/A

ADDITIONAL BENEFITS OF MEMBERSHIP

This corporate category offers exclusive visibility in this sector at events and seminars across the world, enhancing your customers' perception of you as an industry authority, on our web site, in the Coalition Handbook and CDROM, by speaking opportunities, access to the Members Only area of our web site, attending the Coalition meetings and most importantly within the workgroups whereby through discussion and personal involvement, using your voting power, you can contribute actively to the development of standards and interfaces.

Full member benefits include:

- Financial incentives: 50 percent discount all "brochure-ware" (such as our annual CDROM Companion to the BPM and Workflow Handbook, advertising on our sister-site www.e-workflow.org), $500 credit toward next year's fee for at least 60 percent per year meeting attendance or if you serve as an officer of the WfMC.
- Web Visibility: your logo on all WfMC pages, inclusion in the WfMC web banner network, a detailed company profile in online member directory as well as in all WfMC publications.
- User RFIs: (Requests for Information) is an exclusive privilege to all full members. We often have queries from user organizations looking for specific workflow solutions. These valuable leads can result in real business benefits for your organization.
- Publicity: full members may choose to have their company logos including collaterals displayed along with WfMC material at conferences / expos we attend. You may also list corporate events and press releases (re-

lating to WfMC issues) on the relevant pages on the website, and have a company entry in the annual Coalition Workflow Handbook

- Speaking Opportunities: We frequently receive calls for speakers at industry events because many of our members are recognized experts in their fields. These opportunities are forwarded to Full Members for their direct response to the respective conference organizers.

ASSOCIATE MEMBERSHIP

Associate and Academic Membership is appropriate for those (such as IT user organizations) who need to keep abreast of workflow developments, but who are not workflow vendors. It allows voting on decision-making issues, including the publication of standards and interfaces but does not permit anything near the amount of visibility or incentives provided to a Full Member. You may include up to three active members from your organization on your application.

INDIVIDUAL MEMBERSHIP

Individual Membership is appropriate for self-employed persons or small user companies. Employees of workflow vendors, academic institutions or analyst organizations are not typically eligible for this category. Individual membership is held in one person's name only, is not a corporate membership, and is not transferable within the company. If three or more people within a company wish to participate in the WfMC, it would be cost-effective to upgrade to corporate Associate Membership whereby all employees worldwide are granted membership status.

HOW TO JOIN

Complete the form on the Coalition's website, or contact the Coalition Secretariat, at the address below. All members are required to sign the Coalition's "Document of Understanding" which sets out the contractual rights and obligations between members and the Coalition.

THE SECRETARIAT

Workflow Management Coalition (WfMC)
Nathaniel Palmer, Executive Director,
759 CJC Hwy, Suite #363,
Cohasset, MA 02025-2115 USA
+1-781-923-1411 (t), +1-781-735-0491 (f)
nathaniel@wfmc.org

Index

Additional BPM Resources

NEW e-Book Series ($9.97 each)

- Introduction to BPM and Workflow
  http://store.futstrat.com/servlet/Detail?no=75

- Financial Services
  http://store.futstrat.com/servlet/Detail?no=90

- Healthcare
  http://store.futstrat.com/servlet/Detail?no=81

- Utilities and Telecommunications
  http://store.futstrat.com/servlet/Detail?no=92

Non-Profit Associations and Related Standards Research Online

- AIIM (Association for Information and Image Management)
  http://www.aiim.org
- BPM and Workflow online news, research, forums
  http://bpm.com
- BPM Research at Stevens Institute of Technology
  http://www.bpm-research.com
- Business Process Management Initiative
  http://www.bpmi.org *see* Object Management Group
- IEEE (Electrical and Electronics Engineers, Inc.)
  http://www.ieee.org
- Institute for Information Management (IIM)
  http://www.iim.org
- ISO (International Organization for Standardization)
  http://www.iso.ch
- Object Management Group
  http://www.omg.org
- Organization for the Advancement of Structured Information Standards
  http://www.oasis-open.org
- Society for Human Resource Management
  http://www.shrm.org
- Society for Information Management
  http://www.simnet.org
- Wesley J. Howe School of Technology Management
  http://howe.stevens.edu/research/research-centers/business-process-innovation
- Workflow And Reengineering International Association (WARIA)
  http://www.waria.com
- Workflow Management Coalition (WfMC)
  http://www.wfmc.org
- Workflow Portal
  http://www.e-workflow.org

More Unique Books on BPM and Workflow from Future Strategies, Publishers (www.FutStrat.com)

2008 BPM & WORKFLOW HANDBOOK

http://www.futstrat.com/books/handbook08.php

Spotlight on Human-Centric BPM

Human-centric business process management (BPM) has become the product and service differentiator. The topic now captures substantial mindshare and market share in the human-centric BPM space as leading vendors have strengthened their human-centric business processes. Our spotlight this year examines challenges in human-driven workflow and its integration across the enterprise.
Retail $95.00

2009 BPM & WORKFLOW HANDBOOK

http://www.futstrat.com/books/handbook09.php

Spotlight on BPM in Government

The question, "How can governments manage change organizationally and be agile operationally?" is answered in this special spotlight on BPM in Government with specific emphasis on the USA government where agencies, armed forces, states and cities are facing almost insurmountable challenges. **Retail $75.00**

BPM EXCELLENCE IN PRACTICE 2009

http://www.futstrat.com/books/eip9.php

Innovation, Implementation and Impact

Award-winning Case Studies in Workflow and BPM

These companies focused on excelling in *innovation, implementation* and *impact* when installing BPM and workflow technologies. They recognized that implementing innovative technology is useless unless the organization has a successful approach that delivers—and even surpasses—the anticipated benefits.
$49.95

BPMN MODELING AND REFERENCE GUIDE

http://www.futstrat.com/books/BPMN-Guide.php

Stephen A. White, PhD, Derek Miers

Understanding and Using BPMN
Develop rigorous yet understandable graphical representations of business processes.

Business Process Modeling Notation (BPMN) is a standard, graphical modeling representation for business processes. It provides an easy to use, flow-charting notation that is independent of the implementation environment.
Retail $39.95

2010 BPM & Workflow Handbook

http://futstrat.com/books/handbook10.php

Business Intelligence

Linking business intelligence and business process management creates stronger operational business intelligence. Users seek more intelligent business process capabilities in order to remain competitive within their fields and industries. BPM vendors realize they need to improve their business processes, rules and event management offerings with greater intelligence or analytics capabilities. **Retail $75.00**

BPM Excellence in Practice 2010:

http://futstrat.com/books/eip10.php

Successful Process Implementation

Award-winning Case Studies in Workflow and Business Process Management

For over 19 years the Global Awards for Excellence in BPM and Workflow have covered virtually every economic environment, from bubble to bust and back again. The first modern process era emerged from the economic downturn of the early 1990s. Then, after years defined by relentless cost-cutting, the new charter for business shifted toward enhancing capacity to address the return of customer demand. **Retail $49.95**

BPMN 2.0 Handbook

http://futstrat.com/books/bpmnhandbook.php

Robert Shapiro, Stephen A. White PhD., Nathaniel Palmer, Michael zur Muehlen PhD., Thomas Allweyer, Denis Gagné *et al*

Authored by members of WfMC, OMG and other key participants in the development of BPMN 2.0, the BPMN 2.0 Handbook brings together worldwide thought-leaders and experts in this space. Exclusive and unique contributions examine a variety of aspects that start with an introduction of what's new in BPMN 2.0, and look closely at interchange, analytics, conformance, optimization, simulation and more. **Retail $75.00**

Social BPM

http://futstrat.com/books/handbook11.php

Work, Planning, and Collaboration Under the Impact of Social Technology

Keith D. Swenson, Nathaniel Palmer, Sandy Kemsley
Keith Harrison-Broninski, Max Pucher, Manoj Das, *et al*

Today we see the transformation of both the look and feel of BPM technologies along the lines of social media, as well as the increasing adoption of social tools and techniques democratizing process development and design. It is along these two trend lines; the evolution of system interfaces and the increased engagement of stakeholders in process improvement, that Social BPM has taken shape.
Retail $59.95

Get 25% Discount on ALL Books in our Store.

Please use the discount code **SPEC25** to get 25% discount on ALL books in our store; both Print and Digital Editions (two discount codes cannot be used together).
http://store.futstrat.com/servlet/Catalog

9517394R0013

Made in the USA
Charleston, SC
19 September 2011